MODERN CAMBRIDGE ECONOMICS

FISCAL AND MONETARY POLICIES AND PROBLEMS IN DEVELOPING COUNTRIES

MODERN CAMBRIDGE ECONOMICS

Editors
Phyllis Deane   Gautam Mathur   Joan Robinson

Also in the series
Phyllis Deane
The Evolution of Economic Ideas
Michael Ellman
Socialist Planning
Joan Robinson
Aspects of Development and Underdevelopment
Amiya Kumar Bagchi
The Political Economy of Underdevelopment

FISCAL AND MONETARY POLICIES AND PROBLEMS IN DEVELOPING COUNTRIES

Éprime Eshag

Senior Research Officer,
Oxford University Institute of
Economics and Statistics,
and Fellow of Wadham College, Oxford

CAMBRIDGE
UNIVERSITY PRESS

CAMBRIDGE UNIVERSITY PRESS
Cambridge, New York, Melbourne, Madrid, Cape Town, Singapore,
São Paulo, Delhi, Dubai, Tokyo, Mexico City

Cambridge University Press
The Edinburgh Building, Cambridge CB2 8RU, UK

Published in the United States of America by
Cambridge University Press, New York

www.cambridge.org
Information on this title: www.cambridge.org/9780521270496

© Cambridge University Press 1983

First published 1983
Reprinted 1985, 1992

A catalogue record for this publication is available from the British Library

Library of Congress catalogue card number: 82-17831

ISBN 978-0-521-24900-3 Hardback
ISBN 978-0-521-27049-6 Paperback

To students who care about the
underprivileged and unemployed

CONTENTS

TABLES

CHART

SERIES PREFACE

The modern Cambridge Economics series, of which this book is one, is designed in the same spirit as and with similar objectives to the series of Cambridge Economic Handbooks launched by Maynard Keynes soon after the First World War. Keynes' series, as he explained in his introduction, was intended 'to convey to the ordinary reader and to the uninitiated student some conception of the general principles of thought which economists now apply to economic problems'. He went on to describe its authors as, generally speaking, 'orthodox members of the Cambridge School of Economics' drawing most of their ideas and prejudices from 'the two economists who have chiefly influenced Cambridge thought for the past fifty years, Dr Marshall and Professor Pigou' and as being 'more anxious to avoid obscure forms of expression than difficult ideas'.

This series of short monographs is also aimed at the intelligent undergraduate and interested general reader, but it differs from Keynes' series in three main ways: first in that it focuses on aspects of economics which have attracted the particular interest of economists in the post Second World War era; second in that its authors, though still sharing a Cambridge tradition of ideas, would regard themselves as deriving their main inspiration from Keynes himself and his immediate successors, rather than from the neoclassical generation of the Cambridge school; and third in that it envisages a wider audience than readers in mature capitalist economies, for it is equally aimed at students in developing countries whose problems and whose interactions with the rest of the world have helped to shape the economic issues which have dominated economic thinking in recent decades.

Finally, it should be said that the editors and authors of this Modern Cambridge Economics series represent a wider spectrum of economic doctrine than the Cambridge School of Economics to which Keynes referred in the 1920s. However, the object of the series is not to propagate particular doctrines. It is to stimulate students to escape from conventional theoretical ruts and to think for themselves on live and controversial issues.

JOAN ROBINSON
GAUTAM MATHUR
PHYLLIS DEANE

PREFACE

The main purpose of this book is to examine the potential of fiscal and monetary policies for promoting economic development in less developed countries (LDCs) and to assess the extent to which this potential is exploited. The book is confined to what have come to be known as developing 'market' economies; it excludes all 'socialist', or 'centrally-planned', countries. There are some one hundred and fifty countries and territories variously designated as 'developing', 'less developed', or 'underdeveloped' market economics. They cover virtually all of Africa, Central and South America, the Middle East and a large part of Asia. Their aggregate population, estimated at over two billion in 1980, accounts for about three-fourths of the world population outside the centrally-planned countries.[1]

The so-called developing world thus consists of a large number of heterogeneous countries, differing significantly from one another in such important respects as area, population, resource endowment, stage of development, per capita income, as well as in social and political institutions. This clearly implies that the development problems encountered by the various countries and the fiscal and monetary policies used to deal with them are by no means identical and are far too numerous to be examined, even in broad outline, in this short monograph. Because of this, we have confined the scope of the book to a broad analysis of the use of fiscal and monetary policies in resolving certain basic problems which are shared, in varying degrees, by almost all developing countries. We have concentrated on three such problems: the inadequacy of LDCs' capital equipment in relation to the size of their labour force and to the area of unused cultivable land; the misallocation of their investment resources; and their vulnerability to internal and external imbalances.

1. Among centrally-planned economies also the population of LDCs. which includes that of China, accounts for a similar proportion of the total.

The procedure generally followed is first to analyse the *potential* of fiscal and monetary policies for dealing with the three sets of problems and then to assess the *actual* use that is made of them in practice. In comparing the 'potential' with the 'actual' use of these policies, due allowance has been made for the relative weakness of the administrative machinery in developing countries which, in practice, limits their freedom of action in the choice of policy instruments.

The broad conclusion emerging from our analysis is that most developing countries fail to exploit adequately the development potential of fiscal and monetary policies. A close examination of conditions in a representative sample of these countries reveals that one important explanation for this is to be found in institutional and socio-political obstacles to the adoption and implementation of the necessary policies and measures. In other words, there is a clear indication that governments, whose character and policies are strongly influenced by the interests of dominant economic and political groups, have, by and large, not been willing to prejudice these interests by exploiting the development potential of fiscal and monetary policies fully. We have found this a very useful thesis which goes a long way to explain realistically a number of shortcomings in government policies discussed in the book.

The above thesis has, in our view, a much wider application: institutional factors and 'vested interests', as distinct from technical economic considerations, also play an important role in shaping economic policies in developed market economies, as well as in socialist countries, at times to the detriment of the majority of the population. In examining the impact of the stabilisation policies of industrial countries on LDCs we have had occasion to invoke this thesis to explain the recent growth in the influence of monetarism and of 'sound finance' in industrial countries, which has resulted in a steady growth in unemployment and a gradual erosion of the welfare state. The book does not deal with the policies of socialist countries, which exercise a relatively small influence on developing market economies. There has, therefore, been no opportunity of considering the influence of vested interests in socialist countries on their economic policies. This should not, however, be construed to imply that these countries do not suffer from institutional obstacles to economic development. It has, in fact, become increasingly clear that the abolition of private property and of capitalist institutions has not precluded the emergence of other types of vested interest inimical to the pursuit of rational socialist policies. There is growing evidence that the centralised authoritarian bureaucracies which have emerged in most socialist countries have, at times, been more concerned with preserving their own powers and privileges than with promoting development along a socialist path.

The book is divided into six chapters. The first two are devoted to the definition of concepts and to an explanation of two economic models, one of income determination and the other of economic development. It is largely within the framework of these two models that the role of fiscal and monetary policies is examined in the succeeding chapters.

Chapter 1, which presents all the important value judgments contained in the book, begins by explaining what is understood here by the concept of 'economic development'. We abstract from social, political, cultural, and technological features of economic development and use the simple index of economic welfare of the community for measuring the progress of development. It is shown that such an index has to be compiled by reference to both the rate of growth and the pattern of distribution of national income. It is then argued that the problems of economic development, so defined, cannot be satisfactorily resolved by the market mechanism and that governments must play an active role in promoting development.

Chapter 2 explains the general approach followed in the book for identifying and analysing the role of fiscal and monetary policies in the management of demand and in financing economic development. It is argued that the Keynesian model of income determination, briefly reviewed in the *first part* of the chapter, provides a suitable framework for the analysis of the role that these policies can play in both industrial and developing economies in influencing the volume of effective demand as well as general price levels. This approach, which is followed closely in the analysis of the problems of internal and external imbalances in Chapter 6, is shown to stand in sharp contrast to that of the neo-monetarists, examined critically in the appendix to the chapter. In the *second part* of the chapter, we review Kalecki's model of financing investment in a 'mixed' economy. The model suggests that fiscal and monetary policies can be used to accelerate the pace of development by raising the ratio of investment, financed by domestic savings and foreign capital, in national income, as well as by helping to direct investment resources into 'essential' projects, as defined in Chapter 1. It is largely within the framework of this model that the role of these policies as well as of foreign capital in promoting economic development is analysed in the succeeding three chapters.

Chapter 3 is devoted to the problem of increasing domestic savings through fiscal measures aimed at restraining public and private consumption. It first examines the pattern of government consumption expenditure for a sample of developing countries by comparing their outlays on 'defence', 'education' and 'health' with one another and with those of the industrial countries of the West. A similar comparison is then made of the ratios of direct and indirect taxes to national income. Later in the chapter we suggest a number of broad guidelines for framing taxation policies and measures in LDCs. Our analysis reveals that most developing countries have failed to promote adequately the growth of domestic savings by curbing useless government consumption outlays and by exploiting the tax potential of the economy, especially in the agricultural sector.

In *Chapter 4* we examine the problem of financing investment through foreign capital. The chapter begins by explaining the dual function of foreign capital in economic development. It then presents a survey of the actual flow of different categories of external capital to developing countries in the 1970s. We conclude by examining the development *potential* of the various types of foreign capital and by explaining the key role played by government policies in determining the *actual contribution* to development made by such capital. The chapter has two appendices, the first of which reviews the recommendations of the United Nations and DAC on foreign aid and on capital flow to LDCs; the second deals with the external debt and with the debt servicing problems of developing countries.

Chapter 5 is on the pattern of investment. It discusses the ways and means by which both fiscal and monetary instruments can be used to direct the flow of investment resources to projects which have a high social priority. It first gives a number of broad guidelines for the choice of investment projects in the public sector. This is followed by an explanation of how various types of fiscal and monetary instrument can be employed to influence the pattern of private investment. The chapter includes a survey of the operations of 'industrial development banks' and of 'agricultural credit institutions' in developing countries. The broad conclusion emerging from our discussion is that most developing countries have not made full use of fiscal and monetary instruments to give adequate priority to essential investment.

Chapter 6 examines the problems of internal and external imbalances in LDCs and the 'relevance' and 'efficacy' of restrictive fiscal and monetary policies for dealing with them. We first identify the various types of imbalance commonly experienced in these countries in terms of the factors responsible for generating them. We then provide a rough sketch of the techniques required for the diagnosis of inflationary pressures and of external disequilibria and discuss the remedies appropriate to each type of imbalance. The second part of the chapter consists of a critical review of the monetarist approach to external imbalances. This part complements the critique of neo-monetarism presented in the appendix to Chapter 2, and like the latter is relevant to both developing and industrial economies. Because the IMF (the Fund) exercises significant influence on the economic policies of many of its members, we have concentrated on its version of monetarism. We have also provided some factual information on the organisation, resources and regular credit tranche facilities of the Fund in order to give the reader a concrete impression of its *modus operandi*. The Fund's 'special facilities', as operated early in 1981, are briefly surveyed in an appendix to the chapter. These facilities are subject to periodic changes, invariably announced in the *IMF Survey* and other publications mentioned in the appendix.

Chapters 3 to 6 contain a number of statistical tables the chief purpose of which is to illustrate the arguments advanced in the text. A number of tables, notably those in Chapter 4, however, serve the additional purpose of providing factual information on capital flows and on the external debt of developing countries in the 1970s. These tables are compiled from the data published in regular periodicals and reports, specified in the tables, through which the interested reader can in future obtain more up-to-date information.

I am extremely grateful to the editors of the series for first persuading me to undertake the task of writing this monograph and then encouraging me to finish it. I am in particular debt to two of the editors, Joan Robinson and Phyllis Deane, who have read all the three drafts of the book and made valuable comments on them; because of the difficulty of communication, the third editor, Professor Mathur, was, unfortunately, not able to see the last two drafts. Next to the editors, I owe the greatest debt to my old friend and ex-United Nations colleague, Sidney Dell, who has read the penultimate draft of the book and commented extensively on both the substance and coverage of the individual chapters. Two other persons, Hans Singer of the Institute of Development Studies, Sussex, and Michael Surrey of the University of Leeds, have, in their capacity as readers for the CUP, read the penultimate draft of the book and made helpful comments on it. But to Michael, my ex-colleague at Wadham College, I owe a special debt for also making a number of useful editorial comments on the text. I have also received helpful editorial as well as substantive comments at various stages of my work from a number of past and present friends, notably Heather Joshi, Susan Hitch, Linda Lewis, Alexa Walker and Shahen Abrahamian, for which I am very grateful.

In writing the book, I have drawn heavily on the specialised knowledge of some of my Oxford friends and other professional colleagues, who have been prevailed upon to read certain parts of the book and give me the benefit of their expertise. I am extremely indebted to all these economists whom I list below, going through the book in order of chapter. I have received most helpful comments from: Amartya Sen, of All Souls College, on Chapter 1; Wlodzimierz Brus, of Wolfson College, on Chapters 1 and 2; John Flemming, of Nuffield College, and Tony Courakis, of Brasenose College, on the appendix to Chapter 2; R. J. Chelliah, of the National Institute of Public Finance and Policy, New Delhi, on 'Tax ratios' in Chapter 3; Solon T. Barraclough, of the United Nations Research Institute for Social Development, Geneva, and Professor Richard Bird, of Toronto University, on 'Direct agricultural taxes' in Chapter 3; Stein Bevan, of DAC Secretariat in Paris, on Chapter 4; Sanjaya Lall of the Institute of Economics and Statistics, Oxford, on 'Direct investment' in Chapter 4; Michael Lipton, of the Institute of Development Studies, Sussex, and Mr J.C. Abbot, of the FAO Secretariat, Rome, on 'Agricultural credit institutions' in Chapter 5; and Messrs Carl P. Blackwell, Arie C. Bouter, Manuel Guitian and A. W. Hooke, IMF staff members, on the second part of Chapter 6 (beginning with 'The IMF monetary approach to the balance of payments'), and on the appendix to that chapter. I should add that comments by the staff members of the international organisations mentioned, namely DAC, FAO, IMF and United Nations, were all made in a 'private and personal' capacity, which I believe rendered them more rather than less valuable than 'official' comments would have been.

I have left to the last the acknowledgement of my heavy indebtedness to my own university employer, the Institute of Economics and Statistics. The book would never have been attempted, let alone finished, had I not been in a position to enjoy fully the research facilities provided by the Institute. I should in particular like to acknowledge the competent services provided by: John Watson, the Librarian of the Institute, his assistant, Doreen Monger, and their staff; Mary Gisborne, the ex-Secretary of the Institute; Catherine Fitzharris, the statistical clerk; and especially Caroline Wise and Caroline Baldwin, the two patient and indefatigable secretaries. The final revisions to the draft were made in New York, and Valerie White, of the United Nations, was kind enough to devote a good deal of her own time to typing them.

It must by now have become clear to the reader, that in writing this monograph, apart from having had ample research facilities, I have by no means lacked the benefit of advice and comments, substantive and editorial, from highly qualified and competent persons. Rightly or wrongly, however, I have not always followed their suggestions, and, because of this, I must alone be held responsible for all the shortcomings and for any errors of omission and commission that may be detected in the book.

ÉPRIME ESHAG

ABBREVIATIONS
(in alphabetical order)

AID	(US) Agency for International Development
BIS	Bank for International Settlements
BOUIES	*Bulletin, Oxford University Institute of Economics and Statistics*
CFF	Compensatory Financing Facility
CMEA	Council for Mutual Economic Assistance
DAC	(OECD) Development Assistance Committee
ECLA	(UN) Economic Commission for Latin America
ECOSOC	(UN) Economic and Social Council
EFF	Extended Fund Facility
FAO	(UN) Food and Agricultural Organisation
Fund, the	International Monetary Fund
GAB	General Arrangements to Borrow
GDP	gross domestic product
GNP	gross national product
ICAD	Inter-American Committee for Agricultural Development
ICOR	incremental capital/output ratio
IDA	(World Bank) International Development Agency
IFS	(IMF) *International Financial Statistics*
ILO	(UN) International Labour Office
IMF	International Monetary Fund
INMIDEL	Industrial and Mining Development Bank of Iran
LDCs	less developed countries
ODA	official development assistance
OECD	Organisation for Economic Co-operation and Development
OPEC	Organisation of Petroleum Exporting Countries
R and D	research and development
SDR	(IMF) special drawing right

SFF	Supplementary Financing Facility
UN	United Nations
UNCTAD	United Nations Conference on Trade and Development
UNDP	United Nations Development Programme
UNIDO	United Nations Industrial Development Organisation
VAT	Value added Tax

SYMBOLS AND TERMINOLOGY USED

——	nil or negligible
...	not available
billion	one thousand million

1

THE MEANING AND THE STRATEGY
OF ECONOMIC DEVELOPMENT

This book, which deals with the fiscal and monetary policies of developing countries, can be said to fall largely within the sphere of what has come to be known as 'normative' economics. Although this is not universally acknowledged, any work concerned with issues of economic policy must inevitably embody certain value judgments, whether or not expressly stated, derived from the moral and political philosophy of the author. These value judgments are generally reflected in the basic assumptions underlying the analysis of policies and often influence the theoretical framework of the analysis. Because of this, we believe that the reader is entitled to be informed in advance of the more important value judgments contained in the book, and this introductory chapter is devoted largely to that purpose.

We first explain what is understood here by the concept of 'economic development' and consider the difficult question of measurement of the rate, or pace, of economic development. We then set out what we regard as important reasons for government intervention and participation in the process of economic development. Lastly, we draw attention to the key role which, in our view, is played by institutional and political factors in determining the course of economic development – a thesis frequently invoked in the monograph.

THE MEANING AND MEASUREMENT OF ECONOMIC DEVELOPMENT

There is no simple definition of 'economic development' which adequately reflects the experience of the countries which are undergoing development.[1] Economic development is a very complex process

---

1. For a discussion of the meaning of economic development, see Gerald M. Meier, *Leading Issues in Economic Development*, second edition, OUP (1970), pp. 5–9. See also Frances Stewart and Paul Streeten, 'New Strategies for Development: Poverty, Income Distribution and Growth', *Oxford Economic Papers*, November 1976.

involving not only economic, but also many social, political, technological and cultural changes. For the purpose of this book, however, one need not provide a comprehensive definition embracing all the important features of development. It would generally be agreed that the primary purpose of seeking development of a country is to increase the economic welfare of its inhabitants by mobilising its productive resources. One could, therefore, define economic development, somewhat narrowly, as the process of increasing the degree of utilisation and improving the productivity of the available resources of a country which leads to an increase of the economic welfare of the community by stimulating the growth of national income.

It follows from the above definition that the progress of development has to be assessed by reference to two separate indicators, namely, the indices of 'production', or 'national income', and of the 'economic welfare' of the community. The former covers what may be designated as the 'growth' aspect of development. The economic welfare indicator, on the other hand, brings to light, as we shall presently see, the pattern of allocation of resources and of the distribution of income among different groups and classes of the community; in a sense, it combines the 'quality' and the 'growth' aspects of development.

The most common index of development used in economic literature is that of growth in per capita GNP at constant prices, or per capita real income. This index, however, covers only the 'growth' aspect of development; it takes no account of the distribution of income. As an indicator of the increase in the economic welfare of the community as a whole, it is adequate only for a homogeneous society whose members all benefit equally from a rise in national income; it is clear that such societies do not exist.[2] Nevertheless, the index is widely used and this is usually justified on the grounds that individuals' utility, or welfare, is unmeasurable and that there is no 'objective' or 'scientific' way of numerically quantifying changes in the welfare of the community that may result from a redistribution of income among its members. Following Pareto, an 'optimum' welfare situation for a community is, therefore, defined as one in which no one can be made better off without someone else becoming worse off.

The impossibility of quantifying economic welfare does not, however, in our view, mean that it is not important and can be ignored, any more than the quality of a good, which is also often unquantifiable, can be ignored in assessing its value. We believe that, although

2. For a detailed discussion, see Amartya Sen, 'Economic Development: Objectives and Obstacles', in Robert F. Dernberger (ed.), *China's Development Experience in Comparative Perspective*, Harvard University Press, Cambridge, Mass. (1981).

utility is not cardinally measurable, it is nevertheless possible to construct an ordinal ranking of the relative magnitude of utility which will accrue to different income groups by a given increment of their income; we assume that this magnitude will be higher for the low than for the high income groups. To take an extreme example, we maintain that the increase in welfare of a starving family from an additional income of, say, £10 per week used to finance its purchases of food would be larger than that of a rich family which spends an equal increment of income on buying, say, an extra bottle of champagne per week. This means that, to construct an index of growth of economic welfare, different weights should be attached to the rise in real income of the various income groups, the lower the income the bigger the weight. It also means that the consideration of income distribution must form an integral part of any acceptable index of economic development if it is agreed that the chief aim of development is to increase the economic welfare of the community as a whole.

This approach to economic welfare is in line with that of the nineteenth-century English utilitarians and of Alfred Marshall. The utilitarians believed that a transfer of income from the rich to the poor would generally increase the aggregate welfare of the community. And Marshall, the founder of the English neo-classical school of economics, specifically recognised that the utility derived from a given amount of additional income is greater for the low than for the high income groups. He writes, 'A shilling is the measure of less pleasure, or satisfaction of any kind, to a rich man than to a poor one . . . The clerk with £100 a year will walk to business in a much heavier rain than the clerk with £300 a year; for the cost of a ride by tram or omnibus measures a greater benefit to the poorer man than to the richer.'[3] It is clear that the refusal of some economists to recognise this fact, as well as their insistence on 'value-free' 'objective' comparisons of economic situations in adopting Pareto's concept of 'optimality', inevitably exert a bias towards the maintenance of the status quo in the distribution of wealth and income.

The process of growth

The rate of growth of national income of a developing country will vary directly with the rates at which its idle resources are brought into production and the productivity of such resources is increased. Economic resources of less developed countries (LDCs) can, like those

3. Alfred Marshall, *Principles of Economics*, Macmillan, eighth edition (1920), p. 19.

of developed countries, be divided into three broad categories – land (including water and minerals), labour and man-made means of production; for the sake of brevity we shall refer to the latter as 'capital equipment',[4] The two most striking characteristics of LDCs which distinguish them from developed countries and which largely account for their low per capita production, are the relatively 'low degree of the utilisation' and the 'inferior productivity' of their land and labour resources. The phenomenon of the underutilisation of these two resources is clearly observed in the presence of a high level of open and disguised unemployment,[5] of large areas of potentially arable uncultivated land and of unexploited water and mineral resources. Their inferior productivity is reflected in the relatively small yields of cultivated land and in a low per capita output of labour in urban occupations as compared with developed economies.

The principal explanation for the above two characteristics of LDCs is the inadequacy of their capital equipment in relation to the size of labour force and to the area of unused cultivable land, a defect that can be remedied only through investment in capital equipment. Another important explanation is to be found in the backward technology and in the relatively poor quality of a labour force lacking in technical, organisational, and administrative skills and suffering from poor health. To remedy this shortcoming too it is necessary to undertake investment in human resources through outlays on health, on education and on the introduction of new technical skills.

As we shall see, in many developing countries a number of institutional factors, such as archaic feudal and semi-feudal land tenure systems, also hamper the utilisation and productivity of land and labour resources. This type of obstacle to the growth of production, however, calls for political solutions with which we shall not be directly concerned.

Leaving aside the institutional factors, it is clear from the above that, 'the process of increasing the degree of utilisation and of improving the productivity of the available resources of a country' in development, entails the *creation* of additional productive resources through investment in capital equipment, in human resources and in production technology, including organisational skills. A large part of this book will be devoted to an examination of the ways and means in which

---

4. The term 'capital equipment' is thus used in this book to signify all man-made means of production, including economic infrastructure, e.g. transport and communication facilities.

5. For a discussion of the question of 'disguised unemployment', see Amartya Sen, *Employment, Technology and Development*, OUP (1975), Chapter 4.

fiscal and monetary policies can be used to encourage the *creation* of such additional productive resources through investment.

The relative size of physical productive capacity, or capital equipment, in industrial and developing countries goes a long way in explaining the fundamental difference between the crucial economic problems facing the two groups of economies. The capital equipment of industrial countries is adequate to provide employment for their entire labour force; the so-called 'structural unemployment', due to a lack of consistency, or harmony, between the patterns of production and demand, accounts for a relatively small fraction of their labour force. The levels of employment and production in these economies is determined primarily by aggregate effective demand; in Kalecki's terminology they are 'demand-determined'. Hence, the *crucial* long-term problem of free enterprise industrial countries is to avoid the loss of production that results from a deficiency in effective demand.

In developing countries, on the other hand, production is primarily constrained by a shortage of productive capacity in the form of capital equipment, noted above, rather than by a deficiency in effective demand; they can therefore be regarded as 'supply-determined'. They face a serious problem of 'structural unemployment', accounting for a significant proportion of the labour force, due largely to the shortage of capital equipment in relation to labour force. The *crucial* long-term problem of these countries is, therefore, the creation of additional productive capacity through investment. Compared with this, the problem of deficiency in effective demand, discussed in Chapter 6, is of *secondary* importance for LDCs, just as the problems of structural unemployment and production bottlenecks are for developed economies.

Economic welfare index

We shall generally measure economic welfare by reference to the standard of living of individuals, as reflected in the volume of their consumption. It is realised that this is a very narrow definition of economic welfare since it takes no account of many other important implications for welfare of economic development; these include the welfare resulting from employment, as distinct from income,[6] and various environmental and cultural features of development which enhance or diminish the welfare of the community. But we abstract

6. See Frances Stewart and Paul Streeten 'Conflicts Between Output and Employment Objectives in Developing Countries', *Oxford Economic Papers*, July 1971, and Amartya Sen, *Employment, Technology and Development*, Chapter 9.

from these and other problems involved in the assessment of welfare.[7] What we require is a concrete index which can be used in practice as a rough indicator of the rate of development and for this the level of consumption of individuals should generally be adequate.

Since the level of personal consumption is determined largely by real income, one can take changes in real income of individuals as indicators of changes in their economic welfare. It would follow from this that the rate of economic development for each individual can be assessed by reference to the rate of growth of his real income. But development policy should aim at increasing the welfare of the community as a whole; this embodies numerous individuals with different levels of income. To ascertain the rate of development of the economy, one requires an average *weighted index* of the growth in GNP, or real income, which in some way reflects the growth of welfare of the entire community.

It would be possible to obtain, as is at times done, a numerical measure of the weighted index of national income by assigning some arbitrary numerical weights to the income of different groups in the community. For example, if the population were divided into five income groups, one could start with a weight of 1 for the richest and end with a weight of 5 for the poorest group. The rate of progression of the weights should vary with the spread of income between the groups; the larger the spread, the steeper the progression. For example, in some developing countries, where members of the richest group are at least as opulent as those in industrial countries, and members of the poorest group live well below subsistence level, one could vary the weights from 1 for the former to say 20, 50, or even more for the latter group. There is, of course, no neutral 'scientific' way of determining these weights; they are arbitrary in the sense that they are decided, implicitly or explicitly, by the policy makers in accordance with their moral and political judgment.

There appears to be no special reason, however, for giving arbitrary numerical weights to different income groups; an ordinal ranking of weights should in practice generally be adequate. One could, for example, estimate a minimum level of acceptable income, or a 'poverty line', for each developing country, and proceed to give a top priority to raising the level of income of those groups that fall below the poverty line, and lower priorities to increasing the incomes of higher income groups; the higher the level of income of a group the lower its

---

7. Readers interested in this subject should refer to Amartya Sen, 'The Welfare Basis of Real Income Comparisons: A Survey', *Journal of Economic Literature*, March 1979.

priority. Although the poverty line can never be clearly and precisely defined, it is nevertheless possible to form a reasonable view of the order of magnitude of the minimum income required to prevent poverty. The reason for this is that the bulk of this income is required to defray the costs of the *minimum* amount of food, clothing, shelter and health services required to maintain an individual alive and in an active healthy condition, and this can be objectively estimated. The other less tangible human requirements, such as *minimum* education and recreation, which are not so easily assessable, account for only a relatively small fraction of the total consumption in developing countries and cannot significantly affect the level of the poverty line. The ILO and World Bank have, for example, made rough estimates of the poverty line for a large number of LDCs. According to these estimates about one-third of the population of developing countries in the mid-1970s was found to live below the poverty line and was designated as 'absolute poor'.[8]

No mention has thus far been made of the temporal aspect of economic development. Governments should be concerned not only with the welfare of the present generation but also with that of future generations. What is considered the best development policy for the present generation may not necessarily contribute most to the welfare of future generations. As explained in Chapter 2 (pp. 55–9), an acceleration in the rate of growth of production would entail an increase in the share of investment and a corresponding reduction in the share of consumption in national income. This will mean a restraint on the rate of growth of current consumption in the interest of increasing the productive capacity of consumer goods in the future.

Governments are thus compelled to apply, at least implicitly, some system of weighting the welfare of different generations in formulating their investment policies. The policy adopted is a matter of 'value judgment' on the part of the authorities, since there is no 'objective' way of comparing the welfare of different generations.[9] The theories which maintain that the rate of interest, in some way, indicates the community's preference for current consumption have little foundation in reality; they have, nevertheless, at times been used morally to justify interest accruing to wealth owners, as was done, for example, by Marshall. Although Keynes was able to demonstrate that interest was a reward for 'illiquidity' and not a reward for 'abstinence', these

8. See OECD, *Development Co-operation, 1978 Review*, p. 41 and Annex 11. See also World Bank, *World Development Report, 1980*, p. 13 for more recent estimates.
9. See A.K. Sen, *Choice of Techniques*, second edition, Basil Blackwell, Oxford (1962), Chapter VIII and Appendix B.

theories continue to be used in one form or another in the current literature.[10]

Essential and inessential investment and consumer goods

In terms of the allocation of investment resources, the foregoing approach would of course entail giving a higher priority to the provision of goods and services required by the lower income groups, namely the majority of the population. For most developing countries this will involve a concentration of resources into production of food and clothing of the type consumed by lower income groups and into provision of low cost housing and simple health and education services needed to raise the standard of living of such groups. For some developing countries an even more urgent and important policy objective than the elimination of extreme poverty is the need to reduce the risk of periodic disasters resulting from droughts, floods, tidal waves, etc. The human suffering that results from these disasters – famine, sickness, epidemics, and so on – is considerably more acute than any experienced by living below the poverty line.[11]

Throughout this book the terms *essential investment* and investment with a *high social priority*, are used somewhat loosely to indicate the type of investment mentioned above, while the terms *inessential investment* and *low priority investment* signify the type which caters to the needs of the minority consisting of the richer members of the community. Similarly the expressions *essential consumer goods* and *necessities* are used to cover those goods and services which constitute the bulk of the consumption of the majority of the population, whereas *non-essentials* and *luxuries* refer to goods consumed mainly by the richer strata of the population.

It is clear that the two categories of investment and of consumer goods mentioned are not fixed in character; the list of 'essential investment' and of 'necessities' will vary from country to country and for the same country from one period to another. Generally, the higher the standard of living of the broad masses of the population, the larger will be the list of essential investment projects and of goods and services included in the category of necessities.

It is also clear that the suggested criteria for classifying investment

10. See Éprime Eshag, *From Marshall to Keynes, An Essay on the Monetary Theory of the Cambridge School*, Basil Blackwell, Oxford (1963), Appendix to Chapter III. See also J.M. Keynes, *The General Theory of Employment, Interest and Money*, Macmillan (1936), Chapters 13–14, especially pp. 174 and 182.
11. See Amartya Sen, in Robert F. Dernberger (ed.), *China's Development Experience.*

projects are too broad to permit the ranking of *all* investment projects in the order of their social priority. Although most projects can be so ranked without much difficulty, some are likely to be of the same order of importance for the promotion of economic welfare and should be grouped in the same rank. It would, for example, be difficult to distinguish between a project aimed at promoting the education of the majority of the population from one that aims at improving its health, and the policy makers will have simply to use their judgment in the allocation of resources between them. This is, however, a relatively minor problem, since investment decisions in such cases are unlikely to exercise an important influence on development. As explained in the following chapters, in practice, the policies which significantly influence the welfare index of development tend to be concerned with the distribution of resources between what are easily identifiable as being 'essential' and 'inessential' investment in terms of the broad criteria mentioned (see also pp. 54–5).

In theory, one should evaluate the increase in economic welfare corresponding to any growth in GNP by examining time series data on the distribution of income between different income groups; the larger the share of the lower income groups in any increment of national income, the larger would be the increase in economic welfare of the community. Unfortunately, hardly any developing countries possess such data and, because of this, we propose to evaluate the welfare aspect of development through an examination of the pattern of investment catering primarily to domestic rather than export markets for which more information is available.

It should be possible to obtain a broad indication of the welfare aspect of the development policy of a country by comparing the amount of its *per capita essential investment* with that of its *per capita inessential investment*. To calculate these per capita figures, each category of investment should be divided by the respective number of people which it is intended to serve. In other words, one would have to divide the value of essential investment by the majority of the population in the lower income groups and that of inessential investment by the remainder of the population.[12] A policy which pays due regard to the welfare aspect of development would ensure that the per capita essential investment is larger than that of inessential investment. Abstracting from any differences in incremental capital/output ratio

12. Investment outlays, such as those on epidemic and flood control projects, which benefit the entire population of a country or region, can, for this purpose, either be excluded from the calculation or be apportioned between the two classes of income groups in the ratio of their population.

(ICOR)[13] the higher is the ratio of per capita essential to per capita inessential investment, the larger will be the growth in economic welfare corresponding to any increase in national income.

Lop-sided development

It will be shown later that in many developing countries the criterion of promoting the economic welfare of the community plays a relatively small part in determining the pattern of investment as compared with other criteria, such as profitability and prestige value of investment. Consequently in many of these countries a relatively large share of investment tends to be devoted to the production of luxuries and to other low priority purposes. Although, for reasons noted above we refrain from resorting to a numerical index of economic welfare, we can still make qualitative distinctions between different types of investment policies, by reference to the ratio of per capita essential to per capita inessential investment. Since policies which attach some weight to the welfare index of development would ensure that the ratio in question is greater than unity, we shall designate as *lop-sided* any development in which this ratio is less than unity; the lower the ratio falls below unity, the greater the degree of 'lop-sidedness'.

STRATEGY OF DEVELOPMENT

According to the orthodox neo-classical theory the problem of development, like most important economic problems encountered by industrial countries, is best resolved by the market mechanism. The theory implies that market forces and competition, unhindered by government intervention, will, in the long run, tend to bring about the maximum rate of resource utilisation and a pattern of resource allocation which produce optimum social welfare, as defined by Pareto. This attitude to development continues to survive in the literature of economics and to influence government policies, although it would not be easy to find a single developing country that is prepared to consign its economic destiny entirely to the free operation of market forces.

It is argued here that economic development, as we understand it, requires active government participation in the management of the

---

13. The ratio of the increment in 'capital equipment' to the increment in 'productive capacity', which will equal the ratio of net investment to the increment in national income when productive capacity is fully utilised.

economy. There are two important reasons for this. *First,* the *laissez-faire* system does not necessarily ensure optimum rates of savings and investment, which are the major determinants of the rate of growth of production. *Secondly,* the pattern of resource allocation which emerges from the operation of market forces is unlikely to be the most appropriate one in terms of promoting economic welfare as defined above. It will be shown that government intervention makes it possible both to raise the volume of savings and investment and to provide a better pattern of resource allocation for promoting economic welfare.

Raison d'être for government intervention

The more important reasons which justify government intervention can be summarised under four broad headings.

1. *Lower efficacy of the market mechanism*

One reason for government intervention and participation in productive activity in developing countries is the generally recognised fact that market forces, whether conducive to development or not, operate less effectively in these than in developed economies. The response of factors of production to market signals in LDCs tends to be not only slow and sluggish but also uncertain in magnitude. This is largely the result of a relatively low mobility of resources, due to a lack of diversified production and skills, a shortage of business skills as well as relatively inefficient systems of transport and communication. Mobility is particularly low in the many developing countries that have experienced prolonged periods of economic and political instability and where in consequence expectations about the durability of any price incentive provided cannot be strong enough to warrant significant reallocation of investment resources.

The relative inefficacy of the market mechanism in the economies of developing countries is especially pronounced in the agricultural sector, which often accounts for the bulk of their production. A large part of agricultural activity is devoted to subsistence farming and this is generally less susceptible to the influence of price incentives. But even when agricultural produce is marketed, it is not clear how quick and significant would be the response of individual farmers to price and profit incentives. This is partly because the farming community is not always strongly motivated by the objective of profit maximisation, although this may well play a greater role in large plantations managed along traditional business lines. In addition, the archaic land tenure system of many LDCs, combined with a limited accessibility to credit of small farmers and with the intervention of middlemen in the disposal of their produce, set serious constraints on the responsiveness of production to price changes (see pp. 201–7).

Because of this lower efficacy of the market mechanism in developing countries, attempts to influence the pattern of investment and production through price incentives have often met with failure. A good example of this is provided by the experience of Argentina in the period 1957–64, when successive devaluations of the currency aimed at stimulating agricultural production through price incentives produced no positive results.[14] As explained later, in such cases a policy of direct government intervention, involving, on the one hand, the provision of subsidised inputs to farmers in the form of cheap seeds, fertilisers, loans and technical assistance and, on the other, the taxation of the potential productive capacity of farms, is more likely to be successful (see pp. 110–12). The knowledge that a certain tax had to be paid on a farm, irrespective of the volume of production, is likely to act as an effective incentive to individual farmers to make maximum use of the subsidised inputs and hence to stimulate productivity.

2.   *Unequal distribution of income*[15]

For many years, informed observers have believed that the inequality of income in most developing countries is considerably greater than in industrialised economies. This can be explained largely by the heavier concentration of wealth, in the form of land and industrial enterprises, in the hands of a small number of families, by a wider disparity in the level of education and skills between the rich and the poor as well as by the absence of an effective system of progressive taxation on incomes and wealth in most developing countries as compared with developed economies. Until recently, however, the data needed to confirm this general impression were very scanty. Since the War a large number of sample surveys of income distribution have been carried out.[16]

14. See Éprime Eshag and Rosemary Thorp, 'Economic and Social Consequences of Orthodox Economic Policies in Argentina in the Post-War Years,' *BOUIES*, February 1965, p. 38.
15. The data included in this section were provided by my ex-colleague, Professor M.J.C. Surrey, of the University of Leeds, before he left Oxford.
16. See, for example, Carl S. Shoup *et al.*, *The Fiscal System of Venezuela*, The Johns Hopkins Press, Baltimore (1959); Ifigenia M. de Navarrete, *La distribución del Ingreso y del desarrollo de México*, Escuela Nacional de Economía, Mexico (1960); Irving B. Kravis, 'International Differences in the Distribution of Income', *Review of*

Before considering the results of these surveys certain reservations about the quality of the data should be noted. *First,* the measurement of 'income' in developing countries is often extremely difficult, particularly because of the problems involved in valuing income received in kind, notably production by subsistence farmers. *Secondly,* at the higher end of the income scale, there is the possibility of deliberate understatement of income in order to avoid payment of tax. *Thirdly,* divergences in prices between rural and urban areas, which tend to be relatively large in LDCs, mean that differences in money incomes may not be a good guide to differences in real incomes. *Finally,* there are problems associated with the fact that the surveys are based on samples which may be rather small and not adequately representative.

Despite these difficulties, it is possible to discern some general patterns in the large number of studies of different countries of which the findings of one of the more recent and comprehensive are briefly noted here. In a survey of 66 countries including a number of socialist and industrialised countries, several broad patterns emerged.[17] As might be expected, the socialist countries had the most nearly equal distribution of income, with on average about 25 per cent of total income accruing to the lowest 40 per cent of households. The developed countries showed a fairly wide range of degrees of inequality, but on average – with 16 per cent of income going to the lowest 40 per cent – they showed less inequality than most of the LDCs.

For the 45 less developed countries taken together, inequality was significantly greater, with the lowest 40 per cent of households receiving on average about 12 per cent of total income. But this average concealed very wide differences. A number of countries showed a reasonably high degree of equality – Sri Lanka, Pakistan, Uganda, Thailand and Korea, amongst others, had more than 17 per cent of income accruing to the lowest 40 per cent. But in about half the countries surveyed the lowest 40 per cent of households received an average of only 9 per cent of total income; these countries included, among others, Kenya, Iraq, Ecuador, Brazil, Mexico, Venezuela and Jamaica.

Similar patterns and variations were found at the upper end of the

Economics and Statistics, November 1960. See also Joint Tax Program, *Fiscal Policy for Economic Growth in Latin America,* Papers and Proceedings of a Conference held in Santiago, Chile, December 1962, The Johns Hopkins Press, Baltimore (1965), especially pp. 20–4 and 70–4.

17. See Montek S. Ahluwalia, 'Income Inequality: Some Dimensions of the Problem', in Hollis Chenery *et al.* (eds.), *Redistribution with Growth,* OUP (1974).

scale. The share of total income taken by the top 20 per cent of households was typically 30–35 per cent in the socialist countries, and of the order of 40 per cent in a typical industrialised country. In most less developed countries, however, the share of the top 20 per cent was appreciably higher and amounted to as much as 60 per cent or more in 13 of them.

These patterns of income distribution relate, it should be stressed, to pre-tax income, that is, income before making allowance for income taxation and transfer payments by the government. Since the impact of progressive income taxation and redistributive transfer payments in reducing disparities in disposable incomes is undoubtedly greater in most of the developed countries than in the less developed countries, even the patterns described above must underestimate the extent to which inequality of distribution in the LDCs outstrips that in the socialist and industrialised countries. As shown later, estimates of distribution of income in the agricultural sector of LDCs show an even wider disparity between the income of the big landlords and small farmers (pp. 114–18).

A further feature observed in most developing countries is the wide disparity of income and of standards of living between regions and between urban and rural areas in general. This can be explained largely by (a) the concentration of the modern sectors of the economy (industry and commerce) and of public administration in the urban areas and in proximity to the major centres of natural resources under exploitation, and (b) the low rate of mobility of the factors of production, noted earlier.

The greater unevenness of distribution of income in developing countries has serious implications for both the volume and the pattern of investment. The relatively large share of the national income accruing to a small section of the population is bound to result in a high level of consumption by that section. By reducing the share of income left at the disposal of the high income groups, for example through a progressive system of taxation of income and wealth, it should be possible for governments to lower the volume of private consumption and raise the level of domestic savings. Furthermore, since a relatively large part of the consumption of the higher income groups is of imported luxury and inessential goods, such measures would also tend to reduce imports and save foreign exchange.

The pattern of resource allocation under the market mechanism of necessity conforms to the pattern of final demand, which in turn is determined by the pattern of income distribution. It is clear that the more skewed and uneven is the income distribution, the more likely it is that resource allocation will be biased towards catering for the needs of higher income groups and more prosperous regions. Without government intervention in the allocation of investment resources, this can, and indeed often does, result in what has been designated as 'lopsided' development (see p. 10 above). A relatively large share of investment resources may, for example, be allocated to the construction of luxury houses and apartment houses and to the manufacture of motor cars and other durable consumer goods, in countries where a significant proportion of the population live below the poverty line and lack basic housing requirements and essential consumer goods.

3 *Divergence between private and social costs and benefits*

The third important reason for government intervention in the economy is the divergences that often exist between the private and social costs and benefits of investment projects. The private entrepreneur is quite naturally concerned only with the cost incurred by him on a project, and with the income received in his decision whether or not to embark on it. He is not expected to, nor does he in practice, attach any weight to what are commonly known as the 'externalities' of his activities, namely the side-effects (positive or negative) of his operations on the rest of the economy. Important examples of externalities of investment projects which are of particular significance to LDCs are: the effect on employment and on the pattern of production; contribution to a balanced development of industries and regions and to an equitable income distribution through the choice of investment projects and technology; environmental considerations; and the effect on foreign exchange outlays and earnings when growth is constrained by balance of payments considerations.[18] These side-effects of investment, whether numerically measurable or not, have important long-term implications for the development of a country and should be given adequate weight in the allocation of resources, although they fall almost entirely outside the sphere of interest of individual businessmen.

It is obvious that if the aim of economic development is to maximise the economic welfare of the community, resource allocation should be based on social and not on private cost-benefit calculations. Fiscal,

18. Other important examples of externalities, such as 'learning by doing' and 'linkages', are discussed below under the heading of 'long-term dynamic considerations'.

monetary and other measures can, as shown in Chapter 5, be used to influence private investment decisions in such a way that they conform to social requirements; this is done by penalising investment activities which have negative side-effects and stimulating those with positive side-effects. Generally, the larger the gap between the private and social costs and benefits, the greater will be the need for government intervention in investment decisions. (See also pp. 174–5).

Bearing in mind the major types of externalities noted above, there are strong reasons to believe that the gap between private and social costs and benefits of most investment projects would generally be larger in developing than in industrial countries. One of the more important reasons for this is that in most developing countries the ratio of unemployment (open and disguised) to labour force is considerably higher than in industrial economies. The private cost of labour, which individual businessmen have to include in their computations, is the actual wage paid to workers, and this would generally have to cover the cost of subsistence even in the case of the least skilled workers. The social cost of the labour employed on any project, on the other hand, consists solely of the opportunity cost of the workers involved, that is, of the loss of production, if any, caused by the employment offered to the workers on the project.[19] This could be very close to zero in those cases where the locally recruited labour force used on a project was previously not productively employed.

One could argue that an important, if not the most important, factor in the development efforts of certain planned economies, such as China, has been their success in mobilising idle labour resources for productive purposes. Although the productivity of the labour force in the tasks assigned to it has been relatively low, it has nevertheless been well in excess of its opportunity cost. This justifies, for example, the use of idle agricultural labour during slack periods to build dams, roads, irrigation schemes, etc. by using even primitive techniques of shovels and buckets. Where the opportunity cost of labour is close to zero and labour accounts for the bulk of inputs, the gain in production will be equal to almost the entire value of the projects constructed.

4. *Long-term dynamic considerations*

In the preceding section a number of reasons were advanced to justify government intervention in the market mechanism on the

19. For a discussion of this topic see Amartya Sen, *Employment Technology and Development*, Chapter 12.

ground that investment decisions should conform to social rather than private cost-benefit considerations. Here we are concerned with the dynamic implications of investment decisions on development over time. It is argued that even an investment policy that may maximise social as distinct from private benefits in the short run may not necessarily be the best policy to follow from a long-run dynamic point of view, and that this provides another reason for government involvement in the economy. The first argument justifying intervention on this ground was advanced by the classical economists themselves, despite their staunch support for the doctrine of free trade. The other two, which are based on the concept of 'externalities', although not entirely unknown to certain unorthodox writers of the nineteenth century,[20] have largely gained ground as a result of work on development in the post-World War II period.

(a) *The infant industry argument*: This is one of the oldest arguments advanced to justify government interference with the free operation of market forces; it was fully recognised by J.S. Mill and certain other classical economists who were aware of the importance of economies of scale.[21] The basic idea was that a newly established industry, operating below the optimum scale of production, should be given a certain degree of protection against its larger and more mature foreign competitors, until it was able to expand and benefit from all the available economies of scale. The protection given to such infant industries could take the form of production subsidies, the erection of tariff barriers, or the imposition of import quotas.

The infant industry argument can be extended to justify protection of the entire industrial sector of the less developed countries. The industrial sector as a whole can be considered to be operating under conditions of increasing returns, in the sense that its productivity is likely to improve with expansion in the course of time. Apart from gains reaped through economies of scale with the growth in the size of individual plants, a number of other factors may account for this growth of productivity. The two most important are: 'learning by doing' and 'linkages'. The former is represented by the gradual emergence of a disciplined industrial labour force and by the

20. Among the nineteenth-century writers who rejected the doctrine of free trade, the two best known are Friedrich List in Germany and H.C. Carey in the United States; see Eric Roll, *A History of Economic Thought*, Faber and Faber, London, first edition (1938), pp. 225–8 and 300–1.

21. See, for example J.S. Mill, *Principles of Political Economy*, ed. W.J. Ashley, Longmans, Green and Co., London (1940), p. 922.

improvement in technical, managerial and organisational skills. The emergence of ancillary industries, linked to the original industries by providing inputs to them and by utilising their outputs, would also contribute to the growth of the overall efficiency of the industrial sector.

It is worth remembering that historically all major industrial countries of today, with the exception of the United Kingdom, resorted to deliberately protectionist policies in the early stages of their industrialisation during the nineteenth century; this is true of France and Germany, as it is of the United States. The United Kingdom, which was the first country to industrialise in the late eighteenth and early nineteenth centuries, enjoyed a comparative advantage in manufacturing and thus did not depend on a protectionist policy. Japan, which industrialised last, relied heavily on non-tariff (administrative) measures to restrict imports, as it does even now to some extent. Moreover, the relatively long distances separating it from Western Europe and North America in a period of high transport costs afforded its industries a natural protection against Western competition.

(b) *Provision of stability through diversification*: The second important dynamic consideration which may justify government intervention in the economy stems from the need to provide stability over time to the economy. The free operation of market forces may at times produce a heavy concentration of production in a small number of sectors. In the case of developing countries this produced in the past specialisation in the production of a small number of primary products in which they enjoyed a comparative cost advantage. Historically, this type of specialisation took place in most colonies of Africa and Asia and in many Latin American countries in the course of the nineteenth century. The natural resources of these countries were exploited with the help of foreign capital and skills and they were transformed into important suppliers of primary products – minerals and agricultural products – to industrial nations.

It is clear that, the less diversified the structure of production is, the more unstable the total value of output is likely to be in response to any change in market conditions. This simple principle is amply demonstrated in recent history. Developing countries, which have concentrated on the production of a few primary products, have periodically been subject to violent economic fluctuations often accompanied by social and political disruption. The most dramatic example of this type of instability is provided by the impact of the

Great Depression in the 1930s on the economies of the producers of primary products, when the real national income of some of them fell by about 30 per cent and the foreign exchange earnings by over 50 per cent in the course of one year.

A large number of other cases can be cited from the more recent history to illustrate the disruptive effects on the primary producing countries of even mild fluctuations in the level of activity of industrial countries (see pp. 215 and 226). The experiences of Sri Lanka, Colombia and Ghana, which specialise largely in the production and export of tea, coffee and cocoa, respectively, following the fall in the prices of these commodities in the course of the 1950s, provide only a few of many such examples. All three countries were compelled to impose severe import restrictions, to revise downwards their investment plans and thereby to depress the level of domestic activity because of an unexpected fall in the price of their major export commodities.[22]

It follows that, because of its contribution to stability of production and income, diversification of economic activity is a desirable objective *per se*. There should therefore be a trade-off between diversification, on the one hand, and efficiency in the allocation of resources as determined by consideration of comparative cost advantage, on the other. It also follows that the authorities must take an active part in determining the pattern of investment if they are to ensure that the objective of diversification, which falls outside the scope of market forces and private entrepreneurs, receives adequate weight in investment decisions. In the case of developing countries this means that the authorities should not only encourage the production of new primary products – agricultural and mineral – but, more important, also promote industrialisation which generally provides the widest scope for the diversification of economic activity.

(c) *Provision of economic autonomy through autarchy*: It is obvious that, other things being equal, the smaller is the ratio of foreign trade in the national product, the greater is the economic autonomy enjoyed by a country. In the extreme case of a closed economy, when a country is entirely self-sufficient and has no foreign trade, it will be completely free to follow any economic policy that it may desire. Thus while foreign trade provides a country with the opportunity of raising productivity through specialisation, it does have a distinct disadvan-

22. For a more detailed discussion of the experience of the three countries mentioned, see Éprime Eshag, *Quantification of Disruptive Effects of Export Shortfalls*, UNCTAD, document TD/B/C.3/AC.3/23 (11 October 1968).

tage in reducing its freedom of action in the pursuit of what may at any time be considered socially desirable economic policies. Therefore, other things being equal, policies of import substitution, which tend to reduce the share of trade in total production, should, in our view, be preferred to those of export promotion which yield an equal saving of foreign exchange.[23] Such considerations would of course be entirely ignored if investment decisions were left to the free operation of market forces.

Shadow pricing

The importance of 'externalities' is now recognised by many policy makers and economists. Some writers have therefore suggested the use of what has come to be known as the technique of 'shadow pricing' in the formulation of investment policy. Although there are substantial differences among writers both on the definition and on the method of application of this technique to project evaluation, it is generally agreed that input valuation should take explicit account of social opportunity costs, and that outputs should be valued in terms of their social worth instead of their market prices.[24] The purpose is to attain an optimum allocation of resources by equating 'social marginal costs' with 'social marginal revenue'. The two better known cost-benefit techniques advanced in recent years are those recommended by OECD and UNIDO.[25] The techniques of project evaluation can be used by the authorities in respect both of governments' own investment and of private sector operations. In the latter case information on social costs and benefits can help the authorities to decide on the extent of encouragement that should be given to various private industrial projects.

In principle, this development is to be welcomed since it draws attention to the importance to economic development of distinguish-

---

23. Not all economists, however, would agree with this proposition. For a discussion of this and other trade strategies for LDCs see Paul Streeten (ed.), *Trade Strategies for Development*, Macmillan (1973), especially Chapter 3. See also I. Little, T. Scitovsky and M. Scott, *Industry and Trade in Some Developing Countries*, OUP (1970), and Harry G. Johnson, *Essays in Monetary Economics*, second edition, George Allen and Unwin (1970), pp. 262–77.

24. For a discussion of the question raised by the use of shadow prices, see Amartya Sen, *Employment, Technology and Development*, Chapter 11.

25. See I.M.D. Little and J.M. Mirrlees, *Manual of Industrial Project Analysis in Developing Countries*, Vol. II, OECD, Paris (1968), and *Project Appraisal and Planning for Developing Countries*, Heinemann Educational Books, London (1974); UNIDO, *Evaluation of Industrial Projects*, United Nations, Sales No.: E.67.II.B.23, New York (1968); Partha Dasgupta and Amartya Sen, *Guidelines for Project Evaluation*, United Nations, Sales No.: E.72.II.B.11, New York (1972).

ing between the concepts of social and private costs and benefits and between static and dynamic considerations. One must, however, at the same time recognise that it is rarely, if ever, possible to give numerical values to all the social costs and benefits of investment projects; it is particularly difficult to quantify objectively the importance of the dynamic considerations mentioned above. This is only partly because of the lack of statistical data in many developing countries. A more important reason is that many of the 'externalities', such as environmental costs and benefits as well as those of balanced regional development, income distribution, diversification and autonomy, which are of particular importance in formulating a long-term development strategy, cannot be objectively quantified. Thus, while it is essential to take into account all these variables, whether numerically quantifiable or not, it is not very obvious how this should be done.

There appear to be two broad approaches to this question. The *first* would involve calculating social costs and benefits for those variables that can be quantified relatively reliably, and then adding all the other variables in the form of unquantified symbols, e.g. A, B, C, etc., to the final equation showing the net social benefit of an investment project. The weight attached to each unquantified variable in relation to the result of the quantified part of the final equation, which will generally be done informally, will inevitably depend on the arbitrary judgment of decision making bodies.

The *second* approach aims at deriving a numerical value for the net social benefit of projects under consideration and would, therefore, require the quantification of all variables. It is important to note that this approach entails the use of value judgment more implicitly, since the numerical values imputed to those variables for which no reliable data are available, or are objectively unquantifiable, will inevitably involve implicit judgments in addition to the explicit ones. This will give the project evaluators more scope for bringing in, consciously or unconsciously, their own personal views, beliefs and judgments, and they may or may not draw attention to this fact in the presentation of their final estimates.[26]

26. Under both approaches, one could assign a range of numerical values, instead of a single value, to some of the variables which cannot be accurately quantified because of lack of information or for the other reasons mentioned. This will involve specifying maximum and minimum values for such variables and comparing the net social benefits of different projects under (i) the most and (ii) the least favourable assumptions. This procedure could, of course, help to resolve some, but not all, decision problems. For a detailed explanation, see Partha Dasgupta and Amartya Sen, *op. cit.*, especially Chapter 12; and Amartya Sen, *Employment, Technology and Development*, pp. 112–14.

There appear to be a number of reasons for preferring the first approach to the second. *First*, it has the merit of greater simplicity and lower costs in terms of its demand on the services of statisticians who are generally in short supply in developing countries. *Secondly*, it expressly acknowledges the use of value judgment in project selection and hence avoids the temptation on the part of project evaluators of claiming a 'scientific' or 'objective' basis for the estimates of social costs and benefits; the users of the second approach are not so free of this temptation. *Thirdly*, the first approach provides the authorities with greater flexibility in the process of project selection, since the relative weights attached to unquantified variables can be altered more freely in response to any change in circumstances if no specific numerical values are imputed to them. In other words, the authorities are less likely to be unduly mesmerised by the 'magic of numbers' created by the process of quantifying all variables.

Fourthly, and probably the most important single advantage of the first approach is that it can take into explicit consideration certain important variables which do not lend themselves to easy quantification. Under the second approach there is a strong temptation to confine the cost-benefit calculations to those variables that are objectively and readily quantifiable and to ignore those which are not, although some of the latter may have a considerably greater significance for the development of a country. One example of this is provided by the OECD *Manual* on social cost-benefit analysis in which the authors justify the omission of most variables concerned with external economies on the alleged ground that they are not very important or are not quantifiable.[27] This attitude is in particular clearly revealed in the discussion of the external economies resulting from the transmission of technology and know-how from one project or industry to the rest of the economy. The *Manual* says: 'Furthermore, if this consideration is to be worth taking into account, there has to be *both* (a) a presumption that this kind of external economy will differ significantly from project to project, or industry to industry, and (b) some way of quantifying the effect.'[28] In other words, it is proposed to ignore such considerations if no way of 'quantifying the effect' can be found.

It is worth noting in this connection that there is a tendency on the part of some economists to lay undue stress on the importance of the knowledge of economics and particularly on quantitative techniques of analysis, including econometrics, in the formulation of economic

---

27. See Little and Mirrlees, *Manual*, Chapter xvi.
28. *Ibid.*, pp. 210–11; emphasis added.

policies. This is, alas, a delusion of self-importance not dissimilar to that of the proverbial currier who, on being consulted as to the best way to fortify a town in danger of a siege, said: 'If you have a mind to have the town well fortified and secure, take my word, there is nothing like *leather*.'[29] In fact the amount of technical economic knowledge required to solve most of the important economic problems in industrial and developing countries is relatively little. The fact that in industrial countries, for example, such problems as unemployment, inflation and inequities in income distribution remain unresolved, is due not to a lack of technical knowledge of economics but to the institutional framework and the social and political forces at work which largely shape the policies and actions of governments (see pp. 50–3 and 239). Similarly, among LDCs, many countries have, as shown in Chapters 3 and 5, a pattern of resource allocation which has a minimal effect in promoting development and caters largely to the requirements of the richer classes. The real explanation for this is to be found in the order of priorities favoured by the ruling classes, which generally differs from that which is dictated by developmental needs. The misallocation of resources is often so glaring that it must be obvious even to the average man in the street that it could not have been caused by simple technical incompetence on the part of the planners or by the absence of refined techniques of project appraisal.

THE KEY ROLE OF SOCIO-POLITICAL FACTORS IN DEVELOPMENT

It is important to draw the attention of readers at this stage to the fact that the foregoing account of development strategy, and indeed a large part of what follows in the book, is in one sense hypothetical. It is based on the assumption that policy makers in LDCs are genuinely and sincerely committed to promoting economic development, as under-stood by us (see pp. 1–8 above). In other words, the approach followed in the book is to set out what the governments of developing countries *should do*, in terms of their development strategy and fiscal and monetary policies, *if* promotion of economic development has a high priority in their policies. This is done, realising fully that only in a handful of countries has the pursuit of such a policy constituted the primary objective of governments. The declared intentions of most

29. See Daniel Fenning, *The Universal Spelling-Book*, London (1792), p. 36 and *Oxford English Dictionary* (1903) Vol. vi, Part 1, p. 161. I am grateful to Dr John Sykes of Oxford University Press for this reference.

governments to promote development have often not been reflected in their actions and policy measures. This, in our view, is largely responsible for a relatively slow and disappointing rate of growth of production in relation to the available potential and for the 'lop-sided' pattern of growth observed in many countries.

The explanation for the observed divergence between the declared aims and the practices of most developing countries is not hard to find. Declarations of intention are readily made, usually for public relations purposes at home and abroad, but the policies followed are determined by a completely different set of factors. As noted earlier in this chapter (p. 2) human societies do not consist of a homogeneous mass of people with harmonious interests managed by an elected committee along the lines of a kibbutz. In each country there are a number of economic classes and income groups often with diverging and at times with conflicting interests, exercising different degrees of active or passive influence on the government. The ruling groups which emerge in these socio-political conditions cannot be expected to act 'neutrally' in the interests of the entire community. Their conception of the community's welfare, and hence their order of priorities, will inevitably be coloured by the moral philosophy of the classes which they represent. Moreover, it is natural that a large proportion of economic and political advisers who serve the ruling groups should be drawn from among those who hold sympathetic or adequately pliable views. Subject to any constraints imposed on their actions by the pressure and threats of other groups in the community, governments are bound, by and large, to act in a way which suits the interests and satisfies the aspirations of the classes and groups which they represent and on whose support they depend for their political survival.

Quality of the administration

A common characteristic of developing countries is their relatively weak administrative machinery as compared with that of most industrial countries. It is reflected in the lower degrees of efficiency and of integrity of the civil service and of politicians. This, we believe, has been a major obstacle to development because the degree of technical competence and of integrity of the civil service is an important factor in determining the limits of useful governmental intervention, and hence of the active role that the authorities can assume in promoting development. Where the authorities exceed these limits, the effect is to hinder rather than to advance development. What this implies is that *in practice* few developing countries are in a position properly to utilise all the policy instruments discussed in the book which can *in theory* be employed to assist development.

One reason for the relative weakness in the administrative machinery in LDCs is that they suffer from a lack of know-how in management and organisational skills as compared with developed countries, a fact explained by lower degrees of education, training and experience. This factor is likely to be of great importance in the 'least-developed' countries of Africa and Asia which have not until recently had adequate educational and training programmes.[30] But it can be of very little significance in the majority of developing countries which have enjoyed a reasonable educational system for two or more decades and which manifestly do not lack the supply of personnel with adequate managerial skills.

A considerably more important factor in determining the efficiency and integrity of the administrative machinery in most countries is, in our view, the nature, or character, of their governments. This in turn depends largely on the political and social conditions prevailing in the country and on its economic structure. There is a closely-knit organic relationship between the economic and social framework of a country, the character of its successive governments over a period, and the quality of its civil service. For example, where the distribution of property and income is very uneven, as is the case in many developing countries, government policies are, as noted above, likely to be biased in favour of the interests of the richer classes of the community. The higher echelons of the civil service, which are responsible for the formulation, interpretation and execution of policy measures, will tend to be drawn largely from the richer classes themselves or from among other professionals prepared to collaborate with these classes.

One effect of this pattern of the recruitment of personnel is to reduce the efficiency of the administrative machinery below its maximum potential, since technical qualifications and merit would play a relatively small part in appointments. Another and more invidious implication of such a socio-economic structure is its vulnerability to corruption. The reason for this is that in some cases governments and their technocratic policy advisers will simply refrain from adopting certain measures which are essential for development purposes but which are prejudicial to their own interests. In other cases, they may *formally* adopt such measures, but, given the inefficiency and corruption of the civil service, are not able to implement them. It can in a

---

30. For a description of 'least-developed' countries, see pp. 164–5.

sense be argued that, in these countries, inefficiency and corruption are tolerated by the authorities because in practice they tend to serve their interests.

All this, as we shall see, is particularly true of the fiscal policies of many developing countries. In some of them, where either there is no strong pressure for development policies because of the weakness of public opinion, or because the governments are able to ignore such pressures owing to their autocratic powers, fiscal measures are simply inadequate for the exploitation of the maximum development potential. In many other countries the authorities are politically compelled *formally* to introduce important fiscal measures, such as a very progressive taxation system, as well as plans for the promotion of essential investment, but *in practice* fail to implement such measures because of the weakness of the administrative machinery.

The emphasis laid on socio-political obstacles to development should not, however, be allowed to obscure the importance of many other serious obstacles to development. It would be rather naive to assume that a change in institutional framework of a country, which brings to power a government genuinely committed to economic development, will by itself resolve most of its development problems. All developing countries, irrespective of the character of their governments, have to face and overcome numerous obstacles that retard their pace of development. Some of these obstacles ensue from the present international economic order which developing countries can do little to change. They include, as we shall see, adverse movements in the terms of trade, fluctuations in export prices, trade restrictions on the exports of LDCs and certain negative aspects of the operations of transnational, or multinational, corporations.[31] There are, in addition, many other development problems which are endogenous in nature but which cannot be rapidly resolved. These include, training of labour force in technical, organisational and administrative skills; creation of new institutions, e.g. co-operative organisations, which can function reasonably efficiently; provision of infrastructure, and regulation of the population growth. It is clear that, no matter how resolute and determined governments may be in promoting economic development, it will take a relatively long time to deal with such problems.

Economic development is thus a long uphill struggle which, as we

---

31. The attention of the industrial countries has recently been drawn to these problems by an independent international commission under the chairmanship of Willy Brandt; see *North-South: A Programme for Survival*, Pan Books, London and Sydney (1980), especially Chapters 11–12.

shall see, is not made any easier by the attitudes of industrial countries. But while fully recognising this fact, we nevertheless believe that in most LDCs the policies pursued by governments themselves are to a large extent responsible for their slow rate of development, as indicated by their growth of production and the pattern of investment. In other words, we maintain that the failure of the authorities to give the development objective the high priority it deserves, has played an important part in their low rate of development in relation to their potential. The data on fiscal and monetary policies of developing countries presented in the following chapters, will, it is believed, amply support this thesis. Particularly important are the data on fiscal policies, since, in our view, of the various indicators of a government's commitment to economic development, fiscal performance, as reflected in taxation and expenditure policies, ranks highest.

2

THE SCOPE AND ROLE OF FISCAL AND MONETARY POLICIES

Fiscal policy consists of measures related to central and local government revenue and expenditure. Monetary policy consists of the measures which affect the supply of money and credit and the rate of interest. Changes in the supply of money and in the rate of interest are generally closely interrelated in the sense that, other things being equal, an increase in the supply of money and credit is likely to produce a fall in the rate of interest, and vice versa. A broader definition of monetary policy adopted here includes also measures taken to change the exchange rate.

An important reason for linking fiscal to monetary measures in the analysis of government policies is that the former have a direct bearing on the supply of money and/or on the market rates of interest. A budget deficit, for example, will have the effect of increasing the supply of money unless the entire deficit is financed by borrowing from the private sector in which case market rates of interest will tend to rise. This explains why monetary policies aimed at restricting the growth in the supply of money almost invariably entail deflationary fiscal measures directed at restricting budget deficit by curbing Government outlays and/or increasing tax revenue (see pp. 260–1).

This chapter is devoted to the examination of the role that can be played by fiscal and monetary instruments in the management of demand and in financing economic development. In the *first part* of the chapter we summarise the Keynesian model of income determination which, in our view, provides a suitable framework for the analysis of the role of these instruments in the management of demand and in the preparation of stabilisation policies designed to deal with inflation and external imbalances. The Keynesian approach to these issues points to policies which differ significantly from those derived through the quantity theory of money in the analysis made by the members of the Chicago school – known also as 'monetarists', or 'neo-monetarists'.

Bearing in mind the growth in the influence of the monetarists among policy makers in recent years, it has been thought useful to scrutinise their basic propositions on price inflation and on movements in production and employment in an appendix (2A); the Keynesian and monetarist approaches to external imbalances are examined in Chapter 6 (see pp. 227–36 and 243–52).

In the *second part* of the chapter we present Kalecki's model of financing investment in a mixed economy. This model provides a useful framework for the analysis of the role of fiscal and monetary instruments in promoting economic development by indicating the use that can be made of them to increase the *volume* and to influence the *pattern* of investment.

BACKGROUND TO THE MODERN APPROACH

Historically, the role assigned to fiscal and monetary policies in different periods has varied with the prevailing views on the proper function of governments in the management of the economy. Under the *laissez-faire* philosophy, which dominated economic thinking in the nineteenth and early twentieth centuries, the role of the government was largely confined to the provision of suitable conditions for the free operation of market forces; in particular, this entailed maintaining law and order, and ensuring the enforcement of business contracts. The fiscal duties of the authorities were, therefore, limited to providing adequate tax revenue to cover the costs of maintaining an efficient civil administration (including certain collective economic and social services) and of the defence of the realm.[1] The government was expected to refrain from deficit financing, which was believed to contribute to price inflation by increasing the supply of money.

Nor did the orthodox economists of the *laissez-faire* era assign any important role to the supply of money and to monetary policies in the management of the economy. Their basic postulate was that monetary measures could not have a durable and lasting impact on production and on the rate of interest, which, in their view, were determined by 'real' factors, namely the quantity and quality of land, labour and capital. It was thought that, since money is not capital, but only 'command over capital', changes in its quantity do not affect the supply of 'real' resources available for investment which determines what was variously designated as the 'real', 'natural', 'normal', or 'equilibrium' rate of interest. Changes in the supply of money affect

1. For more details, see Ursula K. Hicks, *Public Finance*, second edition, CUP (1955), pp. 14–27.

only the 'market' rate of interest and this may, for a time, fall below or rise above the 'natural' rate. A divergence between the two rates, however, results in an increase or decrease in the volume of credit and in a rise or fall of prices, respectively, through the operation of the quantity theory of money; such price movements will continue until the 'market' rate of interest is brought into line with the 'natural' rate.[2]

The function of money was to facilitate business transactions, or, as Hume put it, money is 'the oil which renders the motion of the wheels more smooth and easy'.[3] The primary duty of the authorities was, therefore, to provide the country with a convenient and easily identifiable currency and to ensure the stability of the exchanges by regulating the supply of money and the rate of interest in accordance with 'the rules of the game' applicable to the gold standard.[4]

These were broadly the views which dominated economic thinking in England from Adam Smith to Marshall. Throughout this period monetary theory and policy remained almost entirely divorced from the general body of economic analysis, which was conducted in 'real', i.e. non-monetary, terms, while the quantity theory of money was the chief instrument of analysis of changes in the price level. As shown below, it was not until the Keynesian revolution of the mid-1930s when the *General Theory*[5] was published that monetary and fiscal theories could be integrated within the general corpus of economic theory. This, as we shall see, provided a foundation for a new approach to the role and scope of monetary and fiscal policies in the management of the economy, including development policies.

There has been a significant extension in the scope of fiscal and monetary policies in the course of the last fifty years largely because of a growing disillusionment with *laissez-faire* philosophy, particularly with the market mechanism as a means of promoting maximum utilisation of productive resources and of ensuring an equitable distribution of income. That the distribution of income under the market mechanism

2. For detailed references to the writings of classical and neo-classical economists, see Éprime Eshag, *From Marshall to Keynes, An Essay on the Monetary Theory of the Cambridge School*, Basil Blackwell (1963), pp. 53–8.

3. See the essay 'Of Money', in David Hume, *Writings on Economics*, ed. Eugene Rotwein, Edinburgh (1955). See also J.S. Mill, *Principles of Political Economy*, ed. W.J. Ashley, Longmans, Green and Co. London (1940), Book III, Chapter VII; and Eshag, *From Marshall to Keynes*, p. 91.

4. The foregoing description of the position of the pre-Keynesian economists is no more than a very rough sketch of economic thinking in England during the nineteenth and early twentieth centuries. The reader interested in more detailed and precise information on this subject should refer to Eshag, *From Marshall to Keynes*, Chapters 3 and 4, especially pp. 53–9 and 73–4.

5. J.M. Keynes, *The General Theory of Employment, Interest and Money*, Macmillan (1936).

was not always morally justifiable was recognised by many classical economists and utilitarians from the early days of the nineteenth century; in particular they did not approve of the share of income accruing to the landlord class. But, as shown below, it was not until the Great Depression of the 1930s that it became apparent, at least to some economists and governments, that the free operation of market forces could also not ensure the full utilisation of productive resources; this clearly called for governmental intervention in the economy. Even more profound in recent years has been the disillusionment with the ability of market forces to resolve the basic economic problems facing less developed countries. Studies conducted by the United Nations and by leading development economists, notably Myrdal, Kalecki and Prebisch since the Second World War, all point to the need for active government participation in the process of economic development for the reasons explained earlier (pp. 11–20).

The instruments of intervention used by the authorities to deal with the above problems vary from country to country although almost invariably they include both general and selective fiscal and monetary measures. The scope assigned to these measures by most of the modern economists can be said to cover the following three broad areas:

1. Redistribution of income,
2. Regulation of the level of economic activity, or management of aggregate effective demand, and
3. Promotion of growth, including economic development in less developed countries.

We shall not be directly concerned in this book with the *first* topic since little use is made of fiscal and monetary measures by LDCs to redistribute income. It should, nevertheless, be noted that fiscal instruments have come to provide a convenient means for the redistribution of income among different sections of the community. In practice this is usually done by combining a progressive taxation system, under which tax rates vary directly with the level of income, with a system of transfer payments and subsidies. Transfer payments, which are confined almost exclusively to industrial countries, are generally made to lower-income groups in such forms as unemployment and sickness benefits, old age pensions and other assistance schemes. Subsidies are used in both industrialised and developing countries to bring down prices of goods and services of mass consumption below their costs. These often include staple foods and some of the essential services provided by public enterprises and government departments, such as transport, health and education.

This book is concerned primarily with the *third* area covered by fiscal and monetary policies, which is introduced in the last section of the present chapter and developed in the succeeding three chapters. The *second* area, namely the management of aggregate effective demand, although less significant for developing countries, is nevertheless not entirely irrelevant to them and is also examined here. Although the *crucial* problem facing LDCs is, as explained earlier (pp. 3–5), that of a shortage of productive capacity, some of these countries are at times unable to utilise even their inadequate capital equipment to the full because of a deficiency in effective demand. Generally, the significance of this problem for LDCs varies with the relative weight of the modern industrial and commercial sector in the economy.

As shown in Chapter 6, which is devoted to an examination of inflation and balance of payments difficulties in developing economies, divergent policies, some of which result in the underutilisation of productive capacity, are in practice prescribed for resolving these problems. Since Keynesian and monetarist theories of income and price determination play an important part in the formulation of the various policies, the following section on the management of demand, together with Appendix 2A, should be useful to readers not fully familiar with these theories. Moreover, a knowledge of the basic propositions embodied in the theory of income determination is useful, even if not indispensable, for a proper understanding of the analysis of the role of fiscal and monetary policies in promoting economic development.

THE MANAGEMENT OF DEMAND AND PRODUCTION

The modern approach to the use of fiscal and monetary instruments for the regulation of economic activity in industrial countries can roughly be traced back to the Great Depression of the 1930s when the free enterprise economies of the world, operating under the market mechanism, were plunged into a deep economic depression. The decline in the level of production and employment in industrial economies led to a fall in demand for the products of primary exporting countries and to a steep drop in their export prices and incomes. The depression dealt a severe blow to the faith of governments in *laissez-faire* philosophy. Many primary exporting countries were forced to abandon the policy of free trade and to encourage industrialisation through import substitution behind tariff walls and through other protectionist measures. A number of governments in industrial countries were also gradually persuaded to abandon hope in the remedial influence of the market mechanism and to take an active part in tackling the problem of unemployment. An important example of the latter was the New Deal legislation introduced in the United States after Roosevelt's election to the Presidency in 1932.

The economic depression, which persisted with varying degrees of severity from 1930 until the eve of the Second World War in 1939, could not be easily explained in terms of the orthodox neo-classical doctrine of the time. This doctrine had stipulated that there is a natural tendency for an economy to move towards *equilibrium* under the free play of market forces; 'equilibrium' being a position in which all factors of production are fully employed at a price equal to their marginal product. To put it differently, the doctrine maintained that the free play of market forces had a natural tendency to eliminate 'involuntary' unemployment of the factors of production. The mass unemployment and widespread excess capacities prevailing in the industrial world had, therefore, to be explained in terms of 'frictions' that impeded the working of the market mechanism. Particular emphasis was laid on the downward rigidity of wages, due to the behaviour of trade unions, as a cause of mass unemployment.[6] More specifically, it was thought that the level of employment in the economy was determined by the demand and supply schedules of labour at different rates of wages and that, but for the rigidity of wages, unemployment would be eliminated by an appropriate downward shift in the supply schedule.

Not all economists were, however, satisfied with the orthodox analysis and explanation of the depression. In Sweden, Wicksell's pupils were groping for a new approach to the question of employment but had not as yet succeeded in developing a comprehensive theory by the time Kalecki and Keynes produced their theories. In England Keynes had, as early as 1929, argued against the 'orthodox Treasury dogma' which stipulated that it was not possible to create 'additional employment' by 'State borrowing and State expenditure'.[7] He had, however, like President Roosevelt, reached this conclusion largely through intuition and common sense rather than on the basis of a comprehensive theory of employment. 'It was not till the summer of 1934', to quote Joan Robinson, 'that Keynes succeeded in getting his theory of money, his theory of wages and Kahn's multiplier into a coherent system';[8] this system was presented in his famous book, *The*

6. There is no clear distinction between 'money' and 'real' wage rates in neo-classical writings, it being implicitly assumed that changes in money wages result in similar changes in real wages as long as the supply of money is properly regulated.
7. See J.M. Keynes, *Essays in Persuasion*, Macmillan (1933), p. 121.
8. See 'Introduction' in M. Kalecki, *Studies in the Theory of Business Cycles, 1933–1939*, Basil Blackwell, Oxford (1966), p. viii.

General Theory of Employment, Interest and Money, published in January 1936.

Before Keynes and his pupils had succeeded in escaping fully from the orthodox neo-classical doctrine and producing their new theory of employment, Michal Kalecki, starting from Marx's scheme of expanded reproduction, had independently developed an almost identical theory in Poland; this was published in Polish during 1933 in an article entitled 'Outline of a Theory of the Business Cycle'.[9] The substance of his theory was later presented in a paper to the Econometric Society in October 1933, published in *Econometrica*, No. 3, 1935. According to Joan Robinson this theory 'contains the basic elements of the theory of savings, investment and employment' and 'in several respects, Kalecki's version is more robust than Keynes''.[10] Historically, it may be worth noting that these papers establish not only Kalecki's independent discovery of what is generally known as 'Keynesian theory' but also his publication priority over Keynes in both Polish and English.[11]

The new approach to the theory of employment followed by Kalecki and Keynes can be said to start from the simple proposition that employment varies directly with production, and production depends on the aggregate effective demand, or gross national expenditure.[12] In industrial economies, which have adequate productive capacity in capital equipment to employ the entire labour force, production and employment will grow in line with the increase in gross national expenditure at constant prices until the labour force is fully employed.[13] Attempts to raise expenditure beyond this point will result in price inflation rather than in growth of production. If gross national expenditure falls short of the level required to employ the entire labour force, part of the labour force will be 'involuntarily' unemployed; such unemployment will persist as long as this expenditure remains unchanged. Neither author could discern any forces inherent in the market mechanism that could be relied on to push the economy to full employment equilibrium.

It is important to emphasise at this stage that the fundamental

---

9. See Michal Kalecki, *Selected Essays on the Dynamics of the Capitalist Economy, 1933–70*, CUP (1971), Essay 1.
10. See Joan Robinson 'Michal Kalecki on the Economics of Capitalism', *BOUIES*, February 1977, pp. 9–10.
11. For a more detailed discussion see Joan Robinson's 'Introduction' in Kalecki, *Studies in the Theory of Business Cycles, op. cit.*, and *BOUIES*, February 1977, *op. cit.*
12. For an explanation of the precise meaning of 'effective demand' in terms of 'expenditure' see pp. 228 below.
13. To simplify the discussion we abstract from what has come to be known as 'structural unemployment', described earlier (p. 5).

difference between the neo-classical and Keynesian theories of employment is not on the issue of the relationship of marginal product of labour to real wages, but on the whole nature of the aggregate demand schedule for labour. According to Keynesian theory, whatever role may be assigned to the schedules of diminishing marginal productivity of labour facing individual firms in determining their demand for labour, the summation of these schedules will not produce a schedule which represents total demand for labour for the economy as a whole. To put it differently, even if one were to assume that real wage rates were equal, or closely related, to marginal product of labour for every firm, it would be the aggregate effective demand which, by determining the level of production and employment of various firms, would determine what the marginal product of labour and hence the real wage for each one of them should be, and not the other way round as was postulated by neo-classical economists.[14] Because of this a fall in real wages in the economy would lead to a fall in effective demand and a fall, rather than a rise, in production and employment.[15] The neo-classical assumption that the micro-theory of demand of a firm for labour could be applied at a macro-level to the economy as a whole in effect suffers from what is known as the 'fallacy of composition', which consists in assuming that what is true of things severally is true of them 'taken together'.[16]

14. This is, of course, the *crucial* difference between the Keynesian and neo-classical theories of employment. It is in a way similar to the difference between the two schools in 'the chain of causality' attributed by them to the interaction between the rate of interest and marginal product, or efficiency, of capital. In the Keynesian model, it is the rate of interest which, by determining the level of investment, also determines the marginal efficiency of capital, and not the other way round (see Keynes, *General Theory*, Chapter 14, especially p. 183).

Attempts at 'synthesising', or 'reconciling', Keynesian with neo-classical theories of employment and interest have tended to confuse the issue by largely ignoring this crucial issue of 'the chain of causality'. See, for example, J.R. Hicks, 'Keynes and the Classics', *Econometrica*, 1937; and Don Patinkin, *Money, Interest and Prices*, Harper and Row, Publishers Inc. (1965). For further references, see M.J.C. Surrey (ed.), *Macroeconomic Themes*, OUP (1976), Chapters 1 and 9.

15. For a graphical illustration of this proposition, see Robinson, *BOUIES*, February, 1977, pp. 13–14.

16. The same fallacy can be discerned in the neo-classical theory of savings, which maintains that an increase in thriftiness on the part of the community as a whole will increase the volume of national savings, just as it does for single individuals.

There is some evidence to suggest that Marshall himself had some doubts about the legitimacy of extending his marginalist analysis of the behaviour of a firm to the economy as a whole. After illustrating the tendency of marginal product of capital and of labour to equal the rate of interest and wage rate, respectively, for individual firms, he adds that such illustrations 'cannot be made into a theory of interest, any more than into a theory of wages, without reasoning in a circle'. See Alfred Marshall, *Principles of Economics*, Macmillan, eighth edition (1920), p. 519.

Keynesian model of income determination

It will be helpful for the subsequent discussion to illustrate here the above model of income determination, henceforth referred to as the 'Keynesian model', in a more precise algebraic form. Gross national expenditure consists of the sum total of consumer and public authorities' current expenditure on goods and services, or private and public consumption, *plus* gross domestic private and public investment, *plus* exports of goods and services and 'factor' (or 'property') income received from abroad and *minus* imports of goods and services and factor income paid abroad. Thus,

$$Y = C_p + C_g + I_p + I_g + X - M \tag{1}$$

where Y stands for gross national expenditure, C_p for private consumption, C_g for public consumption, I_p for gross domestic private investment, I_g for gross domestic public investment, X for export of goods and services and factor income received from abroad, and M for import of goods and services and factor income paid abroad. (For brevity X and M are henceforth usually referred to simply as 'exports' and 'imports', respectively).

The various components of expenditure generate identical streams of private and public incomes, the sum total of which constitutes gross national income and must equal gross national expenditure. Gross national income is in turn partly consumed by the private and public sectors and the remainder is saved.

$$Y = C + S \tag{2}$$

$$C = C_p + C_g \tag{3}$$

$$S = S_p + S_g \tag{4}$$

where C stands for total consumption, i.e. the sum of private and public consumption, S for gross national savings, S_p for gross private savings and S_g for gross public savings. For the sake of brevity, the terms 'income', 'savings' and 'investment' are henceforth used to indicate 'gross income', 'gross savings' and 'gross investment', respectively.

If we substitute in equation (2) for C and S from equations (3) and (4) and compare the result with equation (1), we get

$$C_p + C_g + S_p + S_g = C_p + C_g + I_p + I_g + X - M$$

or

$$S_p = -S_g + I_p + I_g + X - M \tag{5}$$

But public savings (S_g) is equal to 'disposable public revenue', defined as public revenue (other than borrowing) from taxation and other sources *less* transfer payments, minus public consumption, so that

$$S_g = T - C_g \tag{6}$$

where T stands for disposable public revenue.

Substituting for S_g in equation (5) from equation (6) we get

$$S_p = (C_g - T) + (I_p + I_g) + (X - M) \tag{7}$$

It is clear that in equation (7) the term $(C_g - T)$, in the absence of capital transfers, represents budget balance on current account; $(I_p + I_g)$ is total domestic investment; and ignoring foreign transfer payments, $(X - M)$ is external balance on current account. The equation can also be presented in the form

$$S_p = (G - T) + I_p + (X - M) \tag{7a}$$

where G stands for total government expenditure and is equal to $C_g + I_g$; the term $(G - T)$ therefore is overall budget balance on current and capital accounts combined.

Combining equations (4), (6) and (7), we can also write,

$$S = I_d + (X - M) \tag{8}$$

where I_d is gross domestic investment $(I_p + I_g)$. For a closed economy, where X and M are zero, we get

$$S = I_d \tag{9}$$

In equation (7) S_p, T and M are all determined predominantly by national income (Y). To simplify the discussion, let us assume that S_p, T and M are linear functions of Y,[17] so that

$$S_p = a_1 + s_p Y \tag{10}$$

$$T = a_2 + tY \tag{11}$$

$$M = a_3 + mY \tag{12}$$

where a_1, a_2 and a_3 are constants; m is the marginal propensity to import; s_p the marginal propensity to save by the private sector, and t the marginal rate of growth of disposable public revenue which will generally approximate closely to the marginal rate of taxation.

17. Strictly, private savings should be related to private disposable income rather than to Y, but this will merely complicate the algebra of the multiplier without adding much to the arguments presented here.

Substituting in equation (7) for S_p from equation (10) we get

$$Y = \frac{(C_g - T) + (I_p + I_g) + (X - M) - a_1}{s_p} \tag{13}$$

This form of presenting the equation of income is useful for analysing separately the impact on national income of changes in private and public investment outlays and in the balances on current budget and on current external accounts. But where the overall budget balance on the combined current and capital accounts is under consideration, the equation can be written in the form

$$Y = \frac{(G - T) + I_p + (X - M) - a_1}{s_p} \tag{13a}$$

It is clear from the above two equations that a change in any of the variables appearing in the numerator will generate a change in national income which is $1/s_p$ larger; $1/s_p$ is therefore designated 'the multiplier'. The three terms $(G - T)$, I_p and $(X - M)$ may for convenience be designated as 'net injections', or as Kalecki preferred to call them 'net non-consumption payments', since the income derived from these items does not have as a counterpart currently produced supplies of consumer goods.[18] They are designated 'net' because government expenditure and exports are taken net of government revenue and of imports, respectively.

Another, and more commonly used, form of presenting the 'multiplier equation' is to show the relationship between national income and the exogenous variables, or 'gross injections', represented by public expenditure, investment and exports. To do this we substitute in equation (7) for S_p, T and M from equations (10), (11) and (12) and obtain

$$Y = \frac{C_g + I_p + I_g + X - a_1 - a_2 - a_3}{s_p + t + m} \tag{14}$$

or

$$Y = \frac{G + I_p + X - a_1 - a_2 - a_3}{s_p + t + m} \tag{14a}$$

This shows that changes in Y produced by a given change in any exogenous variable will be $1/(s_p + t + m)$ times larger; here the expression $1/(s_p + t + m)$ represents 'the multiplier'.

It is worth pointing out at this stage some of the implications of the

18. See *Inflationary and Deflationary Tendencies 1946–1948*, United Nations, Sales No.: 1949.II.A.1, p. 6.

Keynesian model, in particular of equation (7a), which have a special bearing on the later discussion. *First*, the three items on the right-hand side of equation (7a), when positive, represent three sources of demand for private savings. In other words, private savings are required to finance the budget deficit $(G - T)$, private domestic investment (I_p) and the balance on current balance of payment account, or foreign investment $(X - M)$. A surplus on the budget balance (when $G - T < 0$) finances domestic investment and the external deficit by an equivalent amount. A deficit on external account (when $X - M < 0$), indicates that an equivalent amount of the budget deficit and domestic investment is financed by foreign borrowing and/or by a reduction in foreign assets, and that the need to generate private savings for the purpose is correspondingly reduced.

Secondly, a given increase in the sum total of the three 'net injections' in equation (7a) must generate an equivalent growth in private savings; a decrease must have the opposite effect. The movements in private savings are of course the consequence of parallel movements in national income produced by changes in these injections. A growth in national income so generated may result from an increase in production of goods and services and/or from a rise in the general price level, depending on the elasticities of supply in the economy.

To take first the two extreme cases: if there are, as often happens in industrial countries, widespread unutilised productive capacities, in the form of unemployed labour and spare equipment, the increase in injections will be accompanied by a growth of production and of real national income without inducing a noticeable rise in prices. At the other extreme, if the productive capacity is almost fully utilised and the elasticity of supply of goods and services is close to zero, the increase in the injections will lead to a rise in the general price level which will raise the market value of the national product and nominal national income adding little to the volume of production and real national income.[19] This category of price rises, which may be called *aggregate demand inflation*, has rarely been observed in normal peacetime conditions. It is largely confined to war and immediate post-war periods when the supply of consumer goods is severely restricted and cannot meet the growing demand generated primarily by budget deficits $(G - T)$ due largely to military outlay.

In practice, it is more usual to have situations in which some sectors of the economy are operating at full capacity while other sectors have

19. As explained earlier, in LDCs the limit to productive capacity is set by the shortage of capital equipment and not labour, as is generally the case in developed economies (see p. 5).

idle productive capacities. In such cases an increase in aggregate demand will result partly in a rise in prices and partly in a growth of production. This type of price rise, caused by localised demand pressures, may be called *sectoral demand inflation*. As explained later, because of their less diversified structure of production, developing countries tend to experience sectoral demand pressures at a relatively low level of economic activity in relation to their productive capacity (pp. 221–2).

Thirdly, a rise in prices caused by the pressures of demand against productive capacities is likely to increase the share of profits and to reduce the share of wages in national income. Because a higher proportion of profits than wages is saved, total private savings will increase. The additional savings generated as a result of the re-distribution of national income in favour of profits are often designated 'forced', as opposed to 'voluntary' savings. This is because wage earners are 'forced' to reduce their consumption owing to a fall in real wage rates caused by the price rise. As shown below, in developing countries this type of redistribution of income often results also from a failure of the supply of wage-goods, notably food, to grow in line with the rise of effective demand.

Fourthly, there is a fundamental difference in the policy implications of equation (7a) for dealing with the *crucial* problems of industrial and developing countries mentioned earlier. The *crucial* problem of industrial countries is to ensure that the sum total of the volume of investment and the other injections specified in the equation, is high enough to absorb the full employment level of savings in order to avoid unemployment. In developing countries, on the other hand, the volume of these injections tends to be too high in relation to the productive potential and the question of taking deliberate measures to stimulate them does not usually arise. For these countries, as we shall presently see, investment is constrained by the availability of 'voluntary' savings (see pp. 55–9 below). Their *crucial* problem is to ensure that an adequate level of investment from a development point of view can be undertaken without causing inflation, or, to put it differently, that the equality of savings with injections is not brought about through 'forced' savings associated with inflation and a redistribution of income from low- to high-income groups.

Another way of illustrating the difference between the positions of less developed and industrial countries, is to look at the 'short-term' role that investment plays in them. For developed countries the key role of investment in the short run is to generate effective demand in order to reduce the waste in production due to unemployment and idle equipment.[20] For this reason it is of secondary importance for them whether effective demand is stimulated through investment or through private and public consumption (including useless expenditure on armaments). In periods of economic depression armament outlays may indeed be preferred to the type of public investment which contributes to an augmentation of the idle productive capacity or to an improvement in labour productivity, which would tend to aggravate the problem of unemployment. Developing countries, on the other hand, require investment for the purpose of expanding their productive capacity which is indispensable for the growth of production. The distinction between the two categories of expenditure is crucial for these countries; since it is essential for them to keep private and public consumption under strict control in order to make room for the maximum rate of investment and of expansion of productive capacity.

FISCAL AND MONETARY MEASURES

In the foregoing model, equations (13a) and (14a) can be used to examine the effects of fiscal and monetary policies on effective demand and national income. Fiscal measures will be reflected in changes in G, if they take the form of changes in public expenditure, or in t and T, if they consist of changes in taxation. In addition, the direct effect of certain selective fiscal measures, such as investment and export subsidies and taxes, will be observed in changes in I_p and X, while tariff changes will affect m and M. In each case there will be a change in effective demand leading to changes in national income.

If the primary economic objective of the authorities were to attain full employment, a rational approach to the use of fiscal measures would have to take into account the state of employment at the time of policy decision. There is, in particular, no intrinsic virtue in a balanced government budget. In a period of unemployment, for example, the volume of public expenditure (G) should be increased and/or taxation (T) reduced, even though this may result in a budget deficit. Opposite fiscal measures should be taken if private investment demand (I_p) and foreign balance ($X - M$) combined are buoyant enough to generate a level of aggregate demand in excess of the full employment level of production. These questions are of primary interest to industrial rather than developing economies. The paramount function of fiscal policies in development, as shown in Chapter 3, is to release resources for the

20. We are not concerned here with the important 'long-term' role played by investment in changing the structure of production and in introducing new technology.

growth of domestic investment by restraining consumption, and this is best explained in terms of the equation $I_d = S + (M - X)$, derived from equation (8) above.

As noted above (p. 28), other things remaining unchanged, a budget deficit will result in an increase and a budget surplus in a reduction in the supply of money. Changes in the supply of money will, as we shall presently see, have certain repercussions on effective demand which have to be taken into account. In most countries, however, the authorities can to a large extent regulate the total supply of money by such means as open market operations, variations in commercial banks' minimum cash and liquidity reserve ratios, compulsory deposits with the central bank and the imposition of ceilings on bankers' loans and credits to the private sector. Since open market operations require a capital market, they are of greater value as a regulatory instrument to developed industrial countries.

The effect of changes in the supply of money on
private demand and on prices

In the Keynesian model, the effects of monetary measures, namely changes in the supply of money and in the rate of interest, on effective demand can be examined by reference to the influence that they are likely to exercise on the variables specified in any of the four equations (13) to (14a) above. Taking equation (13a),

$$Y = \frac{(G - T) + I_p + (X - M) - a_1}{s_p}$$

for example, it is clear that G and T, and hence $(G - T)$ are determined by the fiscal policy of the authorities although they have a direct bearing on the supply of money and on interest rates. What is required, therefore, is to analyse the impact of monetary measures on the other variables of the equation, namely s_p, I_p and $(X - M)$, within the framework of general theories of 'savings' (or 'consumption'), 'private investment' and the 'balance of payments', respectively.

Regarding the balance of payments, the two important factors determining the value of export and import of goods and services and hence of $(X - M)$ with which we need be concerned here are movements in national income and in the prices of tradable goods (see pp. 230 and 234–5). Given the government's fiscal policy $(G - T)$, the effect of monetary measures on $(X - M)$ can, therefore, be traced by examining the influence exercised by such measures on 'private demand' (consumption and investment) through s_p and I_p and on 'internal prices' along the lines indicated below.

To analyse the impact of a change in the supply of money on private demand and on internal prices it is essential to take a case in which the change in the money supply itself is not caused, or accompanied, by a movement in any other variable (including fiscal policy). In other words, one should take a case in which all factors, other than money, which might influence private demand and prices, remain initially unchanged, so as to isolate the *direct* effects of changes in money from those of changes in other factors. Open market operations, in which the monetary authorities buy from or sell to the public government bonds, provide a good starting point for such an analysis, since in the first instance their influence is confined to the supply of money and to rates of interest, with no associated direct changes in income or in prices of goods and services. In the case of developing countries, which may lack markets in government debt, one could equally start from a position in which the commercial banks are operating at minimum legal reserve requirements and the authorities, by raising the level of such reserve requirements, can force the banks to reduce the volume of their credit.

In most other cases, however, changes in the supply of money are not only accompanied by, but actually caused by, movements in other economic variables. This is true, for example, of changes in the supply of money which result from the budgetary and the balance of payments position. It is also true of those changes in the volume of bank deposits which are made in response to changes in the demand of borrowers for bank credit. In such cases, variations in the supply of money must be considered as *passive*, and it would be wholly illegitimate to regard them as the *cause* of any movements in income and prices which may accompany them. As shown in Appendix 2A, the failure to distinguish between cases in which changes in the supply of money *cause* changes in income, and the more frequent cases in which changes in the supply of money are the *effect* of changes in income, has been a major source of confusion in dealing with the problem under consideration by monetarists.

We therefore begin our analysis by taking a simple case of open market operations in which the authorities increase the supply of money by buying securities from the public. The purchase of securities will tend to lower interest rates by bidding up the price of bonds; and at the same time there will be an increase in bank deposits and in the cash reserves of commercial banks and other financial institutions. Other things remaining unchanged, this will increase the willingness of the banks and other institutions to lend to the private sector for both consumption and investment purposes; they will tend to raise the ceiling of credit made available to borrowers and to lower the rate of interest charged on loans. There will also be an increase in the general liquidity of the money market which will make it easier for corporations to raise capital through the issue of shares and bonds. Thus the effect of the purchase of securities by the authorities will be to lower the *cost* and increase the *availability* of credit. Very similar results will follow from a reduction of legal cash and/or liquidity reserve requirements of commercial banks at a time when banks are unable to satisfy the demand for loans of their credit-worthy customers because of a shortage of reserves. For the sake of brevity the terms 'loans' and 'borrowing' are henceforth used to cover bank loans and advances as well as other forms of finance raised in the capital market.

We now proceed to consider the likely impact of a change in the supply of money, brought about in the above manner, on private consumption and investment expenditures as well as on the general level of prices. We do this by examining the way in which the principal factors determining these three variables are likely to be influenced by a change in the supply of money. Since the purpose is merely to illustrate the Keynesian approach and to indicate the broad conclusions that result from it, we use only a very simplified version of the theories of 'consumption', 'investment' and 'price determination'. The propositions presented here can be said to be widely accepted by the great majority of economists outside the Chicago school which, as shown in Appendix 2A, has, in any case, adopted a completely different approach for dealing with this problem.

Monetary policy and private consumption

It would be generally agreed that in the short run when, in Keynes's terminology, all 'objective' and 'subjective' factors determining the propensity to save, other than income, can be assumed to remain constant, the primary determinant of movements in private consumption is the change in real disposable personal income.[21] Allowance has, of course, to be made for lags in the reaction of consumption to changes in income, and for the influence of past experience and of expectations about future incomes and prices on current consumption. Many of the hypotheses advanced since Keynes on the behaviour of private consumption, such as Duesenberry's 'relative income' and Friedman's 'permanent income' hypotheses, amount in substance to an elaboration and refinement of Keynes's

---

21. See Keynes, *General Theory*, Chapters 8 and 9.

basic proposition with which we need not be concerned here.[22]

Given the level of real personal disposable income, the supply of money can influence private consumption *directly* through its impact on the propensity to consume; the *indirect* effect of a change in the money supply on real disposable income and on consumption through its influence on domestic and foreign investment is discussed separately later. Perhaps the most important way in which the supply of money exercises a *direct* influence on private consumption is through its effect on the purchases which can be made on credit under hire-purchase, or consumer credit, schemes. It is obvious that the degree of stringency of hire-purchase terms – that is, the rate of interest charged and, in particular, the requirements on the down-payment and on repayment period – will have an important effect on the level of sales, a fact which has been clearly demonstrated in practice.

In assessing the practical importance of this influence of monetary policy, however, it should be remembered that sales made on hire-purchase are generally confined to consumer durables (long-lasting goods) which represent an addition to the physical wealth of the purchasers and should strictly be classified as investment rather than consumer goods; these sales account for only about 10–15 per cent of total consumers' expenditure in industrial countries and for considerably less in LDCs. It may in addition be noted that although changes in the supply of money would influence the availability and cost of credit for hire-purchase sales, more powerful and predictable effects can generally be obtained by direct government measures which alter the terms of agreements relating to the down-payment and to the repayment period, independently of changes in the supply of money.

Apart from the monetarist claim of a direct link between the supply of money and private expenditure, examined in Appendix 2A, there are two other ways in which it might be thought the supply of money could *directly* influence the propensity to consume.[23] The *first* is derived from Keynes's observation on the effect of windfall capital gains on

22. For references and a brief review of these and other consumption theories see Surrey (ed.), *Macroeconomic Themes*, Chapter 2; see also M. J. Farrel, 'The New Theories of the Consumption Function', *Economic Journal*, December 1959.
23. It is not proposed to discuss separately here the so-called 'Pigou effect' according to which an increase in the real value of money balances, due to a fall in prices of goods and services, would tend to raise the propensity to consume. The effect on private expenditure, including consumption, of a growth in 'real balances', due to a rise in the supply of money, is discussed in Appendix 2A. For a detailed discussion of the 'Pigou effect' see Axel Leijonhufvud, *On Keynesian Economics and the Economics of Keynes*, OUP (1968), especially pp. 315–30.

consumption.[24] It is maintained that the fall in the rate of interest which generally accompanies an increase in the supply of money will often raise the money value of the wealth of property owners, in particular of those who earn fixed incomes from bonds and real estate, and that the windfall capital gains so generated will tend to raise their consumption. But this type of capital gains will to a large extent be offset by the losses of the debtors, thereby neutralising the positive effect of a fall in the rate of interest on private consumption; they are, in any case, unlikely to have more than a temporary 'shock' effect on saving and consumption propensities. It would thus seem unreasonable to attach much weight to the *direct* influence that can be exercised in this way on the propensity to consume by changes in the supply of money.

Secondly, it is suggested by some that an increase in the supply of money which is generally accompanied by a fall in the real rate of interest, would tend to raise the propensity to consume by lowering the rate of return on savings, and that a fall in the supply of money would have the opposite effect.[25] This proposition, which was one of the important tenets underlying the theories of saving, investment and interests of the classical economists, was accepted – though with some reservations – by neo-classical economists like Marshall. He writes,

But though saving in general is affected by many causes other than the rate of interest: and though, the saving of many people is but little affected by the rate of interest; while a few, who have determined to secure an income of a certain fixed amount for themselves or their family, will save less with a high rate than with a low rate of interest: yet a strong balance of evidence seems to rest with the opinion that a rise in the rate of interest, or demand price for saving, tends to increase the volume of saving.[26]

There is to date no reliable factual 'evidence' on the relationship of saving propensity to the rate of interest, and it is almost certain that Marshall could have had none when he was writing in 1920.[27] One may safely assume that, *even if* there were a positive correlation between the real rate of interest and the propensity to save in the short run, it is unlikely to be important enough to be worth consideration.

24. See Keynes. *General Theory*, pp. 92–3.
25. The term 'real rate of interest' is used here to signify the 'market rate of interest' minus the change in the GNP price index.
26. See Marshall, *Principles of Economics*, pp. 533–4; see also *ibid.*, pp. 232–6.
27. Marshall did use his conclusion to justify morally the payment of interest to wealth owners, by saying that interest was a just reward for 'waiting'. See Eshag, *From Marshall to Keynes*, pp. 49–50 and 71.

Monetary policy and private investment

Although the supply of money may have no significant *direct* effect on private consumption, it may in some cases play a more important *indirect* part in determining the level of national income and hence of consumption by influencing private investment. For this reason, the study of the effect of changes in the supply of money on private investment deserves special consideration.

It would be agreed, on the whole, that the volume of private domestic investment in any period is determined primarily by the anticipated profitability of investment (the marginal efficiency of investment) on the one hand, and the supply of finance available on the other. An increase in the supply of money can influence private investment in two ways: (a) by increasing the *availability* of finance and thus raising the ceiling of borrowing available to the individual investor, and (b) by lowering the real rate of interest, or the *cost* of finance. A reduction in the supply of money will have the opposite effect. It is useful to keep these two influences (of the 'availability' and of the 'cost' of finance) separate from each other, although they are closely interlinked because an increase in the availability of credit is generally accompanied by a fall in the rate of interest, and vice versa.

The two important factors which are likely to influence the degree of sensitivity of business investment to monetary policy are the liquidity position of firms and the extent of their dependence on outside credit to finance their operations. It is clear that, other things being equal, the higher the liquidity of firms and the larger the share of investment financed by internal resources are, the less sensitive their investment decisions to a given change in the supply of money will be.[28] There will also be some differences between the sensitivity of different types of investment to changes in the 'cost' of borrowing, depending primarily on the degree of reliability attached to the estimates of their net future returns. These factors largely explain, for example, the relatively greater sensitivity of residential construction, as compared with manufacturing investment, to changes in the availability and cost of finance.

Mention should also be made of investment in stocks, or 'inventory investment'. This type of investment differs from fixed investment in that it is not directly productive in the sense of increasing the productive capacity of firms. Stocks are generally held as an essential

28. For a more detailed discussion of this subject, see Éprime Eshag, 'The Relative Efficacy of Monetary Policy in Selected Industrial and Less-developed Countries', *Economic Journal*, June 1971.

concomitant of production as well as to guard against an unforeseen increase in demand and against future rises in costs and prices. It is clear that, other things being equal, producers will wish to minimise the amount of their capital which is tied up in stocks, because of the opportunity cost of the resources invested in them. In any given conditions, therefore, an increase in interest rates, which raises the implicit cost of holding a given level of stocks, will tend to restrain investment in stocks. The post-war experience has, however, shown that major fluctuations in inventory investment have been dominated by the effects of present and anticipated changes in production, demand and prices rather than by interest rates. A good example of this is provided by the inventory cycle experienced among industrial countries in the course of the Korean conflict, i.e. in 1950/51 and 1951/52.[29]

Apart from its direct impact on private domestic investment, monetary policy can also exercise an indirect influence on foreign investment, or the balance of payments $(X - M)$, and hence on the level of domestic activity, in an open economy with floating exchange rates. A tightening of monetary policy, for example, which raises internal rates of interest in relation to those prevailing abroad, will tend to stimulate the inflow of foreign financial capital and to lead to an appreciation of the rate of exchange. This will have the effect of reducing import prices in domestic market and of raising export prices abroad, causing a fall in the volume of exports and a rise in the volume of imports and so a fall in real national income.

In studying the relationship between the supply of money and investment, it is important to note the lack of symmetry between the efficacy of an 'increase' and of a 'decrease' in the supply of money in conditions of slump and boom, respectively. Experience has shown that it is generally easier to curb private investment in a boom by following a sufficiently tight monetary policy (reducing the supply of money) than it is to stimulate investment by adopting an easy money policy in a period of depression. The mere fact that investment finance is made available in larger quantities and on cheaper terms is unlikely to have a significant effect on business investment when firms are holding gloomy expectations about the future; in cases of extreme pessimism, even interest-free loans may have little or no effect in encouraging private investment activity. By contrast, a sufficiently tight monetary policy can choke off some investment even if expectations are very buoyant.

29. See United Nations, *World Economic Report, 1952–53*, Sales No.: 1954.II.C.1, New York (1954), pp. 6–10.

We have so far been concerned solely with the effects of a change in the availability and cost of finance on private demand, assuming that the consumption and investment demand schedules remain unchanged; the two schedules show the relationship of private consumption and investment to income and the rate of interest, respectively. In other words, no account has been taken of the possible impact of a change in the supply of money on these schedules themselves. Both schedules are, however, likely to shift, if a given change in the supply of money were to alter consumers' and businessmen's expectations regarding the future course of prices, incomes, and especially government policies, and this will affect private demand. The significant growth in the influence of the Chicago school on the attitudes and policies of businessmen and of governments in recent years, discussed below, has, therefore, added a new important dimension to the question under consideration. It is worth noting in this connection that, even if consumers and businessmen were themselves entirely unconvinced by the monetarist doctrine and policies, the mere expectation on their part that the authorities are likely to adopt a monetarist line in response to changes in the supply of money will inevitably influence their consumption and investment decisions.

Monetary policy and the price level [30]

There is nothing in the Keynesian approach to suggest the existence of a *direct* link between the supply of money and the level of prices. Prices of goods and services change only because of changes in demand or supply conditions in the market. In considering the relationship between monetary policy and price changes, it is therefore necessary to examine how changes in monetary policy can influence demand and supply conditions.

On the demand side, it is necessary first to consider how a change in the supply of money will affect aggregate effective demand through its influence on private consumption and investment in the various ways outlined above. It is then to be ascertained what effect any such change in demand will have on prices. In manufacturing and service sectors, this will depend primarily on the productive capacity of firms in relation to the current demand for their output, and will vary from one period to another. A rise in demand is obviously more likely to lead to a

---

30. This section, which is concerned only with the relationship of the supply of money to prices, is extracted from the more general discussion of price determination in Chapter 6 (pp. 231–4) to which the reader should refer.

rise in prices when firms are operating at or near full capacity than when they are suffering from idle capacity. A fall in demand has generally little or no effect on prices in these sectors.

The relationship between the supply of money and the price level is even more tenuous when supply, or cost, factors are responsible for price changes. Interest payments do, of course, constitute a part, albeit a minor one, of costs; a fall in interest rates, associated with an increase in the supply of money, will, however, tend to lower rather than raise costs and prices, and vice versa. In manufacturing and service sectors, the three more important factors on the supply side which can produce a rise in costs are: a rise in money wage rates in excess of the increase in labour productivity; fiscal measures which raise indirect taxes or reduce subsidies, and a rise in import prices of inputs due to a devaluation or to a rise in the world price of imported goods.[31] Given the level of aggregate demand, such changes in costs will raise the level of prices. In other words, when the aggregate supply schedule is pushed upwards because of rising costs, prices will tend to rise even if the supply of money and the level of aggregate demand are kept constant or are declining. The most recent illustration of this proposition is provided by the experience of many industrial countries of the West during the period 1973–80 in which unusually high rates of inflation have been accompanied by a stagnation of effective demand and production; a new term, 'stagflation' has been coined to describe these conditions.

The counter-revolution against Keynes

The debate on the Keynesian model of free enterprise economies, reviewed above, continued for some years after the publication of the *General Theory*. But it was the Keynesian analysis which primarily inspired the highly successful policies adopted in the UK during the Second World War which succeeded in financing war expenditure without engendering serious inflationary conditions. The Keynesian approach was also closely followed in the immediate post-War period to keep both unemployment and inflation to a minimum during the transition from a war to a civilian economy. The instruments used were primarily fiscal measures and direct controls. Throughout this period little resort was made to monetary measures in regulating the volume of effective demand, although the rates of interest were deliberately held down, partly to restrict the share of income accruing

---

31. As noted earlier (p. 48), under a system of floating exchange rates, interest rates can indirectly influence the exchange rate and import prices.

to the *rentier* class and partly to stimulate private investment activity.

During the immediate post-War years, the Keynesian approach gained widespread popularity among the younger generation of economists. Many of them assumed that Keynes had succeeded in overthrowing the neo-classical doctrine of equilibrium and in discrediting, once and for all, the quantity theory of money as an instrument of analysis of movements in the level of employment, production and prices. But this assumption has proved to have been over-optimistic. The neo-monetarist school, reviewed in Appendix 2A, has had a considerable success in recruiting a number of academic economists.[32]

More important, however, is the fact that the neo-monetarists have come to enjoy a growing influence among the governments of both industrial and developing countries, especially in the formulation of anti-inflationary policies. This can, for example, be seen in the UK where the Keynesian approach had dominated the economic policies of the Conservative and Labour parties during and immediately after the War, but since the mid–1970s, the orthodox doctrine of 'sound finance', has formed the common plank of both parties. They have come to view with disfavour any growth in budget deficit, more or less irrespective of the prevailing level of unemployment. Both the Labour government of 1975–9 and the Conservative government that succeeded it, have strongly emphasised the key role that should be assigned to controlling the rate of growth in the supply of money and hence the role of the budget balance, which influences the supply of money, in combating inflation.

As explained in Appendix 2A, the theoretical edifice of the Chicago school rests heavily on two old pillars – the quantity theory of money and the neo-classical (Walrasian) model of general equilibrium, refuted earlier (see pp. 32–4 above). As regards the quantity theory, it will be demonstrated that such arguments as have been advanced to explain the alleged *causal link* between the supply of money, on the one hand, and national income and prices, on the other, are based on what are manifestly highly unrealistic and indeed absurd assumptions on the behaviour of the private sector as it affects its demand for money (see pp. 65–73).[33]

32. The Chicago school propaganda tends to exaggerate the extent of this success. For example, at one stage Friedman claims that 'agreement has been reached' among economists 'on the fallaciousness' of Keynes's theory of employment. See M. Friedman, *A Theoretical Framework for Monetary Analysis*, National Bureau of Economic Research, Occasional Paper 112, New York (1971), pp. 15 and 44.

33. Later in the book we show that the same is true of the Chicago school approach to the balance of payments (see pp. 244–7).

In view of the above facts, it is impossible to explain the growth in the popularity of the neo-monetarist school without taking into account certain important changes that have taken place in social and political conditions since the end of the War. During the early years of the Keynesian Revolution, the memory of the Great Depression of the 1930s and the experience of the War had generated in industrial countries strong social pressures for the pursuit of full employment policies and for the introduction of the welfare state; the 1945 landslide election victory of the Labour Party in the UK provides a good illustration of this. This climate of public opinion made the adoption of Keynesian full employment policies for a time politically unavoidable despite the persistent opposition of certain important business and financial circles committed to the doctrines of *laissez-faire* and 'sound finance'. The pressure of these circles for the restoration of the market mechanism and for the adoption of 'sound finance' policies was, however, progressively intensified and in time (in the UK after the mid-1960s) their campaign succeeded in gradually reducing governments' commitment to the policies of full employment.

There can be little doubt that the Chicago school has served the cause of this campaign, which is still in progress, by providing it with a suitable economic theory, and that the school, in turn, owes much of its popularity to the publicity it has received in the course of the campaign. It other words, we believe that the real explanation for the successes of neo-monetarists in influencing government policies in recent years is to be sought, not in the discovery of serious flaws in the Keynesian analysis, but in the shift of political power from the supporters of full employment and the welfare state to the advocates of the free enterprise system and the market mechanism. It is this swing of the political pendulum away from the direction of full employment, where it stood in the immediate post-War period, rather than the theoretical soundness of the basic propositions of the neo-monetarist school, that largely explains the growing acceptance of their arguments by policy makers.

It is worth noting that, although Keynes did not, Kalecki did foresee the emergence of strong influential opposition after the War to full employment policies.[34] Writing as early as 1943, Kalecki predicted that important business interests would successfully oppose the

34. See 'Political Aspects of Full Employment' in *Political Quarterly*, No. 4 (1943), reprinted in an abridged form in Kalecki, *Selected Essays on the Dynamics of the Capitalist Economy*. For comments on this article see *BOUIES*, February 1977, Joan Robinson, p. 16; G.D.N. Worswick, p. 27; Sidney Dell, p. 35; and Éprime Eshag, pp. 81–2.

policy of *maintaining* full employment through government spending. The reasons for this opposition were subdivided by him into three categories.

(i) the dislike of Government interference in the problem of employment as such; (ii) the dislike of the direction of Government spending (public investment and subsidizing consumption); (iii) dislike of the social and political changes resulting from the *maintenance* of full employment.[35]

The opposition to the *maintenance* of full employment would, he says, 'induce the Government to return to the orthodox policy of cutting down the budget deficit' which will prevent the *maintenance* of full employment.[36] He adds, however, that 'in the slump, either under the pressure of the masses, or even without it, public investment financed by borrowing will be undertaken to prevent large-scale unemployment';[37] this is a good prediction of the 'stop–go' policies followed in the UK since the mid-1950s. Kalecki was even able to foresee the emergence of the Chicago school by suggesting that the opposition to full employment 'would probably find more than one economist to declare that the situation was manifestly unsound'.[38]

FINANCING OF ECONOMIC DEVELOPMENT

The central topic of this book is the role of fiscal and monetary policies in economic development – the creation of additional productive resources through investment in capital equipment, in human resources and in production technology (see pp. 4–5 and 31–2). Ignoring for the present changes in the incremental capital/output ratio (ICOR)[39] and any underutilisation of capacities due to deficiencies in effective demand, it can be postulated that the higher is the ratio of investment to national income the larger will be the rate of growth of productive capacity and of employment and production. For brevity, we shall generally use henceforth the term 'ratio of investment' to indicate the proportion of investment in GNP, and the term 'rate of investment' for the flow of investment in a given period.

The progress of economic development, as defined by us, should, however, be measured by the rise in a *weighted index of GNP*, which takes into account the distribution of income between different income groups and thus provides an indication of the growth in the economic welfare of the community as a whole. We have seen that, generally, the

35. Kalecki, *Selected Essays on the Dynamics of the Capitalist Economy, op. cit.*, p. 139.
36. *Ibid.*, p. 144.
37. *Ibid.*
38. *Ibid.*; 'the situation' refers to the condition of full employment.
39. For a definition of ICOR, see p. 10, fn.

larger is the proportion of 'essential' investment in total investment, the bigger will be the share of a given increment in national income accruing to lower-income groups, and, therefore, the greater the increase in economic welfare of the community corresponding to that increment in national income (see pp. 8–10).

It follows from the above that our primary task is to examine the way in which fiscal and monetary policies can be used to accelerate the pace of economic development, (a) by increasing the ratio of investment, and (b) by directing investment resources to 'essential' projects with high social priority. To do this, it is essential first to identify the major obstacles to raising the ratio of investment in developing economies without reducing the share of lower-income groups in national income.

Kalecki's model

Kalecki's model of financing economic development in a mixed economy, which is closely followed here, provides a simple way of dealing with the problem under consideration.[40] In this model, the index of growth in GNP is taken as a measure of the rate of economic development when, and only when, the rise in this index is not accompanied by a fall in real per capita income of the lower-income groups, including wage-earners. This, according to Kalecki, means that two basic conditions have to be satisfied if an unweighted GNP index is to be accepted as an indicator of the pace of development.

(a) At any given level of the money wage rate, the prices of wage goods, which in developing countries consist predominantly of 'necessities', in particular of staple food, must not rise because of inflation.

(b) Taxes on lower-income groups and on 'necessities' should not be increased, which implies that only taxes on higher-income groups and on 'non-essentials' should be raised for the purpose of restraining private consumption.[41]

40. See Michal Kalecki, *Essays on Developing Economies*, The Harvester Press (1976), Essay 7. Kalecki does not give a precise definition of 'mixed economies'. It is, however, clear that he has in mind a typical developing economy in which, although the bulk of production and of distributional activities are controlled by private enterprise, certain key production activities are undertaken by public enterprises, and in which the government plays an active role in promoting development through its investment, fiscal and monetary policies.

41. Kalecki actually assumes that no taxes are levied on lower-income groups or necessities at all (*ibid.*, p. 98), but it should be sufficient to assume that taxes are not raised above their current level.

For a definition of the terms 'necessities' or 'essentials', and of 'non-essentials' or 'luxuries', see p. 8 above.

It can be seen that in this model consumer goods and services are divided into two broad categories, 'essentials' and 'non-essentials', and the community into two broad groups, lower- and higher-income groups. This is done in order to simplify the formal model which, despite this simplification, serves, as we shall see, the important purpose of identifying the crucial problems encountered in financing an accelerated rate of development. It is realised, of course, that in real life the population of any developing country comprises a large number of income groups, ranging from the lowest, living below subsistence level, to the highest, which often enjoys as large an income as that accruing to the richest classes in developed countries; similarly consumer goods and services range from the most to the least essential. The assumption that there are only two income groups and two categories of consumer goods will, therefore, be dropped when we come to consider operationally the taxation policies of LDCs in Chapter 3. It will be shown that the most that can be done in practice through taxation policy to ensure that the *weighted index of GNP* rises in line with the growth of production is to implement a progressive system of taxation under which the proportion of income paid in direct and indirect taxes by different income groups rises directly with their per capita income (see pp. 100–1 and 104).

The question which the model attempts to answer can be phrased in two different forms. (a) 'What are the financial constraints to an acceleration of the rate of growth of production which will not infringe the two conditions postulated earlier?' Or, (b) 'what determines the maximum rate of growth of production that can be achieved without infringing the two conditions?' For the sake of brevity we shall at times refer to this maximum rate of growth and to the rate of investment corresponding to it as 'warranted' rate of growth and 'warranted' rate of investment, respectively. The reader should be warned that the term 'warranted' as used here has a somewhat diferent connotation from that used by Harrod. In Harrod's writings, which are concerned with industrial countries, the expression 'warranted rate of growth' indicates the rate corresponding to the full employment level of savings.[42]

According to Kalecki's model there are two distinct constraints on the warranted rates of investment and growth in LDCs; one is related to total savings and consumption and the other to the supply of necessities. *The first constraint* consists of the need to restrict total consumption adequately to permit the allocation of the desired volume

42. See R.F. Harrod, *Towards a Dynamic Economics*, Macmillan (1948), Lecture Three.

of resources to investment without generating price inflation. The higher the target rate of growth, the higher must be the ratio of investment and the lower the share of consumption in national income. Given the incremental capital/output ratio, a constant rate of growth requires constant shares of investment and consumption in national income. An acceleration in the rate of growth, on the other hand, entails a falling share of consumption in national income, or a slower rate of increase in consumption than in national income; a deceleration will have the opposite implication. Any rate of growth in production will thus have a corresponding rate of growth in consumption which will avoid price inflation. The rise in consumption should be restricted to this rate by means of taxation of higher-income groups and of expenditure on non-essentials. Kalecki maintains that, although this is not an easy task, for most developing countries it should not present an unsurmountable obstacle to the achievement of higher rates of growth than those currently being recorded.

A more serious obstacle to the achievement of higher warranted rates of investment and growth in developing countries is, according to Kalecki, presented by the *second constraint*, namely the supply of necessities. Any increase in national income will result in a corresponding rise in the money income of labour force and in demand for necessities. It is clear that the higher the rate of growth, the greater will be the rate of increase in income of wage- earners and in demand for necessities. In a closed economy, assuming no change in money wage rates, as long as the production of necessities can be increased in line with the increase in demand without raising the average cost of production, prices of necessities and the real income of wage earners will remain unchanged. If the demand for necessities exceeds the supply, prices of these goods will rise and the purchasing power of wages will decline proportionately, and this will infringe the first condition postulated in the model.

Bearing in mind the fact that there is a limit to the rate at which the total supply of necessities (from domestic production and imports) can be increased, the maximum warranted rate of growth will be constrained to a level at which the increase in demand for necessities can be met by an equal rise in their supply at the ruling prices. It is because in most LDCs the growth in the production of staple food, which accounts for the bulk of the supply of necessities, is severely hampered by deep-rooted institutional obstacles, such as archaic land tenure systems, that this presents a more serious constraint to the achievement of higher warranted rates of growth; the negative role in development of these institutional factors will be considered more fully later in this book (see pp. 112–18, 201–7 and 218–21).

Formal model

The foregoing arguments can be stated with greater precision by the aid of the following chart used by Kalecki in his model. Assume that

r stands for the rate of growth of real national income in both sections of the chart.

c_n stands for the rate of growth in demand for necessities at constant prices in Section A.

c stands for the permissible rate of growth of total consumption at constant prices in Section B.

OQ and $O'Q'$ are 45° lines drawn through the origin in Sections A and B, respectively.

In Section A, the line OBK shows the functional relationship between c_n and r. It is assumed that at certain low rates of growth in national

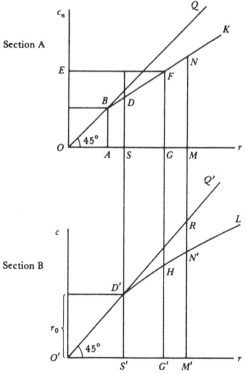

Chart 2.1. Relation between rates of growth of production, permissible consumption and demand for necessities

Source: Kalecki, *Essays on Developing Economies*, pp. 101–5.

income (up to OA) the income elasticity of demand for necessities (e_n) is unity ($e_n = c_n/r = 1$) and coincides with the 45° line along the length of OB, but that at rates of growth larger than OA, e_n will be smaller than unity. To simplify the argument, assume e_n remains constant, so that c_n is a linear function of r, represented by the straight line BK with a slope of less than unity; assume also that the amount of necessities consumed by high-income groups remains constant, so that changes in the supply of these goods affects the consumption of low-income groups only.

In Section B, the line $O'D'L$ shows the functional relationship between r and c; it shows at each point the rate at which total consumption should be allowed to grow to permit the corresponding rate of growth in national income indicated in the chart. Assume that initially the rate of growth is $r_0 (= O'S')$. As long as this rate is unchanged, the share of investment and consumption in national income will also remain unchanged and, therefore, consumption can be allowed to rise at the same rate as income, i.e. $c = r_0$, point D' being located on the 45° line $O'Q'$.

If it is then desired to increase the rate of growth (r) to, say, $O'M'$ for a given period, it will be necessary to constrain the rate of growth of total consumption to $M'N'$, which is lower than $O'M'$. This means that, during the period in question, the average rise in investment will be higher than the rise in national income which in turn will be higher than the rise in consumption. The higher is the new rate of growth in relation to r_0, the larger will be the difference between r and c. Once the target rate of growth is attained, national income, investment and consumption, can all grow at the same rate as long as the rate of growth remains unchanged. The relation of the curve $D'L$ to the 45° line $D'Q'$ indicates the extent to which c has to be checked, through taxation and/or other measures, for each target rate of growth in national income, during the transition period when r_0 is raised to a higher rate of growth, in order to permit the allocation of adequate resources to investment without engendering inflationary price rises.

The three rates of growth (c_n, c and r), as defined above, are formally interrelated in a way that if one is given the other two can be determined. This can clearly be seen from the two sections of the chart which are drawn so that origins O and O' fall on the same perpendicular line. The points of intersection of any perpendicular line with the horizontal axes and with the lines OBK and $O'D'L$ show the values of r, c_n and c, respectively. For example, if $r = OM$, the perpendicular line NMM' would intersect the lines OBK and $O'D'L$ at N and N', respectively, giving the value MN for c_n and $M'N'$ for c. But this is no more than a formal relationship between the three rates of growth. Kalecki rightly maintains that for most developing countries it is the rate of increase in the supply of necessities that should be considered as given and hence as the determinant of the warranted rates of growth of investment and production. This is because of the institutional obstacles to raising the supply of staple food mentioned earlier.

The foregoing argument can be illustrated in terms of the two sections of the chart. Abstracting for the time being from foreign trade and capital, assume that the maximum rates of growth in the production and supply of necessities is OE in Section A. Draw a horizontal line from point E to find the point of intersection F with the line BK. Then draw a perpendicular line from F and find the points of intersection G and G' with the two horizontal axes and H with line $D'L$. This determines the maximum warranted rate of growth at OG ($= O'G'$) and the corresponding permissible rate of growth of consumption at $G'H$, as r is raised from $O'S'$ to $O'G'$.

Under the same assumption, if r had been raised to OM, by devoting a correspondingly higher share of available resources to investment, the rate of increase of demand for necessities at constant prices would have been MN, which is larger than GF ($= OE$) the maximum assumed rate of growth in the supply of these goods. This would push up the prices of necessities depressing the level of real wage rates and thereby infringing the basic postulate of the model noted above. What happens in fact is that a rise in r from OG to OM increases the level of employment without raising the supply of necessities and this results in a fall in real wage rates. Because the total real income and consumption of low-income groups remains unchanged at the level reached when r was equal to OG, the increase in production generated by raising r to OM will be accompanied by a rise in the share of profits in national income.

The additional profits earned as a result of the redistribution of income in favour of capitalists will be partly saved and partly consumed. The increment in savings will help to finance part of the investment thereby reducing the need to restrain the growth of total consumption (c) by means of taxation. Such additional savings can properly be designated as 'forced savings' since they result from a fall in real wage rates and in per capita consumption of employed labourers at whose expense an equivalent amount of investment is financed. They are similar in character to the 'forced savings' generated in industrial countries when planned investment exceeds planned savings at full employment, and prices rise, leading to a fall in real wages and in private consumption (see p. 40 above).

There is, however, an important difference between the causes and effects of the two types of forced savings. In industrial countries, it is the supply of labour that constitutes the bottleneck in the growth of aggregate production. Because of this, in a closed economy, a rise in investment must be accompanied by a corresponding fall in the supply of consumer goods and hence in total private consumption. In developing countries, on the other hand, the bottleneck consists of the supply of necessities which is generally encountered when, apart from the unemployed labour, there may also exist some idle equipment capacity available for the production of non-essential consumer and investment goods. This means that, even after the appearance of the bottleneck in question, an acceleration in the rate of investment will lead to a rise of production and of real national income. In the limiting case, when the supply of necessities is completely inelastic, the entire growth in national income will accrue to profits.

That portion of the additional profits, which is not saved, will be used to increase the consumption of non-essentials. It can be seen from Section B of the chart that when r is increased from $O'G'$ to $O'M'$, c can rise from $G'H$ to $M'N'$ still leaving adequate resources to finance the higher investment ratio. But since the rate of growth of the supply of necessities remains unchanged at OE ($=GF$), the increase in total permissible consumption (c) can be attained only by a higher rate of consumption of non-essentials. This will tend to encourage investment in industries which produce luxury goods and generally cater to the demand of higher-income groups. Thus although the rate of growth is higher than the warranted rate, the growth itself is 'lop-sided'. Clear signs of this type of 'lop-sided' growth, in such forms as rapidly expanding durable consumer goods industries and luxury housing construction, can be seen in most developing countries.[43]

It is worth noting that the process of redistribution of income in favour of profits as a result of raising r above the rate warranted by the supply of necessities cannot be reversed by raising money wage rates. A rise in money wage rates will produce proportionate increases in the prices of necessities, leaving real wage rates unchanged, because the supply of necessities cannot be increased faster. In addition, increases in money wage rates will tend to push up the cost of production and hence the price of non-essential goods. In such conditions, persistent attempts by wage-earners to maintain their real income by raising money wage rates are likely to lead to a wage – price spiral of inflation.

Foreign trade and capital

The foregoing discussion of Kalecki's formal model has been confined to a closed economy in which the supply of necessities is determined by and is equal to their domestic production. In an open

---

43. For a definition of 'lop-sided' growth, see p. 10.

economy it would be possible to supplement the production of necessities by the importation of such goods. It is obvious that if during any period imports of necessities can be increased faster than their domestic production, the total supply of necessities will rise more rapidly than their production; the reverse will happen if imports rise more slowly than home production.

Generally, in the absence of steadily growing inflow of foreign capital, most developing countries will not be able to finance a high rate of growth in the imports of necessities. This is because of a rise in demand for imports other than necessities, notably investment goods and raw materials, in the course of development, combined with the difficulties of increasing exports discussed later (see pp. 195–6 and 222–6). The great majority of LDCs, therefore, will find it difficult to maintain a non-inflationary rate of growth significantly higher than that warranted by the growth of domestic production of necessities.[44] It is, in any case, the rate of increase in the total supply of necessities, as determined by the maximum combined rates of growth of their home production and of imports, that will determine the warranted rate of growth. If the rate of growth is pushed above this level, developments similar to those outlined above, as regards the distribution of income between wages and profits and the pattern of investment, will take place.

It is worth noting also that the mere availability of foreign exchange will not by itself ensure an adequate rate of growth in the supply of necessities and other commodities to prevent price inflation if the rate of growth of national income is pushed up above a certain level. This is because of the emergence of bottlenecks in port and transport facilities, which slow down the rate of increase of supplies in the distribution channels. This type of inflation has been experienced in recent years by a number of the oil-rich countries who embarked on ambitious investment and public expenditure programmes after the steep rise in petroleum prices at the end of 1973.[45]

Foreign credits can be used not only to increase the importation of necessities but also to finance other imports required for the modification of the structure of production in a way that permits an acceleration in the rate of warranted growth. They can, for example, be used to increase the rate of growth of domestically produced necessities

44. This does not apply to the richer members of OPEC (discussed in Chapter 3) and to a small number of developing countries, such as Singapore, Hong Kong and South Korea, as long as their export earnings continue to grow rapidly enough to finance a growing volume of imports.
45. See, for example, the analysis of the inflationary process in Iran since 1974, in Industrial and Mining Development Bank of Iran, *Annual Reports*, 1975/76 and 1976/77 (sections on the 'Iranian Economy').

and to eliminate other bottlenecks. At the same time, as explained earlier, the importing of foreign capital contributes to the financing of domestic investment thereby reducing the need to restrain the rate of growth of total consumption through taxation of higher-income groups (see p. 39 above). This means that consumption of non-essentials by higher-income groups can grow at a faster rate as a result of foreign credits. Depending on the policies followed by the authorities, it is perfectly feasible to have a situation in which foreign credits merely serve the purpose of stimulating the consumption of non-essentials without making any contribution to development. The role of foreign capital in development will be examined more fully in Chapter 4.

So far the discussion has been focused entirely on the relationship between the supply of necessities and the rates of investment and of growth in national income. As noted earlier, however, investment is not the sole determinant of private income: changes in the other two 'net injections', namely the budget deficit and the export balance, act in a way similar to investment in determining private income and the demand for necessities. Inflationary pressures may thus develop as a result of a rapid increase in the budget deficit and/or the export balance which produce a higher rate of growth in national income and in demand for necessities than that warranted by the supply of necessities. Such situations, which at times arise because of a rapid growth in the budget deficit due to an expansion of government consumption outlays, are perfectly compatible with a stagnant or even declining rate of domestic investment.

Despite its simplifications, Kalecki's model throws considerable light on the central problems of financing of development and of inflationary pressures experienced by developing countries. Moreover, although it is primarily designed to cover the position of mixed developing economies, it has considerable relevance also to the inflationary problems encountered by centrally-planned socialist economies in the course of development. Unlike some economic models, it lends itself to empirical tests based on national accounts and related statistical series, notably those covering sectoral production and employment, wage rates and prices. As shown later, long before the formalisation of the model, Kalecki used this approach to analyse the inflationary experience of mixed and socialist economies engaged in accelerated economic development during the post-War years (see pp. 218–20).

THE ROLE OF FISCAL AND MONETARY POLICIES IN
DEVELOPMENT

Kalecki's model also provides a rough but suitable framework for a
discussion of the role of fiscal and monetary policies in economic
development. It will be recalled that the model lays down two
necessary conditions for achieving a target rate of growth of production without engendering price inflation and a decline in real
wages. *First*, the rate of increase of total consumption has to be
restrained sufficiently to make adequate resources available for the
requisite investment. This means that the volume of 'voluntary', as
distinct from 'forced', savings, together with foreign loans and credits
must be adequate to finance the requisite investment. *Secondly*, the rate
of growth of the supply of necessities must be adequate to satisfy the
increase in demand for such goods. The basic role of fiscal and
monetary policies in promoting economic development can thus be
conveniently analysed by examining the use that can be and is in
practice made of these policies in attaining the following two objectives
implied by the above conditions:

1. Provision of adequate resources through (a) voluntary savings and
   (b) foreign capital to finance the target rate of investment, and
2. Expansion in the supply of necessities at a rate appropriate to the
   target rate of growth of production.

This we do in the next three chapters.

Chapter 3 is devoted to the examination of the problem of restricting
public and private consumption in order to provide adequate
resources in the form of voluntary savings for investment purposes. We
first consider the various categories of public consumption with
reference to their impact on economic development. This provides
some indication of the opportunities available in most developing
countries for restricting the growth of public consumption without
damaging their development prospects. As far as private consumption
is concerned, its growth can be significantly influenced by government
taxation measures, and the second part of Chapter 3 is devoted to an
examination of taxation policies and problems of LDCs.

In *Chapter 4* we examine the role of foreign capital in financing
development. We discuss the advantages and disadvantages of
financing investment through various types of foreign capital and
provide some factual information on the volume, composition and
direction of capital flows to LDCs in the 1970s.

Chapter 5 covers the second objective mentioned above, namely that
of increasing the rate of growth of the supply of necessities. It examines

the use that can be made of fiscal and monetary measures to influence the pattern of investment. It is clear that the larger the share of investment resources channelled into industries responsible for the production of necessities, the larger will be the rate of growth of the production of these goods for any given rate of growth of national income. But although the supply of necessities constitutes the most important single obstacle to an acceleration of the rate of growth in production, it is not the sole impediment to growth. Supply bottlenecks in other important sectors of the economy, notably in infrastructure, such as transport and power, can also retard the rate of growth. What is required therefore is a 'balanced' growth between the major sectors of the economy which prevents a persistent occurrence of serious production bottlenecks in the course of development. This together with the other considerations related to the choice of investment projects, discussed earlier (pp. 15–20), have been taken into account in the discussion of policies in this chapter.

Kalecki's model, which is confined to the central problem of financing development, abstracts from what has come to be known as Keynesian unemployment, namely the failure to make full use of existing productive capacities because of a deficiency in aggregate effective demand. As noted earlier in this chapter (p. 32) although this does not represent the *crucial* problem facing developing countries, it is not entirely irrelevant to them; it is particularly important for those countries where modern industrial and commercial activities generate a significant proportion of total national income. *Chapter 6* is largely devoted to an examination of the problem of underutilisation of productive capacity caused by resorting to deflationary fiscal and monetary policies to deal with price inflation and with balance of payments difficulties.

It is worth noting in conclusion that fiscal and monetary measures are not always the only, nor indeed the most appropriate, policy instruments for dealing with the problem of stimulating economic development. In most developing countries, for example, the best and often the only way of raising significantly the rate of growth of production of food crops, the most important single component of necessities, is to implement large-scale land reform programmes. Similarly price controls combined with the rationing of consumer goods may often be a more effective way of restraining the growth of consumption and of safeguarding the standard of living of lower-income groups than taxation. But such measures, although mentioned from time to time, fall outside the scope of this book which is concerned with the role that can properly be played by fiscal and monetary policies in the process of development.

APPENDIX 2A: THE NEO-MONETARIST APPROACH

The most important challenge to the Keynesian approach to the management of demand, briefly outlined in the text, has come from Milton Friedman and his followers, known variously as the 'Chicago school', 'monetarists' and 'neo-monetarists'. In the late 1950s, some twenty years after the publication of the *General Theory*, Milton Friedman initiated a new method, or technique, for examining the role played by changes in the supply of money in the economy. This consisted of time series regression analysis between the supply of money, on the one hand, and production and prices, on the other; in the case of the UK and the US, the statistical data used cover almost a century, from about 1880 to 1970. The statistical correlations derived from these time series regressions are assumed to provide a solid 'scientific' indication of the impact of changes in the supply of money on production and prices.

It would be outside the scope of this book to examine the various versions of monetarism advanced by the followers of the Chicago school, or to refer to all their publications. The most that can be done here is to take a brief look at Friedman's own work by presenting the important conclusions he draws from regression analysis, and to examine such explanations as he has provided for the alleged causal link between the variables mentioned.[46]

The key propositions of monetarism

The more important conclusions derived from statistical regressions that are relevant to our discussion have been described by Friedman as 'the key propositions of monetarism'; he has summarised them as follows:[47]

(1) On the average, a change in the rate of monetary growth produces a change in the rate of growth of nominal income about six to nine months later;

---

46. Some of Friedman's better-known works include: M. Friedman, 'The Quantity Theory of Money – A Restatement' in M. Friedman (ed.), *Studies in the Quantity Theory of Money*, University of Chicago Press (1957); M. Friedman and A. Schwartz, *A Monetary History of the United States, 1867–1960*, Princeton University Press (1963); M. Friedman, 'The Role of Monetary Policy', *American Economic Review*, March 1968; *The Optimum Quantity of Money and Other Essays*, Macmillan (1969); *A Theoretical Framework for Monetary Analysis*, National Bureau of Economic Research, Occasional Paper 112, New York (1971); and *Money and Economic Development, The Horowitz Lectures of 1972*, Praeger Special Studies in International Economics and Development (1973). The last publication presents in charts a clear and simple summary of some of the data collected, see pp. 11–27.

A useful survey of the monetarist literature and theories is provided by Robert J. Barro and Stanley Fischer in 'Recent Developments in Monetary Theory', *Journal of Monetary Economics*, North-Holland Publishing Co., 2 (1976).

47. See Friedman, *The Horowitz Lectures of 1972*, pp. 27–38; words in brackets added.

['nominal income' meaning the money value of national income, or net national product at current market prices.]

(2) The changed rate of growth of nominal income typically shows up first in output and hardly at all in prices.

(3) On the average, the effect on prices comes some nine to fifteen months after the effect on income and output, so the total delay between a change in monetary growth and a change in the rate of inflation, averages something like 15 to 24 months.

It is clear from above that, in the *short run*, a change in the rate of monetary growth for Friedman plays an important part in determining nominal income by influencing first production and later prices. In his own words, 'I regard the description of our position as "money is all that matters for changes in *nominal* income and for *short-run* changes in real income" as an exaggeration but one that gives the right flavour to our conclusions.'[48] As explained below, however, it is claimed that the effect of the supply of money on production will be transitory in nature; what happens to production in the long run depends on 'real factors' and not on the rate of growth of money which will affect only prices. Friedman concludes from the above propositions that, '*inflation is always and everywhere a monetary phenomenon* in the sense that it is and can be produced only by a more rapid increase in the quantity of money than in output'.[49]

The first point to note is that it is not very surprising to find statistical correlations such as those produced by Friedman, especially by varying time-lags between changes in money and in nominal income, as he does. It is relatively easy to explain the historical correlations between the supply of money, on the one hand, and nominal income, on the other, without invoking the causal link between the two variables claimed by Friedman. For example, in the Keynesian formulation of the demand for money,

$$M = M_1 + M_2 = L_1(Y) + L_2(r),$$

(where M stands for total supply of money, M_1 and M_2 for transaction and speculative balances, respectively; Y for nominal income, and r for the rate of interest), it is known that the function L_1 is a relatively stable one, in the sense that transaction balances (M_1) bear a close positive relationship to nominal income (Y).[50] It follows that, with a continu-

48. See Friedman, *A Theoretical Framework for Monetary Analysis*, p. 27.
49. See Friedman, *The Horowitz Lectures of 1972*, p. 28; see also *ibid.*, pp. 40–1.
50. See Keynes, *General Theory*, pp. 199–201. The notations M_1 and M_2 are those used by Keynes and have a different meaning from that generally given to them in current monetary and financial publications; the same applies to notation M_3 mentioned later (p. 73).

ing rise in nominal income, which has taken place in the UK and US (the two major countries studied by Friedman) since 1870, there has been a more or less parallel increase in M_1. In the absence of a steady rise in the total supply of money (M) there would have been a persistent reduction in the speculative balances, or hoards (M_2), and a corresponding upward pressure on interest rates. Such economies as could have been effected in the use of transaction balances through the creation of money substitutes, would in these conditions have been unlikely to have offset this tendency indefinitely.

The reason why historically there have been no such prolonged periods of continuous rise in interest rates is largely because increases in M have generally resulted from and have accompanied the growth of Y, e.g. through budget deficits, balance of payments surpluses, bank lending, etc. When in the normal course of events changes in M have not kept pace with Y, the monetary authorities in the UK and US have in the past usually taken deliberate measures to increase the total supply of money to prevent a continuous rise in the rates of interest.[51] The introduction of specific 'targets' for the rate of growth in the supply of money since the early 1970s in the UK represents a major departure from past policies on the part of the government.

Our primary interest here, however, is with the explanations given by Friedman for the alleged *chain of causation* indicated in the above propositions and not with the statistical analysis and other empirical data used by him – some of which have been strongly disputed.[52] Statistical studies of the type used by the Chicago school can by themselves, of course, provide no positive evidence as to the chain of causation between the quantity of money on the one hand, and production and prices on the other. It is universally recognised that the statistical concept of correlation is quite neutral as regards causation. It is entirely possible that it is changes in income and prices which cause changes in money rather than the other way round, or that changes in all the three variables are generated by other factors not included in the statistical analysis.[53] It is obvious that a rational

---

51. See N. Kaldor, 'The New Monetarism', *Lloyds Bank Review*, July 1970.
52. See, for example, Kaldor's rejection of Friedman's claim concerning the US monetary policy during the Great Depression, Kaldor, *op. cit.*, pp. 12–14.
53. Attempts have been made to discover statistical evidence which might indicate the *likelihood* of a chain of causality between changes in the supply of money and in nominal income, by examining the chronological order of changes in the two variables. As explained below, such studies cannot be expected to throw much light on the *causal* relationship between the two variables; in this case they seem to have produced divergent results for the UK and the US. See David Williams, C.G.E. Goodhart and D.H. Gowland, 'Money, Income, and Causality: The UK Experience', *American Economic Review*, June 1976.

examination of the causal relationship between these variables must be conducted within the framework of some theories of income and price determination along the lines followed by us in the text (see pp. 42–50 above). But although Friedman has not done this, he has provided some explanation for the causal links claimed by him which needs to be briefly examined here.

Excess money balances

The explanation given by Friedman for the causal relationships indicated in his 'key propositions' are expressed in terms of the Cambridge version of the quantity theory of money.[54]

$$M = kPy \qquad\qquad (1)$$

from which it follows that,

$$M = kY \qquad\qquad (2)$$

and

$$\frac{M}{P} = ky \qquad\qquad (3)$$

where M is the quantity of money; k stands for the proportion of national income held in the form of money and is the inverse of 'income velocity of circulation'; y is national income at constant prices; Y is nominal national income; P is the implicit price index used to convert nominal to real national income, and M/P stands for the purchasing power of the stock of money, henceforth called 'real balances'. He says,

> The quantity theory of money takes for granted that what ultimately matters to holders of money is the real quantity rather than the nominal quantity they hold and that there is a fairly definite real quantity of money that people wish to hold under any given circumstances. Suppose that the nominal quantity that people hold at a particular moment of time happens to correspond at current prices to a real quantity larger than the quantity that they wish to hold. Individuals will then seek to dispose of what they regard as their *excess money balances*; they will try to pay out a larger sum for the purchase of securities, goods and services, for the repayment of debts, and as gifts than they are receiving from the corresponding sources.[55]

He adds that this increase in expenditure leads in due course to a rise in nominal income.

54. See Friedman, *A Theoretical Framework for Monetary Analysis*, p. 9.
   For a comparison with the Cambridge versions of the quantity theory equations, see Eshag, *From Marshall to Keynes*, pp. 20–1.
55. *Ibid.*, pp. 2–3; emphasis added.
   This is almost identical with Marshall's analysis of the 'demand for money' and with his presentation of the quantity theory, although, unlike Friedman, he regarded this theory as being a mere tautology; see Eshag, *ibid.*, pp. 1–4 and 11–12.

The same argument is advanced elsewhere when he writes, 'the attempt by holders of money to restore or attain a desired balance sheet after an *unexpected increase in the quantity of money* will tend to raise the price of assets and reduce interest rates', which would encourage both investment and consumption outlays.[56] Similarly, when comparing Keynesian with monetarist approach, he says, 'The Keynesians tend to concentrate on a narrow range of marketable assets and recorded interest rates.' 'We, on the other hand, stress a much broader and more "direct" impact on spending.'[57]

It is difficult to understand what the concepts of 'excess money balances' and 'unexpected increase in the quantity of money' used by Friedman signify in real life. One can imagine some individuals at times finding themselves holding 'excess money balances' when, for example, they receive 'unexpected' cash gifts or bonuses, which they are likely to spend in part or in whole on consumption, as suggested by Friedman. It is clear, however, that such gifts and bonuses would amount to a 'windfall capital gain' which, as Keynes had explained, would tend to stimulate consumption.[58] There is in fact no reason to expect that the effect on total consumption of cash gifts and bonuses will differ significantly from that of the receipt of gifts and bonuses in kind of equivalent value. For example, a woman who is planning to spend, say, £10 on meat in a week is as likely to increase her total expenditure if she receives in that week an unexpected cash bonus of £10 from her employer as she would if she were, instead, unexpectedly to receive the meat, which she had ordered, as a gift from her admiring butcher.

To illustrate the *direct* effect of cash balances on expenditure, Friedman, on one occasion, gives the example of a helicopter which flies over a community and drops bank notes from the sky which are picked up by the public. He first assumes that the helicopter performs this deed only once, and then takes the case in which the helicopter flights become a continuous process which become fully anticipated by everyone.[59] It is true that in this example what follows will be, more or less, along the lines suggested by Friedman – expenditure and nominal national income will increase and, depending on the availability of idle productive capacity and the behaviour of imports, real output and prices may also rise. But even in this highly artificial example, the *real* reason for the growth of expenditure in the first case is that individuals

---

56. See Friedman, *A Theoretical Framework for Monetary Analysis*, p. 28; emphasis added.
57. *Ibid.*
58. See Keynes, *General Theory*, pp. 89–90.
59. See Friedman, *The Optimum Quantity of Money and Other Essays*, pp. 4–14.

who pick up the notes would (literally) have had a 'windfall' capital gain. The same people would be likely to increase their total outlays, more or less in a similar manner, if, instead of collecting bank notes, they were to pick up goods, or share certificates, or even real estate deeds parachuted by the helicopter. In the second case, when the picking up of notes 'becomes fully anticipated by everyone', the individuals will treat the value of such notes as a permanent rise in income and will for this reason increase their expenditure. It will make no significant difference to the expenditure behaviour of, say, a wage-earner, whether he receives the additional notes in his weekly pay package, or is assured of picking them up weekly in his back garden.

Changes in the supply of money

Whatever may be said about Friedman's helicopter example intended to explain the direct causal link between the supply of money and private demand, the question will remain: how can people in the *real world* find themselves holding 'excess money balances', or experience an 'unexpected increase in the quantity of money'? To examine this question we must consider how the so-called 'monetary base', or 'high-powered money', as well as 'total stock of money' are increased in real life. 'High-powered money' is defined by Friedman as currency held by the public plus commercial banks' cash reserves, and 'total stock of money', as currency held by the public plus all deposits (time and demand) held by the public with commercial banks;[60] it will make no difference to our argument if time deposits, i.e. savings accounts, were excluded from the stock of money.

There are *four* main channels through which the amount of 'high-powered money' can be increased. *Two* of these, namely budget deficits not covered by borrowing from the private sector, and surpluses in the private sector's transactions on the current account of the balance of payments, constitute 'net injections' in the Keynesian model (see equation 13(a) on page 38 above). It will be readily agreed that any increase in the supply of money and in private expenditure brought about through these two channels is the *effect* rather than the *cause* of the increase in income.

The *third* way in which the supply of 'high-powered money' is increased are open market operations involving purchases of securities from the private sector by monetary authorities. We have already explained how such operations may influence private demand and prices by lowering the cost and increasing the availability of credit (see pp. 44–50 above). We shall now consider whether they are also likely

60. See Friedman, *The Optimum Quantity of Money*, p. 41, and *The Horowitz Lectures of 1972*, p. 11.

to increase private demand for the reason given by Friedman, i.e. by generating an 'excess supply of money'.

The important point to note about open market operations is that the money balances acquired by individuals as a result of the sale of their bonds constitute part of their wealth which they have voluntarily transformed from one category of asset to another; such money balances are fundamentally different from transaction balances. The sale of securities by itself would neither add to the wealth of the individuals nor increase their income. There is, therefore, no reason to expect the bond sellers to increase and the buyers to decrease their consumption outlays simply because they have, for some reason or other, decided to change the proportion of the wealth held in the form of cash. If, for example, as is often the case, individuals decide to sell their bonds because they anticipate a fall in bond prices, they are unlikely to treat the proceeds of the sale of the bonds as being in 'excess' of what they desire to hold. Similarly, when the bonds are sold with a specific purpose of acquiring money to finance consumption or investment outlays, the decision to undertake such expenditure must precede the acquisition of additional cash. It would be somewhat perverse, to put it mildly, to suggest that in this case the increased expenditure which follows the sale of the bonds is *caused* by 'excess money balances'.

The *fourth* channel for increasing the stock of 'high-powered money' is the inflow of foreign capital, as measured by the surplus on the private sector's capital account of the balance of payments. The inflow of foreign capital can take a variety of forms the most important of which are foreign loans and credits, portfolio investment, including deposits with private banks, and the finance procured for direct investment. The initial impact of all these flows is similar to that of open market operations discussed above; they increase the amount of 'high-powered money' without influencing national income and expenditure.[61] Even when such capital is imported with the specific purpose of financing direct investment, or other outlays, which eventually raise national income, the intention, or the plan, to undertake the outlays in question must precede its inflow. What is also evident is that the additional money created through the inflow of foreign capital cannot be regarded as being in 'excess' of what the domestic and foreign wealth owners desire to hold.

The increase in the supply of 'high-powered money' brought about through any of the four channels mentioned would, other things remaining unchanged, raise the ratio of bankers' cash reserves to their

---

61. Foreign loans and credits used to finance imports and other external liabilities serve to prevent a reduction in 'high-powered money' rather than to increase its supply.

deposits. This would *enable* the banks to increase the volume of loans advanced to their clients; the loans would increase bank deposits and the total stock of money. It is clear, however, that such increases in loans and deposits must take place in response to the desire and request of the bankers' clients; in other words, it is the decision to acquire additional money to finance some expenditure that is the *cause* of the new deposits created and not the other way round. It is again rather difficult to see how the money so created can be regarded as generating for borrowers either 'excess money balance', or an 'unexpected increase in money balances'.

The foregoing survey of the major factors responsible for the growth in the stock of money throws considerable doubt on the validity of Friedman's claim concerning 'the chain of causality' between the supply of money and nominal income as well as on the entire concept of 'excess supply of money' used to explain the alleged chain of causality. It has been shown that the total stock of money can increase, either because of a rise in injections and national income, or because of the desire of the public to hold larger money balances – generally to satisfy their speculative motive or to provide finance in advance of an anticipated expenditure. Although the money balances held for these purposes are additional to normal transaction balances, they do not by any means constitute an 'excess supply of money' in Friedman's sense.

The distinction between 'transaction' and other balances, especially 'hoards', which represent a 'store of value', is crucial to an understanding of the relationship of the stock of money to national income. The importance of distinguishing between the two categories of money balances was fully recognised by many nineteenth-century writers, such as Henry Thornton, Fullarton, Bagehot, Robert Giffen and Marshall.[62]

Although the earlier versions of the quantity theory at Cambridge failed to differentiate 'hoards' from 'transaction balances', this defect was remedied in the later versions of the theory.[63] 'Hoards' play a key role, for example, in Robertson's 1926 analysis of the relationship between the quantity of money, on the one hand, and economic activity and prices, on the other.[64] Similarly, Keynes had, by 1930, become completely disillusioned with the significance of the traditional, including his own, versions of the quantity theory, and found it necessary to draw a sharp distinction between 'Income-deposits', 'Business-deposits' and 'Savings-deposits', which he represented by

62. For references, see Eshag, *From Marshall to Keynes*, pp. 2–3 and 13–14.
63. *Ibid.*
64. See D.H. Robertson, *Banking Policy and the Price Level*, P.S. King and Son, London (1926), especially Chapters V and VI.

symbols M_1, M_2 and M_3, respectively.[65] He writes, 'But the relationship between the total annual receipts of income-receivers and the average stock of money held for all purposes is a hybrid conception having no particular significance';[66] he was referring, of course, to the concept of 'income velocity of circulation'.

What the neo-monetarists have done in this case is in effect to revert to the earlier simple form of the quantity theory; a procedure justified by the existence of a high statistical correlation, observed between total stock of money and national income and prices. It is true that in dealing with an individual's demand for real balances (M/P), Friedman suggests that this is a function of a number of variables which, apart from real income, include expected rate of interest, expected rate of inflation etc., but he finds little practical use for this approach in providing an aggregate demand function for money.[67] The operational version of the neo-monetarist theory used particularly in the formulation of anti-inflationary policies, discussed below and in Chapter 6, remains the simple quantity theory as expressed in equations (1) to (3) above in which all types of money balances are lumped together.

Laissez-faire *aspect of neo-monetarism*

The revival of the quantity theory by neo-monetarists is closely associated with their advocacy of *laissez-faire* philosophy in policy matters.[68] This entails a rejection of Keynesian theories of employment and of interest and a return to the neo-classical doctrine of equilibrium.[69]

According to Friedman, what happens to production, employment and the real rate of interest in the long run depends on 'real' factors and cannot be changed by monetary policy except 'temporarily' and

65. See J.M. Keynes, *A Treatise on Money*, Vol. II, Macmillan and Company (1930), Chapter 24. In his *General Theory* he combines the 'income' – and 'business' – deposits into a single category named 'transaction' balances. (see p. 66 above).
66. Keynes, *A Treatise on Money*, Vol. II, *op. cit.*, p. 24.
67. See Friedman, *A Theoretical Framework for Monetary Analysis*, pp. 11–15.
68. Friedman in particular has been very explicit in his antagonism to government interference with the operation of market forces and in his support for a free enterprise system. See, for example, M. Friedman, *Capitalism and Freedom*, The University of Chicago Press (1962), and *Dollars and Deficits*, Prentice Hall (1968), pp. 1–16.
69. See R.W. Clower, 'The Keynesian Counter-Revolution: A Theoretical Appraisal', in F. Hahn and R. Brechling (eds.), *The Theory of Interest Rates*, Macmillan (1965). Detailed extracts from this work are published in Surrey (ed.), *Macroeconomic Themes*, pp. 400–21.

except by causing serious disturbances in the economy.[70] He says that there is a 'natural' rate of interest, determined by the productivity of capital, and a 'natural' rate of unemployment corresponding to the level 'that would be ground out by the Walrasian system of general equilibrium equations'. By increasing the rate of growth in the supply of money, the authorities can, 'for a time', hold the real 'market' rate of interest below its 'natural' rate, as well as reduce unemployment below its 'natural' rate. This will, however, it is claimed, cause economic disruption by engendering price inflation, and eventually the rates of interest and unemployment will revert to their 'natural' levels.[71] In his own words, 'there is always a temporary trade-off between inflation and unemployment; there is no permanent trade-off'.[72]

It can be seen that Friedman's propositions on the role played by 'real' and 'monetary' factors in the economy are in both substance and form identical with those postulated by the *pre-Keynesian* (mostly nineteenth-century) classical and neo-classical economists reviewed earlier in this chapter (see p. 29); we have also shown that the same is true of his analysis of 'demand for money' (see p. 68, fn. 55).[73] It is not, however, immediately obvious exactly what Friedman means by 'natural rate of unemployment' since no such rate can, as he puts it, be 'ground out' by the Walrasian general equilibrium equations. His discussion of the subject also indicates that he is not referring to what is commonly known as 'structural' unemployment, described earlier. What this 'natural rate of unemployment' must mean for him is the rate of unemployment that, according to the neo-classical theory of employment, would, as we have explained, result from an excess of real wage rate over the full employment wage rate on the assumption that real wage rates are completely rigid.

Policy prescriptions

According to Friedman, it is not advisable, nor indeed practicable, to direct monetary policy at attaining the 'natural' rates of interest and unemployment, since these rates cannot be estimated 'accurately and readily' and will, in any case, 'change from time to time'.[74] Similarly, although the rate of growth in the supply of money

70. See M. Friedman, 'The Role of Monetary Policy', *American Economic Review*, March 1968, pp. 1–14.
71. *Ibid.*, pp. 5–11.
72. *Ibid.*, p. 11.
73. In view of this fact it is somewhat surprising to see some monetarists labelling Keynesians as 'old fashioned'.
74. See Friedman, *American Economic Review*, pp. 10–11.

has a direct bearing on the rate of inflation, he does not consider price level as a suitable guide for monetary policy. This is because 'monetary action takes a longer time to affect the price level' and because 'both the time-lag and the magnitude of effect vary with circumstances'.[75] Generally, he considers 'discretionary monetary policy' as a 'poor instrument' for dealing with short-term problems of unemployment and inflation.[76]

The best policy for developed countries, which would prevent 'money itself being a major source of economic disturbance', is, in Friedman's view, to maintain 'a steady rate of growth' in the total supply of money.[77] To 'achieve rough stability in the level of prices of final products', he estimates that the supply of money should be allowed to grow at 3 to 5 per cent per year;[78] in a later publication a rate of growth of 2 per cent per year is suggested.[79] It follows from the above, as it did for the orthodox neo-classical economists, that governments need not and indeed, to avoid economic disruption, should not take any action to attain a specific target of employment; the level of employment should be allowed to be determined by the free operation of market forces.

As for developing countries, Friedman believes that 'the best policy' for most of them would be to unify their currencies with the currencies of some large, relatively stable developed countries with which they have close economic relations, and 'to impose no barriers to the movement of money or prices, or interest rates'.[80] 'Such a policy', he says, 'requires not having a central bank';[81] it will, of course, also involve a renunciation of economic autonomy. 'The second best policy' in his view ('which has far greater political feasibility in the present climate of opinion') is similar to that prescribed for developed countries. This would 'require a central bank to produce a steady and moderate rate of monetary growth' in order to prevent an 'erratic' and 'rapid' rate of inflation.[82] In Chapter 6, we discuss the 'efficacy' and 'relevance' of this policy prescription for dealing with inflation and with balance of payments difficulties in LDCs.

Regarding fiscal policy, this, for Friedman, plays an important part only in 'determining what fraction of total national income is spent by

---

75. *Ibid.*, p. 15; see also Friedman, *The Horowitz Lectures of 1972*, p. 39.
76. See Friedman, *The Horowitz Lectures of 1972*, p. 39.
77. See Friedman, *American Economic Review*, pp. 12 and 16.
78. *Ibid.*, p. 16.
79. See Friedman, *The Optimum Quantity of Money*, p. 46.
80. Friedman, *The Horowitz Lectures of 1972*, p. 59.
81. *Ibid.*
82. *Ibid.*

government and who bears the burden of that expenditure.'[83] Apart
from this, the role of fiscal policy for neo-monetarists is to be judged by
reference to its impact on the supply of money. 'Government
spending', according to Friedman, 'may or may not be inflationary. It
will be clearly inflationary if it is financed by creating money.'[84] If, on
the other hand, the spending is financed 'by taxes or by borrowing
from the public', it will not be inflationary.[85] It follows from this that,
as far as the effect on inflation is concerned, a neutral budget should
ensure that the annual rate of growth in the supply of money is kept
within the limits mentioned above.

It is worth noting that the quantity theory as used by neo-
monetarists tends to obscure the important distinction between the
concepts of 'income' and 'money' which is crucial to any meaningful
analysis of the role of money in the economy. This is particularly
noticeable in some of the neo-monetarists pronouncements on fiscal
matters. Friedman's statement, quoted above, for example suggesting
that government spending is not inflationary if it is financed by
borrowing from the public, clearly implies that the expansionary effect
on aggregate effective demand of an increase in private 'income'
(caused by government spending) will, in some way or other, be
completely offset by the contractionary effect of an equivalent
reduction in the supply of 'money' resulting from borrowing from the
public.[86] It may be worth noting also that, since early 1979 in the UK,
this proposition has served as a rather 'convenient' theory justifying
the sale of nationalised industries to the private sector on the grounds
that such sales will restrain inflation by restricting the rate of growth of
the supply of money.

One may venture to suggest that one reason for the general
receptiveness of the public to neo-monetarists' ideas is that in the eyes
of the man in the street, also, there is no clear distinction between the
two concepts; the words 'money' and 'income' are more or less
synonymous in common parlance. Indeed it takes considerable effort
to convince even bright first-year undergraduates in Economics that
individuals' total cash balances need not be closely correlated with
either their wealth or their income.

83. *Ibid.*, p. 29.
84. *Ibid.*
85. *Ibid.*
86. It has also been suggested that government spending financed by the issue of bonds
    may not be expansionary, because the public will not perceive government bonds as
    'net wealth' unless their value exceeds the capitalised value of the implied stream of
    future tax liabilities. See Robert J. Barro, 'Are Government Bonds Net Wealth?',
    Journal of Political Economy, November/December 1974. This suggestion has,
    however, too little to do with the attitude of the bond holders to their wealth in real
    life to deserve serious consideration.

FINANCING ECONOMIC DEVELOPMENT (1) DOMESTIC SAVINGS

In this and the following chapter we shall be concerned with the first constraint on accelerating economic growth, namely the provision of adequate resources to finance requisite investment without engendering inflation (see pp. 55–6). It is obvious that the total supply of such resources is equal to the sum of 'voluntary', as distinct from 'forced', national savings and net capital receipts from abroad, as indicated by the following identity derived from equation (8) on page 37[1].

$$I_d = S + (M - X).$$

The supply of investible resources can thus be augmented by raising the level of voluntary savings (S) and/or by increasing the inflow of foreign capital ($M - X$). For the present we abstract from interaction between the two streams of resources discussed later (pp. 125–30). This chapter is devoted to an analysis of the role played by fiscal and monetary measures in determining the volume of voluntary savings; the role of foreign capital is discussed in the next chapter.

Since savings equal national income less private and public consumption outlays, it follows that measures that succeed in restraining the growth of the two categories of consumption, without retarding the growth of production, will also raise the ratio of savings to national income. Leaving aside for the present the balance of payments constraint on government policies, examined in Chapter 4, the authorities are in a position to offset any contractionary impact of the curbs on consumption by corresponding increases in public investment. The restriction of consumption need not therefore have an adverse effect on the growth of production by depressing aggregate effective demand. Production may, however, be affected, positively or

1. For a definition of the terms 'forced' and 'voluntary' savings see p. 40.

adversely, from the supply side, partly because some fiscal measures may influence incentives to work or to produce. In addition, certain types of government expenditure classified as consumption, such as outlays on education and health, influence the quality of the labour force, while others, such as expenditure on 'economic services', explained below, make a direct contribution to production. Such side effects must be taken into consideration as we explore the possibilities of curbing public and private consumption in this chapter.

PUBLIC CONSUMPTION

Governments of developing countries, like those of any other, are obliged to incur regular expenditure in the course of discharging their normal functions. The volume and pattern of such expenditure will vary with the number of functions undertaken by the authorities, and with the efficiency of administration.

Public expenditure is conventionally divided into two broad categories in national income statistics, namely, *current* and *capital*. The distinction between these two types of outlay is usually made by reference to the criterion of creation of productive physical wealth. Capital expenditure consists of those government outlays that result in the enlargement of the physical productive capacity of the economy either directly through government *investment,* or indirectly by the provision of *investment grants* to the private sector. Generally, all defence outlays, even those made on fixed installations and equipment, e.g. on the construction of barracks and warships, are included in current expenditure, as they are not considered directly productive.

Current expenditures are subdivided into *consumption* expenditure and *transfer* payments. Consumption consists of current, i.e. non-investment, outlays on goods and services by public authorities which directly affect demand and production. Subsidies, pensions, social benefits and other payments, which affect demand indirectly through their influence on the real income of the private sector, are classified as transfer payments; we shall here be concerned solely with government, or public, 'consumption' and 'investment' outlays.

We shall now examine briefly the major categories of government consumption by reference to their social and economic functions. The purpose is to explore the opportunities available for raising the volume of savings through curbs on government consumption without retarding development. We distinguish between four broad categories of public expenditure which account for the bulk of government consumption. These are: general administration and internal security; economic services; education and health; and defence.

1. *General administration and internal security.* In most countries the maintenance of administrative machinery, of law enforcement agencies and of internal security establishments together account for a large share of public expenditure. It is clear that the management of the day-to-day functions of the central government and local authorities plays an important role in determining the efficiency of any economy. Similarly, the provision of security to persons and property and the assurance of the enforcement of contracts constitute basic preconditions for the orderly functioning of society under any political system. This type of expenditure should of course have top priority in any government budget, although its scale should be limited to the minimum required to ensure adequate services.

Regarding government administration, the highest priority in public expenditure should be given to the training and provision of an efficient and reliable civil service machinery. This will produce no more than an instrument for the execution of government policies, but without it there can be no assurance of success in any field of governmental operations, including those related to expenditure and to revenue collection. In general it is preferable to have a small, well-trained and well-paid civil service rather than one consisting of a large mass of employees of heterogeneous quality with low salaries and financially dependent on corrupt practices. In many LDCs it may be economically profitable to retire a large section of the existing civil service on a national pension scheme rather than to retain them in their official employment. But, as noted earlier, governments' willingness and ability to improve the quality of the administrative machinery depends in practice very much on the socio-political structure of the economy and on the character of the governments themselves (see pp. 25–6).

There is also a direct link between the character of individual governments and the expenditure incurred by them on the provision of internal security and on the enforcement of laws. It is clear that the more autocratic (or the less democratic) the government, the less popular or acceptable its laws and decrees are likely to be. This means that the amount of expenditure incurred on the enforcement of law, in the form of outlay on the uniformed and secret police forces, and on courts and prisons, is likely to be higher. Moreover, apart from meeting the need to apprehend criminals and to enforce ordinary civil contracts, autocratic governments need additional security forces (police and gendarmerie) to contain internal political opposition.

2. *Economic services.* This category of public expenditure covers
outlays on the maintenance of economic infrastructure, such as
transport, communication, water and power, which in most developing countries are owned and managed by the public sector. In
addition, the authorities often provide free of charge technical advice
to industry, commerce and agriculture which constitute part of
economic services. It is clear that outlay on economic services can play
an important part in the promotion of development and should have a
high claim to the resources available for government consumption
purposes. In practice, governments which undertake to play a larger
role in promoting development, tend to devote a relatively greater
share of resources to the provision of these services.

3. *Education and health.* Government 'current' expenditure on education and health, although conventionally classified under consumption, in fact amounts to investment in human resources since it
contributes to an enlargement of productive capacity by improving
the quality of the labour force (see p. 4). Thus, apart from general
social welfare considerations, there are important economic reasons for
giving the outlay on these services the same social priority as that
accorded to investment; it is hardly necessary to underline the
significance for development of a healthy, educated and trained labour
force. To ensure that maximum economic benefit is derived from
educational outlays, however, it is important to see to it that the
education and training policies adopted are relevant to the social and
economic requirements of the country. For example, in the majority of
developing countries, programmes for the training of technical and
professional personnel, such as skilled craftsmen, engineers, accountants and statisticians, should receive a much higher priority than they
receive in industrial countries.

4. *Defence.* Unlike the other categories of government consumption,
defence outlay makes little or no direct contribution to development
and can only be rationally justified by threats of external aggression.[2]
It is clear that this category of expenditure should be kept to the
minimum required to ensure the external security of the individual
countries. It should, in this connection, also be noted that, in practice,
military outlays need not necessarily contribute more to the security of
a country than the expenditure incurred on promoting development.
This is clearly illustrated by the experience of Iran which over many
years in the 1970s spent considerably more on defence and internal

2. Some indirect contribution to development may be made by certain outlays, e.g.
investment in infrastructure, such as transport facilities, undertaken for defence
purposes.

security than on economic development and which, nevertheless, underwent a major political upheaval towards the end of the decade and was later seriously threatened by internal disintegration and by foreign incursions on its territory.

Expenditure on defence, education and health

To compare the relative importance attached by the various developing countries to the four categories of expenditure noted above, one would have to examine their share in total government consumption. Although there is no conceptual difficulty in doing this, the available data do not, unfortunately, permit a meaningful evaluation of the share of the first two categories, namely 'general administration and internal security' and 'economic services'. The reason for this is that budgetary systems and accounting practices vary from country to country and there are significant differences in the definition and coverage of these two classes of expenditure. Such information as is available, however, confirms the points noted earlier, namely that the countries with autocratic and dictatorial régimes devote a higher proportion of their expenditure to internal security, and that the share of expenditure on economic services varies with the scope of government involvement in development.

It is, however, possible to make a rough comparison between some countries of the share of resources devoted to the last two categories of government expenditure – 'education and health' and 'defence'. Table 3.1 shows the relative weights of 'defence', 'education' and 'health' in GNP, as well as the share of 'defence' in total government consumption for a selected number of developing countries. The countries have been listed alphabetically by geographic area; the sample is a random one but includes all the large countries for which the relevant data were available. A special section has been assigned to Israel and its neighbouring Arab countries because of their unusually high defence outlays resulting from conditions of conflict or armed truce in the Middle East. By way of comparison, similar figures are presented for a sample of industrial countries of the West. Except where otherwise indicated in the footnotes to the table, the percentages shown in the table are derived from government expenditure in two consecutive years during the period 1974–8.

Before considering the data presented in the table, it is necessary to draw the attention of the reader to certain reservations concerning their quality. Owing to paucity of data on 'transfer payments' in developing countries, the coverage of the table is confined to 'government final consumption expenditure' under all the three headings. For some of countries shown in the table it was possible to obtain the requisite information from the United Nations national accounts publications mentioned in the 'source'. For the countries which lacked this information, only 'defence' outlay by the central government is shown; except where otherwise indicated, these are derived from the budgetary data published by the IMF and need not strictly correspond to 'final government consumption'. Partly because of this difference in the coverage of the figures, and partly because of variations in accounting practice from country to country, the figures presented in Table 3.1 are not exactly comparable between countries and no significance should, therefore, be attached to small differences between them.

Looking first at the data for the ratios of defence expenditure to GNP in the first column of the table, it can be seen that in *Africa*, these ratios are smallest for Ethiopia, Ghana and Tunisia, although even for these countries they are of the same order of magnitude as those of such neutral industrial countries of western Europe as Austria and Finland. The other five African countries covered by the sample register higher percentages of defence outlay, equal to or larger than those of the majority of NATO members; this ratio is particularly high in Kenya, Morocco and Nigeria.

The highest ratios of defence expenditure to GNP outside the Arab–Israeli conflict region are recorded in *Asia* which accounts for almost two-thirds of the population of developing countries. It can be seen from the table that, with the exception of the Philippines and Sri Lanka, the ratio of defence expenditure to GNP is higher in each of the other six Asian countries covered by the sample than the average ratio for the eight NATO members shown in the table; the percentages of defence outlay are especially large for Iran,[3] Malaysia and Pakistan.

In *Latin America*, Mexico spends only about one-half per cent of its domestic production on defence; all other countries included in the sample show considerably higher ratios of defence outlay. These range from about 1 per cent of GNP for Brazil to well over 3 per cent of GNP for Chile, and are comparable in magnitude to the percentages recorded by the neutral industrial countries of the West.

The table shows that the average ratio of defence expenditure to GNP for the 24 developing countries of Africa, Asia and Latin America is of the same order of magnitude as that of the eight members of

3. In Iran, the defence outlays have been cut drastically since the overthrow of the Shah's régime early in 1979.

Table 3.1 : *Selected developing and industrial countries : government final consumption expenditure on defence, education and health[a]*

	Defence	Edu- cation	Health	Defence (Percentage of government
		(Percentage of GNP)		consumption)
I Africa				
Country				
1. Ethiopia	1.9	...	...	18
2. Ghana	1.6	3.4	1.4	13
3. Kenya	3.3	6.0	1.9	18
4. Malawi	2.1	...	...	20
5. Morocco	6.4	...	...	30
6. Nigeria	4.4[b]	...	...	35
7. Sudan	2.4[c]	3.0	1.3	18
8. Tunisia	1.5	...	...	9
Average, Africa	3.0	4.2	1.5	20
II Asia				
Country				
1. India	3.2	0.9	0.5	32
2. Iran[d]	14.1	3.0	1.2	63
3. Korea, Republic of	3.9	0.2	—	37
4. Malaysia	4.6	...	...	28
5. Pakistan (exclud- ing Bangladesh)	5.2	...	...	52
6. Philippines	2.9	...	...	29
7. Sri Lanka	0.7	2.7	1.4	6
8. Thailand	3.3[c]	2.8	0.6	26
Average, Asia	4.7	1.9	0.7	34
III Latin America				
Country				
1. Argentina	1.6	...	...	16
2. Bolivia	2.0	3.4	0.5	16
3. Brazil	1.1	...	...	12
4. Chile	3.6	...	...	28
5. Honduras	1.8	3.4	2.1	15
6. Mexico	0.6[b]	...	...	5

Table 3.1 (*cont.*)

	Defence	Edu-cation	Health	Defence (Percentage of government consumption)
		(Percentage of GNP)		
7. Paraguay	1.4	...	...	21
8. Venezuela	2.4	4.5	1.9	16
Average, Latin America	1.8	3.7	1.5	16
Average, Africa, Asia and Latin America	3.2	3.0	1.2	23
IV Arab–Israeli conflict region Country				
1. Egypt	5.1	...	...	22
2. Iraq	7.4[e]	...	...	...
3. Israel	27.1[b]	3.7[b]	1.3[b]	77
4. Jordan	16.0[c]	3.4	0.8	59
5. Syria	15.4[b]	...	...	74
Average, Arab–Israeli conflict region	14.2	3.5	1.1	58
V Industrial countries A. Neutral countries				
1. Austria	1.2	3.6	4.2	7
2. Finland	1.4	5.4	4.1	7
3. Sweden	3.3	5.8	6.7	12
4. Switzerland	2.0	...	...	16
Average, neutral countries	2.0	4.9	5.0	11
B. NATO members				
5. Belgium	2.8	6.8	...	16
6. Canada	1.7	...	...	8
7. Denmark	2.2	5.9	4.6	9

Table 3.1 (*cont.*)

	Defence	Edu-cation	Health	Defence (Percentage of government consumption)
		(Percentage of GNP)		
8. Germany, Federal Republic of*f*	2.8	...	...	14
9. Italy	1.7	4.2	0.7	11
10. Netherlands*f*	3.0	...	...	16
11. Norway	3.1	5.7	2.5	16
12. United Kingdom	4.7	4.4	4.6	23
13. United States	5.2	4.8	1.1	29
Average, NATO members	3.0	5.3	2.7	16
Average, industrial countries	2.7	5.2	3.6	14

Source: United Nations, *Yearbook of National Accounts Statistics, 1979*; IMF, *International Financial Statistics*, various issues, and *Government Finance Statistics Yearbook*, Vol. IV, 1980.

Except where otherwise indicated by the footnotes, in the case of the countries for which only the 'defence' percentages are shown, the figures are derived from government budgets published in the IMF, *Government Finance Statistics Yearbook*; in all other cases, the data represent 'final government consumption' as published in the United Nations, *Yearbook of National Accounts Statistics*.

a Except for Ethiopia, Iraq and Korea, average of the two most recent years for which data were available during 1974–8. For Ethiopia, average of two years ending 7 July 1974; for Iraq, average of two years ending 31 March 1975; and for Korea, average of 1972 and 1973.

b Percentage of GDP.

c Derived from the budget figures published by the IMF.

d Derived from official national publications.

e Derived from United Nations, *Statistical Yearbook*, 1978; excludes outlays financed from US grants.

f 'Final government consumption', as published by the United Nations.

Note: The average lines show the unweighted arithmetic mean of the country percentage figures.

NATO, and is about 50 per cent larger than the corresponding ratio for the four neutral industrial countries.

Exceptionally large ratios of defence expenditure to GNP, ranging from about 5 per cent for Egypt to over 25 per cent for Israel, are registered in the *Arab–Israeli Conflict Region*. These unusually high levels of outlay are financed largely by oil revenues in the case of Iraq, and by external loans and grants in the case of other countries.

Another and perhaps more significant way of assessing the fiscal policy of developing countries is to compare the ratio of resources devoted by them to what can generally be regarded as largely useless defence outlays with that allocated to education and to health, which, as explained earlier, play a key role in promoting development. It can be seen that, for the *Arab–Israeli Conflict Region*, the outlays on defence range from about 20 to 80 per cent of government consumption and are four to five times larger than the combined expenditure on education and health in Israel and Jordan – the two countries for which the relevant data are available. For the three countries in *Africa* and the three in *Latin America* with complete data, the outlay on defence is lower than that on education but, except in Honduras, larger than expenditure on health. Outside the Middle East, the picture is gloomiest in *Asia*, where in three out of the five countries with complete data (India, Iran and Korea) the share of defence in GNP is appreciably higher than that of education and health combined; all the available evidence suggests that the same is true of Pakistan. It is worth noting that these include some of the largest developing countries which together account for over one-third of the population of LDCs.

It can be seen from the last column of the table that the average share of defence expenditure in government consumption for the Asian countries (34 per cent) is about twice as large as the average for the eight NATO countries; the corresponding figure for the 24 African, Asian and Latin American countries combined (23 per cent) is also about 50 per cent higher than for the NATO countries.

It is possible to obtain a very rough estimate of the order of magnitude of the total defence expenditure of developing countries included in Table 3.1 by converting individual national expenditures into US dollars at official exchange rates and aggregating the figures. According to our estimate, the average annual defence outlay for the countries shown in the table amounts to over $27 billion, of which well over 50 per cent appertains to the eight Asian countries and over 20 per cent to the Arab – Israeli conflict region; the sixteen African and Latin American countries together account for just over 25 per cent of the total. The combined defence expenditure of all developing countries would of course be significantly higher than that of the countries included in the sample. Nevertheless, the defence expenditure by these countries alone is some 35 per cent larger than the average annual Official Development Assistance of about $20 billion received by LDCs from various sources during the years 1974–8 covered by the table.[4]

When comparing the level of defence outlays in LDCs with those of industrial countries, it is essential to remember the important difference between the position of the two groups of countries noted earlier (see pp. 40–1). For developing countries, where investment is constrained by a shortage of savings, this expenditure has the effect of retarding development by reducing the volume of savings. In addition, purchases of arms from abroad, which often account for a significant share of defence outlay, constitute a serious drain on their scarce foreign exchange resources. In industrial countries, on the other hand, where production in peace time is generally restrained by a shortage of effective demand, expenditure on defence can serve the purpose of sustaining and stimulating economic activity. Moreover, the export of arms to developing countries often provides some industrial countries with a lucrative source of foreign exchange earnings. We are concerned here only with the economic implications of armament expenditure in LDCs and not with the dubious political morality of competitive arms sales by both the free enterprise and socialist industrial states to developing countries. It may, nevertheless, be worth noting some of the factors which would seem to render many developing countries such eager customers for the purchase of arms.

As noted earlier, defence expenditure can be rationally justified only in those cases where countries are genuinely threatened by external aggression. But apart from the countries involved in the Middle Eastern conflict, very few can be said to suffer from such threats, although some do have long-standing territorial or frontier disputes, generally of minor economic significance. Yet we have seen that the great majority of developing countries devote a significant proportion of their resources, comparable in magnitude to that of the rich industrial countries of the West, to defence. Moreover, in many of them, defence outlays command a higher priority than investment in human resources in the form of expenditure on education and health. This would suggest that there may be other reasons, not directly

4. See, OECD, *Development Co-operation, 1980 Review*, p. 177.
  For a definition of Official Development Assistance see pp. 133–4 below.

related to genuine security needs, which underline the defence policies of some governments.

We are not in a position to impute specific motives to the defence policies of individual governments; nor would it be proper to do so in this book. But the following factors may help to explain the relatively high levels of defence expenditure in at least some developing countries. *First*, military forces are at times used to reinforce the internal security forces for the purpose of suppression of political opposition. This is particularly true of the autocratic régimes which lack adequate support among the politically active sections of the population. *Secondly*, for some governments involved in frontier and territorial disputes, the objective of resolving such disputes in their own favour by threat of force justifies a relatively high level of defence expenditure. *Thirdly*, in some cases, governments seem to be attracted by the mere prestige of possessing a range of modern sophisticated armaments. *Fourthly*, once, for whatever reason, some countries begin to arm, they pose a potential threat to neighbouring states, thus setting up a chain reaction of competitive armament which more often than not tends to diminish rather than enhance the security of each one of them.

The foregoing analysis of the pattern of government consumption, although incomplete and based on rather inadequate data, does suggest that LDCs as a whole tend to devote an unnecessarily large proportion of their scarce resources to what is often useless military expenditure. A reduction in this expenditure would, in the case of most of them, increase the volume of resources available for development purposes without noticeably diminishing their security. That this is not done would suggest that considerations other than economic development tend to exercise an undue influence on government policies in practice.

FISCAL POLICY AND PRIVATE CONSUMPTION

We now examine the way in which fiscal and monetary measures can be used to increase domestic savings by restricting the growth of private consumption. Because private consumption accounts for a considerably larger proportion of national income than investment, even a relatively small reduction in its rate of growth can have a significant impact on the rates of growth of voluntary savings and investment. It may be worth illustrating this point by means of an arithmetic example. Consider a typical underdeveloped country in which private consumption accounts for 70 per cent and investment and public consumption each for 15 per cent of total production, and assume that GNP and all the three components of expenditure are rising at 3 per cent a year. If the rate of growth of private consumption was then reduced by only half a percentage point (from 3 to 2.5 per cent) adequate resources would be released to raise the rate of growth of investment by over two percentage points – from 3 to over 5 per cent – permitting a proportionate increase in the rate of growth.

It is worth noting that fiscal and monetary measures provide only an indirect means of restraining the growth of private consumption. As noted earlier, the same purpose can, in theory at least, be achieved more directly and equitably through a system of rationing of consumer goods combined with price controls (see p. 64). But few developing countries have the administrative machinery to run such a system efficiently,[5] which partly explains why it is generally confined to periods of emergency and to a few basic necessities. But even in such cases rationing and price controls have rarely been administered efficiently; the result has more often been the emergence of black markets in rationed goods.

Of the two sets of measures, fiscal and monetary, it is fiscal measures that have to bear the brunt of regulating private consumption. Monetary policy can exercise very little *direct* effect on private expenditure except in the case of goods purchased on consumer credit; the latter, which are confined largely to durable consumer goods, account for a relatively small share (less than 5 per cent) of total private consumption in LDCs (see pp. 44–6). Taxation measures, on the other hand, directly affect consumption through their influence on either the amount or the purchasing power of private disposable incomes. Direct taxes reduce the amount of private disposable income and indirect taxes its purchasing power by raising the prices of goods and services on which taxes are imposed. In the remainder of this chapter, therefore, we shall be concerned exclusively with the use of fiscal measures, notably taxation, for the purpose of regulating the growth of private consumption.

Taxation target and potential

Leaving aside its use for redistribution of income with which we are not concerned here, taxation performs two important and distinct functions in the strategy of economic development that should be taken

---

5. One of these countries is Sri Lanka, discussed later (see pp. 177–8).

into consideration in setting a taxation target. *The first* and perhaps the more important function of taxation is to restrain the growth of private consumption in order to increase the *volume* of resources available for investment purposes. As explained earlier, the higher is the target rate of growth of production, the more rigorous must be the curbs on consumption necessary to avoid inflation (see pp. 55–6). The decisions on taxation and growth targets are, therefore, closely interlinked. Abstracting from foreign capital, it is the taxation target, reflecting the decision of the authorities on how much current consumption should be restrained to promote investment and future consumption, that largely determines the warranted rate of growth of production.

The second important function of taxation is to transfer resources from the private to the public sector. Other things being equal, the larger is the ratio of taxation to GNP, the higher will be the share of resources available to governments to meet their current and capital expenditure. Where government revenue exceeds its current expenditure, as is generally the case in most developing countries, any increase in tax revenue will raise the volume of savings available for investment purposes in the public sector. This will enable the authorities to play a larger role in determining the overall *pattern* of investment in the economy discussed in Chapter 5.

The potential of developing countries for raising tax revenue is often judged by reference to their average per capita income which is relatively low in most of them. Per capita income, however, is far from being a satisfactory indicator of taxation potential, since it takes no account of the distribution of income. A more satisfactory indicator of tax potential is provided by the volume of national income accruing to those groups of the population whose standard of living is above subsistence level and which should be made to bear the bulk of the taxation burden; particularly important in this regard is the share and level of income of the richest groups of the community. The relatively large inequalities of income in LDCs, discussed earlier (pp. 12–15), would, therefore, suggest that the taxation potential of these countries is appreciably higher than is indicated by their per capita income. This point will be illustrated below by reference to the distribution of income in the agricultural sector of some developing countries.

The actual amount of tax revenue collected depends only partly on the taxation potential of the individual countries and on the targets of taxation set by the authorities. No less important is the *ability* of governments in practice to collect taxes. Given the potential and the target of taxation, the success of the authorities in exploiting the tax potential and in attaining the target will depend on a number of factors of which the following three are particularly important.

1. *Efficiency of Fiscal Machinery*. Since taxes have to be collected through the civil service, success in this effort will depend to an important extent on its standards of integrity and efficiency. As noted earlier, the most important single factor affecting the quality of the administration in most developing countries is the character of governments and this, in turn, is determined by the social, political and economic characteristics of the countries (see pp. 24–6). There is, therefore, no simple and painless way of improving the performance of the administration significantly, since such improvement will generally entail appropriate changes in their politico-economic structure, a subject with which we are not directly concerned here.

2. *Production and Marketing Structure of the Economy*. There are two important ways in which the structure of production and commerce can influence the ability of governments to exploit the taxation potential to the desired level. *First*, it is more difficult to levy taxes on the subsistence than on the monetised sector of the economy; hence, other things being equal, the larger is the share of the subsistence agriculture in the economy, the more difficult will it be to exploit the taxation potential. *Secondly*, as explained below (pp. 107–9), it is generally easier to estimate the profits of large public mining and manufacturing corporations for taxation purposes than those of family enterprises and of small traders and producers, which account for a relatively large share of production in LDCs. In most countries, public companies are required by law to keep a record of their business transactions and to publish audited accounts and balance sheets for the information of shareholders and of the public in general as well as for submission to the tax authorities. Furthermore, the management of public companies, which is responsible for the publication of accounts and for the payment of taxes, is at least partially divorced from the shareholders and is likely to have less incentive for tax evasion than that of family enterprises.

3. *Importance of Foreign Trade*. The extent of dependence of a country on foreign trade can be measured by the ratio of exports or imports to total production. This will vary with the degree of specialisation in production and with the availability of productive resources. Generally, the larger the geographical size of a country is, the greater its natural, if not its capital and labour resources are likely to be, and hence the smaller its degree of dependence on foreign trade will be. This is on the whole true of both industrial and developing countries. For example, among industrial countries the ratio of exports of goods

and services to GNP varies from about 8 per cent in the US to just under 30 per cent in the UK and to almost 50 per cent in Holland. Similarly, in developing countries this ratio varies from about 5 per cent in India to 20 per cent in Sri Lanka and to over 40 per cent in Zambia.

Given the quality of fiscal machinery, it is on the whole easier for governments to collect indirect than direct taxes. This is particularly true of import tariffs and export duties which, as we shall presently see, account for the bulk of indirect taxes collected. Apart from smuggling, which is of relatively minor importance in most countries, exports and imports pass through a small number of ports and frontier posts in each country which the authorities can keep under close supervision and control for taxation purposes. It follows, therefore, that, other things being equal, the higher the ratio of foreign trade to national income is, the easier it will be to raise the ratio of taxation revenue to national income.

Tax ratios

A number of attempts have been made to relate statistically the yield of taxation in different countries to various characteristics which might have been thought to affect their taxable potential – per capita income, the size of the agriculture sector and the share of foreign trade in national income, for example.[6] The main conclusion of these studies, including our own investigation, is that the ratio of taxation to national income is correlated positively with the share of foreign trade and negatively with the share of agricultural production in GNP, while per capita income is, as shown below (p. 97), statistically unimportant.[7] In addition, the studies show that even the best regression equations obtained cannot account for more than one-half of the observed variance of tax ratios among LDCs. This is not surprising of course, because some of the important variables, such as the efficiency of the fiscal administration and government fiscal policies, being objectively unquantifiable, have been excluded from these regression analyses.

Table 3.2 shows the tax ratios in a selected number of developing

6. See, in particular, the studies conducted by the IMF: Raja J. Chelliah, 'Trends in Taxation in Developing Countries', *IMF Staff Papers*, July 1971, and Raja J. Chelliah, Hessel J. Baas and Margaret R. Kelly, 'Tax Ratios and Tax Effort in Developing Countries, 1969–71', *IMF Staff Papers*, March 1975.
7. I am grateful to Professor M.J.C. Surrey, of the University of Leeds, for this regression analysis.

countries excluding members of the Organisation of Petroleum Exporting Countries (OPEC) which, because of their special revenue position, have been treated separately in the following section. We have also excluded other countries in which governments derive a significant proportion of their income from the exploitation of mineral resources. The reason for this is that it is not clear that government revenue from mineral exploitation, whether received under the heading of 'income tax', 'royalty' or 'profit share', strictly constitutes a part of 'national income' (correctly defined) appropriated by the exchequer. It could legitimately be argued that such revenue should be regarded as a 'capital' receipt since it represents, in essence, the proceeds of the sale of a national asset in the form of a depleting natural resource.[8] The amount of this revenue has, in any case, generally little or no bearing on governments' 'effort' or 'success' to restrain private consumption through taxation.

The countries have been listed alphabetically and by geographical area; by way of comparison similar data are shown for a number of industrial countries. Section A of the table shows the ratios of total tax revenue and of direct and indirect taxes to GNP, and Section B the share of direct and indirect taxation in total tax revenue. Wherever possible tax revenue covers all taxation, including social security contributions, appertaining to 'general government',[9] but, in any case, it generally includes taxation raised by the central and state governments as well as provincial authorities. Despite the attempt to make the data as comparable as possible, there are likely to be some differences between the countries as regards the definition and coverage of direct and indirect taxes and, for this reason, no significance should be attached to small differences in the tax ratios shown in the table.

It can be seen from Section A of Table 3.2 that the average ratio of total tax revenue to GNP ranges from just over 10 per cent in *Latin America* to about 15 per cent in *Africa* and *Asia*. The average ratios of both direct and indirect taxes to GNP are remarkably similar in the latter two continents, and are significantly higher than those for *Latin America*. Of the 27 developing countries included in the Table, only in Tunisia, which raises a relatively large revenue through social security contributions, does the ratio for total tax revenue noticeably exceed 20 per cent. There are, on the other hand, 7 countries

8. See G. Stuvel, *System of Social Accounts*, Clarendon Press, Oxford (1965), pp. 207–8.

9. For a definition of 'general government' see United Nations, *A System of National Accounts*, Series F, No. 2, Rev. 3 (1968), p. 79.

Table 3.2: *Selected developing and industrial countries: direct and indirect tax ratios*[a]

	Section A (Percentage of GNP)			Section B (Percentage of tax revenue)	
	Total tax revenue	Direct taxes	Indirect taxes	Direct taxes	Indirect taxes
I Africa					
1. Egypt	12.8	5.1	7.6	40	60
2. Ethiopia	9.7	2.7	6.9	28	72
3. Ghana	12.1[b]	2.4	9.7	20	80
4. Ivory Coast	20.2	2.8	17.4	14	86
5. Kenya	18.1	6.6	11.5	36	64
6. Morocco	15.3	4.3	11.0	28	72
7. Sudan	12.3	1.7	10.6	14	86
8. Tanzania, United Republic of	15.9	5.0	10.9	31	69
9. Tunisia	22.1	8.8	13.3	40	60
Average, Africa	15.4	4.4	11.0	28	72
II Asia					
1. Burma	8.4	3.7	4.7	44	56
2. India	13.7	2.7	11.1	20	80
3. Korea, Republic of	16.9	4.7	12.2	28	72
4. Malaysia	16.9	4.8	12.2	28	72
5. Pakistan	12.6	1.6	11.0	13	87
6. Philippines	13.7	3.3	10.3	24	76
7. Singapore	15.3	7.2	8.2	47	53
8. Sri Lanka	17.8	3.4	14.3	19	81
9. Thailand	13.1	2.2	10.9	17	83
10. Turkey	17.8	6.1	11.7	34	66
Average, Asia	14.6	4.0	10.7	27	73
III Latin America					
1. Argentina	16.9	6.9	10.0	41	59
2. Brazil	9.5	2.9	6.6	31	69
3. Colombia	10.0	4.9	5.1	49	51
4. Dominican Republic	15.5	4.7	10.8	30	70
5. Guatemala	8.2	1.3	6.9	15	85
6. Honduras	10.6	2.6	8.0	25	75

Table 3.2 (*Cont.*)

	Section A (Percentage of GNP)			Section B (Percentage of tax revenue)	
	Total tax revenue	Direct taxes	Indirect taxes	Direct taxes	Indirect taxes
7. Nicaragua	9.9	1.0	8.9	10	90
8. Paraguay	6.0	0.8	5.1	14	86
Average, Latin America	10.8	3.2	7.7	27	73
Average, developing countries	13.7	3.9	9.9	27	73
IV Industrial countries					
1. Austria	39.1	22.2	16.9	57	43
2. Belgium	39.8	28.6	11.3	72	28
3. Canada	32.1	19.2	12.9	60	40
4. Denmark	43.3	27.3	16.0	63	37
5. France	36.5	21.9	14.6	60	40
6. Germany, Federal Republic of	37.5	24.5	13.0	65	35
7. Italy	30.7	19.8	11.0	64	36
8. Japan	21.7	15.1	6.6	70	30
9. Netherlands	47.5	35.7	11.8	75	25
10. Norway	48.3	30.2	18.1	63	37
11. Sweden	46.0	31.6	14.4	69	31
12. United Kingdom	36.0	23.0	13.1	64	36
13. United States	29.2	20.1	9.1	69	31
Average, industrial countries	37.5	24.5	13.0	65	35
Average, excluding social security contributions	27.8	14.8	13.0	52	48

Source: See Table 3.1

[a]Single years during 1970–75; the year chosen for each country is the most recent one for which the data were available.

[b]Excludes mineral duty which amounted to less than 0.5 per cent of GNP.

Notes: (i) 'Total tax revenue' comprises social security contributions included in 'direct taxes'. (ii) The 'average' lines show the unweighted arithmetic mean of the country percentage figures.

(Ethiopia, Burma, Brazil, Colombia, Guatemala, Nicaragua and Paraguay) in which this ratio is as low as 10 per cent or even less. It is also worth noting that of the 8 Latin American countries included in the sample, in only 2 (Argentina and Dominican Republic) is the ratio of total tax revenue to GNP appreciably higher than 10 per cent.

Section B of the table shows considerable differences between individual developing countries in the share of direct taxes in total tax revenue. It varies from a range of 10–15 per cent in Ivory Coast, Sudan, Pakistan, Guatemala, Nicaragua and Paraguay to 40 per cent or more in Egypt, Tunisia, Burma, Singapore, Argentina and Colombia. It can also be seen that, on average, direct taxes account for just over one-fourth of total tax revenue for the countries included in all the three less developed continents.

It is instructive to compare the tax ratios of developing countries with those obtaining in the industrial countries shown in the last section of the table. It can be seen that the ratios of both direct and indirect taxes to GNP are significantly higher in industrial than in less developed countries. But particularly pronounced is the difference in the ratio of direct taxes between the two groups of countries, the average of which amounts to 4 per cent for all developing countries compared with 25 per cent for industrial countries. A part of this difference is accounted for by social security contributions included in direct taxes which are appreciably higher in industrial countries. But even if these contributions were excluded from direct tax revenue in the latter countries, the ratio of direct taxes to GNP would, as indicated by the last line of the table, still amount to 15 per cent for them. This is about four times higher than the ratio of direct taxes, *including* social security contributions, to GNP for developing countries. It is this wide gap between direct taxation ratios that largely accounts for the significant difference between the ratios of total tax revenue to GNP for the two groups of countries, shown in the table: 14 per cent in developing countries compared with nearly 40 per cent in industrial countries, or just under 30 per cent if social security contributions are excluded.[10]

10. The average ratio of tax revenue to GNP for developing countries as a whole shown in Table 3.2 does not differ significantly from that published in an IMF study in 1974. According to this study, which covered a larger sample of 47 countries, the average ratio of tax revenue, including social security contributions, to GNP during the three years 1969–71 amounted to 16 per cent and, excluding social security contributions, to 15 per cent (see *IMF Survey*, 3rd June 1974, p. 162). One reason for a somewhat higher tax ratio shown by the IMF study is that its sample, unlike ours, includes a number of mineral exporting countries, such as some members of OPEC, for which relatively high-tax ratio are recorded.

The pronounced difference between the ratios of tax revenue to GNP in developing and industrial countries can be explained only partly by the fact that per capita income and the taxation potential of the latter countries are appreciably higher. A second important reason for this difference is the failure of developing countries to exploit their tax potential at a rate comparable to that of industrial countries. This is particularly true of the taxation of land in developing countries, where, as explained later in this chapter, because of a highly unequal distribution of land ownership and of income, there exists a large tax potential which governments have by and large failed to utilise (see pp. 112–18).

A comparison of tax ratios in Africa and Latin America would help to illustrate the point that per capita GNP is not a decisive factor in determining tax ratios. According to United Nations estimates, in 1974 the per capita national income in Africa was at least 60 per cent lower than that of Latin America ($360 in Africa compared with $950 in Latin America)[11] and yet, as shown in Table 3.2, the average ratios of both direct and indirect taxes were appreciably higher in Africa during that period. Since, according to all the available evidence, distribution of income is more unequal in Latin America than in Africa, the potential of direct taxation in the former continent compared with the latter must be even larger than is indicated by the ratios of their per capita national income. It would therefore be reasonable to conclude that the primary reason for a lower ratio of direct taxation in Latin America is the failure of the authorities to exploit the existing tax potential to the extent that African countries have done.

Organisation of Petroleum Exporting Countries (OPEC)

The steep rise in the world petroleum prices at the end of 1973 resulted in a sudden and pronounced increase in the foreign exchange earnings of the oil-rich Middle Eastern countries. These, together with a number of other oil exporting countries, have organised themselves into a 13-nation producers' association known as OPEC. It can be seen from Section A of Table 3.3 that the total oil revenue of OPEC was estimated at about $116 billion for 1976, of which almost $100 billion accrued to 9 members with a per capita oil revenue in excess of $600 and the remainder to the other four countries with an appreciably lower revenue per head of population; for short, countries in the first

11. See United Nations, *Yearbook of National Accounts Statistics 1976*, Vol. II.

Table 3.3 :   *OPEC: oil revenue and tax ratios*

| | Section A | | | Section B[a] | |
| | Oil revenue in 1976 | | | Non-oil tax revenue as per cent of | |
	Total revenue in $m[b]	Popula- tion in '000	Per capita revenue in $[c]	Government consumption	Defence expendi- ture
Country[d]					
Richer members of OPEC					
1. Saudi Arabia	33,500	9,240	3,630	19	40
2. Iran	22,000	33,590	650	37	61
3. Iraq	8,500	11,510	740	...	54
4. Kuwait	8,500	1,060	8,020	...	...
5. Venezuela	8,500	12,360	690	46	300
6. Libya	7,500	2,550	2,940	31	44
7. United Arab Emirates	7,000	656	10,670	...	...
8. Qatar	2,000	98	20,410	...	...
9. Gabon	800	534	1,500	...	...
Other members of OPEC					
10. Nigeria	8,500	64,750	130	...	...
11. Algeria	4,500	17,300	260	89	...
12. Indonesia	4,500	139,620	30	...	...
13. Ecuador	800	7,310	110	...	...
TOTAL	$116,600				

Source: See Table 3.1 ; also UN, *Monthly Bulletin of Statistics*, and Shell Briefing Service, *Oil and Gas in 1976*, Newgate Press Ltd., England (June 1977).
[a] Single years during 1974–76
[b] Rounded to the nearest $100 million.
[c] Rounded to the nearest $10.
[d] Countries in each group ranked according to total oil revenue.

group are referred to as 'the richer members of OPEC'.[12] The highest per capita revenue accrued to the relatively small producers with sparse population, notably Kuwait, Qatar and United Arab Emirates; in the latter two countries as well as in Saudi Arabia there is no clear demarcation line between the exchequer revenue and the personal fortunes of the ruling families.

Section B of the table shows the ratio of the non-oil tax revenue to total government consumption and to its component of defence for those members of OPEC for which the relevant data were available. All government income from the sale of petroleum at home and abroad has, for reasons mentioned above (p. 93), been excluded from tax revenue, although indirect taxes on domestic sales of petroleum are included.

Among the richer members of OPEC a very large proportion of oil revenue has been used to finance government consumption expenditure, which has been growing at an unusually steep rate primarily as a result of a rapid expansion of defence outlay. According to the published information, during the two years following the rise in oil prices in 1973, government consumption rose at an average annual rate of 100 per cent or more in Qatar and Saudi Arabia, at about 70–80 per cent in Iran and Libya and at 30–40 per cent in the other countries. It can be seen from Table 3.3 that in none of the richer members of OPEC for which the relevant data are available does the non-oil tax revenue cover even one-half of government consumption. Moreover, in all these countries, apart from Venezuela, tax revenue falls far short of even the outlay incurred on defence; it covers as little as 40 per cent and only about 60 per cent of defence expenditure of Saudi Arabia and Iran, respectively.

The fiscal policies of the members of OPEC, in particular of its richer members, have a number of serious economic and political implications which should be noted here. *First*, a significant part of oil revenue is at present being used to finance, directly or indirectly, private consumption of luxuries and government defence outlay. This amounts in effect to an exchange of a most valuable natural resource, which is being steadily depleted, for the purpose of augmenting the welfare of the richer groups of the community and for acquiring military advice and equipment from abroad. A rational fiscal policy

12. By 1979, the total oil revenue of OPEC had reached $200 billion, of which over $160 billion was received by the richer members. The per capita oil income of all these countries, with the exception of Iran, was well over $1000 in 1979. In Iran, despite a severe cut in the production and export of oil, total oil revenue for that year ($21,000 million) was only moderately lower than in 1976.

would have ensured that government consumption was financed exclusively by non-oil tax revenue, so that the entire oil revenue could have been allocated to financing present and future investment to create new productive capacities in replacement of the depleting oil resources.

Secondly, the low level of direct taxation has contributed to a steady growth in the disparity between income and wealth of the richer and poorer classes in most countries. This is likely to aggravate the existing social tensions and could lead to political upheavals similar to those witnessed in Iran during 1978–9.

Thirdly, because of the 'lop-sided' nature of growth, due largely to the unequal distribution of income, production of necessities in most countries has not kept pace with the growth in domestic income. Consequently, imports of such goods have been rising steadily and have accounted for a growing share of total consumption. This has had the effect of placing these countries in a highly vulnerable position *vis-à-vis* their trading partners, since a serious interruption in the flow of imports is likely to engender acute economic difficulties for them.

It is not clear whether all OPEC members are fully aware of the long-term implications of their present fiscal policies. What is, however, reasonably clear is that their major industrial trading partners, who find these policies highly desirable in terms of their own short-term economic and political interest, have to date been somewhat reluctant to use their influence to bring about a significant change in them.

GUIDELINES ON TAXATION

In setting up a taxation system for any country it is essential to take into account its economic, social and political characteristics; particularly relevant are the structures of production and trade and the quality of the administrative machinery. As these vary significantly among LDCs, it would clearly be impossible to propose a standard system of taxation that is likely to suit all of them. All that can be done here is to suggest certain broad guidelines for framing different types of taxation measures. Before doing so, we consider briefly the basic elements of taxation strategy.

Essential characteristics of a taxation system

1. *Equity.* To prevent 'lop-sided' growth, taxation policy must give adequate weight to the welfare aspect of development discussed in

Chapter 1 (see pp. 5–8). Measures designed to restrict the growth of private consumption should be directed, in the first instance, at the consumption of the higher income groups. Generally, the severity of the curbs imposed on consumption should depend on the level of per capita income, varying in their effect from a mere restraint in the rate of growth of consumption for lower income groups to an actual reduction of consumption for the richest groups. More specifically, this will involve, as we shall see, the implementation of a progressive system of direct taxation from which the large section of population whose income is below subsistence level is exempted. As for any increases in the indirect taxes levied for revenue purposes, these should bear more heavily on luxuries and semi-luxuries than on necessities. It is clear that the smaller is the proportion of total tax revenue collected from the lower income groups, the larger will be the rate of increase in economic welfare index corresponding to any rate of growth of production.

2. *Incentives to Production.* It is important to take into account the side-effects of the various tax measures on production (see p. 78 above). Material incentives appear to be necessary in the present, and foreseeable future, stages of social evolution to stimulate effort on the part of individual producers. This does not, however, imply that production effort is, in every case, positively correlated with material reward and that an increase in tax need necessarily reduce such effort. It is generally recognised that, with growth in income, the desire for leisure may outweigh that for additional material reward. An increase in wage and salary rates may in some cases reduce rather than increase the supply of labour. Similarly, a rise in agricultural prices and in peasant income may at times lead to a slackening of production effort. In such cases increases in taxation would stimulate rather than retard production. Moreover, even when producers' effort is positively correlated with material reward, the effect of an increase in tax rates on production will depend largely on the type of taxation levied. A rise in tax rates assessed on the basis of the volume of production or income, for example, is likely to have a negative effect on producers' effort, whereas an increase in lump-sum taxes, such as land taxes and licence fees, discussed below, may have a positive effect.

3. *Simplicity of the tax system.* It has been noted that most developing countries lack an efficient and reliable administration for the assessment and collection of taxes. Because of this, it is important to have a taxation system that is simple and readily understood by both collectors and payers of taxes, even if simplicity is achieved at the cost of some inequity in the distribution of the burden of taxation. The

desire to attain a high degree of equity by some developing countries has often resulted in the enactment of very complicated systems of taxation which have been costly to administer and open to evasion. In addition, the criteria used for tax assessments should be clearly and easily identifiable, to enable both the civil servants and the taxpayers to compute tax liability with reasonable certainty. To leave the assessment of taxes to the judgment of tax inspectors is likely to open the fiscal system to arbitrariness and corruption.

4. *Growth in taxation revenue.* To permit a faster rate of growth in investment than in private consumption, taxation revenue should be income-elastic, that is, it should rise faster than national income. There are, broadly, three channels open to the authorities to ensure that tax revenue is income-elastic. *First*, the introduction and practice of a progressive system of direct taxation under which the marginal rates of tax exceed the average tax rate. This will ensure a faster increase in the revenue received from direct taxation than in private incomes. It should, however, be borne in mind that the higher the marginal tax rates are, the greater the temptation for tax evasion is likely to be. This is simply a practical argument against introducing very steep rates of progression in direct taxes which, by encouraging evasion, may adversely affect tax revenue. *Secondly*, the introduction of new taxes with the growth in national income, in order to create additional sources of revenue. *Thirdly*, increases in the rates of taxation, whether direct or indirect, to bring about a faster rate of growth in tax revenue than in private income and expenditure.

5. *Stability of revenue.* It is important to make sure that total tax revenue is, as far as possible, relatively stable and not subject to violent short-term fluctuations. The element of uncertainty due to fluctuations of revenue makes planning of public investment very difficult. Moreover, upward swings in government revenue are likely to encourage wasteful expenditure on current and capital accounts, whereas downward swings generally result in a cut in the public investment programme rather than in current expenditure. This is because it is politically more difficult to dismiss public employees or to cut down their wages and salaries than it is to curtail government investment programmes. An important way of ensuring stability in exchequer revenue is the *diversification* of its sources. The more numerous and diversified the sources of public revenue are, the smaller the amplitude of fluctuations in total revenue is likely to be.

Diversification of tax revenue, however, presents serious difficulties for many developing countries which rely heavily on the production and export of one or two primary commodities, as illustrated by the case of Ghana in the late 1950s. Until 1958 the chief source of tax revenue in Ghana was an export tax on cocoa; in 1957/58 this source of revenue accounted for almost 50 per cent of tax collected and for about 40 per cent of total government revenue. As a result of a sudden fall in the price of cocoa in world markets and in tax revenue derived from cocoa exports after 1958, the authorities were faced with the critical problem of raising adequate revenue to cover their outlays. New sources of tax revenue were introduced with the advice of Lord Kaldor, which made up for the decline in revenue derived from cocoa. But these measures had to be introduced rather speedily and proved to be very unpopular with the taxpayers, who were not accustomed to them. The civil disturbances which followed the new tax measures were partly responsible for strengthening the opposition to Dr N'Krumah's government, which was eventually overthrown in 1966.[13] There are many other examples, such as those of Colombia and Sri Lanka in the 1950s and 1960s, of the economic disruption caused by a steep fall in a major source of tax revenue.[14] These examples point to the need for a gradual introduction of new sources of tax revenue in many developing countries.

Taxation measures

Indirect taxes

Of the two main categories of taxes, direct and indirect, the latter are easier to collect. As noted above (p. 92) this is particularly true of import duties and of export and excise taxes, which account for the bulk of revenue in most developing countries. State monopolies and nationalised industries provide an even easier and simpler method for raising revenue, although in practice nationalised industries, which generally provide essential consumer goods and services, are often run at a loss. The two types of indirect taxes which do present serious collection problems are retail sales tax and value added tax (VAT). This is because of the administrative difficulty of verifying the turnover of a large number of small manufacturers and retailers who tend not to keep adequate records of transactions. There is therefore little point in imposing such taxes in most developing countries, which lack the fiscal machinery for their efficient administration.

13. See, Éprime Eshag and P.J. Richards, 'A Comparison of Economic Developments in Ghana and the Ivory Coast since 1960', *BOUIES*, November 1967.
14. For details, see Éprime Eshag, *Quantification of Disruptive Effects of Export Shortfalls*, UNCTAD, document TD/B/C.3/AC.3/23 (11 October 1968).

Import tariffs and excise duties: The policy generally followed in respect of import tariffs and excise duties is to impose relatively high rates of tax on luxury and semi-luxury goods and low rates on essential consumer goods. Indirect taxes on the latter are, however, likely to yield a considerably higher revenue for the exchequer simply because a significantly larger share of total consumption expenditure is incurred on such goods. Many governments, therefore, tend to rely heavily on the income received from these taxes and show little hesitation in raising the tax rates on essential consumer goods to finance a shortfall in the exchequer revenue. This practice has been partly responsible for increasing inequality in the distribution of income and for 'lop-sided' growth of some countries.[15]

Export taxes: The other major type of indirect taxes levied in most developing countries consists of taxation of marketed agricultural products. These taxes are generally imposed on cash crops exported abroad, although there are a few instances of taxation of agricultural produce sold in internal markets which, because of their small and diminishing contribution to government revenue, are not considered here.[16] Broadly, three principal methods are used for taxing agricultural exports.

The *first* consists of 'explicit' export taxes, specific or *ad valorem*, levied on actual exports. This method is used, for example, by Sri Lanka for taxing exports of tea, rubber and coconut products, and by some Latin American countries, such as Costa Rica, El Salvador and Guatemala for their coffee exports.

The *second* method is through the establishment of state marketing boards, which have the monopoly of buying crops for export; the excess of the export over purchase price represents a tax on such crops. Examples of this technique of taxation are to be found in West Africa (Ghana and Nigeria) for cocoa;[17] the same technique was used in Kenya (for cotton) and in Uganda (for cotton and coffee) before their independence in the early 1960s.[18]

The *third* method for taxing agricultural exports is through the exchange rate system. Here the foreign exchange earnings of exporters of agricultural goods are compulsorily converted into domestic

---

15. For further discussion of tariff policies in LDCs see pp. 180–2.
16. For details see Richard M. Bird, *Taxing Agricultural Land in Developing Countries*, Harvard University Press, Cambridge, Mass. (1974), pp. 52–5.
17. See, Eshag and Richards, *BOUIES*, November 1967.
18. Kenya has at present a number of agricultural marketing boards, but these are not used for taxation purposes. See Judith Heyer, J.K. Maitha and W.M. Senga (eds.), *Agricultural Development in Kenya*, Nairobi, OUP (1976), Chapter 10.

currency by the authorities at a rate lower than the average market rate of exchange; the difference between the buying and selling rates of foreign exchange earnings amounts to a tax on exports. This technique, which was especially popular in Latin America in the post-War years, is used less frequently nowadays, partly because of the IMF disapproval of multiple exchange rates discussed later.[19]

Despite their serious drawbacks mentioned below, export taxes constitute the most popular and effective method of taxing the agricultural sector, largely because of the ease with which they can be imposed and collected. Smuggling of exports is the only way in which they can be evaded and this does not usually happen on a large scale. In a sample of 68 developing countries taken by Bird for the 1960s, 58 countries were found to resort to export taxes of some form or other. The share of these taxes in total tax revenue ranged from 5 to 9 per cent in 13 countries, from 10 to 20 per cent in 16, and was over 20 per cent in 2 countries.[20] As shown later (p. 112) for most LDCs, these ratios are appreciably higher than those of direct agricultural taxes.

In addition to being simple and easy to administer, all three forms of export tax also provide a convenient instrument for stabilising internal incomes. This is done by adopting sliding-scale schedules in the case of the 'explicit' export taxes, by changing the purchase price used by marketing boards, or by varying the exchange rate applicable to exports. In fact, in the case of some marketing boards, such as the Ghanaian Cocoa Marketing Board, founded in 1947 by the British colonial authorities, the initial purpose was to use the Board primarily for the stabilisation of internal prices and incomes, although in later years it came to serve also as an important source of exchequer revenue.[21]

Export taxes, as compared with properly formulated direct land taxes discussed later, have three serious drawbacks. *First*, they are levied on *actual* production for export markets, rather than on the production *potential* of agricultural land, and, as such, provide no financial incentive to increasing land yields through investment and through a more intensive cultivation of land. *Secondly*, export taxes, although paid by merchants, must eventually be borne by producers. They are, therefore, proportionate to the volume of production of

19. See p. 263 below.
   For further discussion of multiple exchange rates, see pp. 184–5.
20. Extracted from Bird, *Taxing Agricultural Land*, p. 32 and the Appendix to that book. The People's Republic of China, included in the original sample, has been excluded here and from the analysis of direct agricultural taxes later in this chapter.
21. See Eshag and Richards, *BOUIES*, November 1967, pp. 357–8.

individual farmers rather than being progressive. *Thirdly*, the revenue received from these taxes tends to be very uncertain and unstable, partly because it varies with international commodity prices which, as explained later, are subject to pronounced short-run fluctuations (see pp. 226 and 231). Another reason is that the volume of production and exports can vary significantly from year to year with the quality of harvests, due to changes in climatic and other conditions. As noted earlier, instability of tax revenue has in the past been an important source of the wastage of foreign exchange and of economic disruption.

Direct taxes outside agriculture

It is in the assessment and collection of direct taxes in developing countries that more serious problems are encountered, especially in agriculture, which usually accounts for the bulk of their production. Because of this, direct taxes in agriculture are examined separately below.

Taxation of wages and salaries. As in the case of industrial countries, wages and salaries in LDCs should be subject to a progressive system of taxation levied at source. There are, however, a number of special factors relevant to such tax measures in developing countries which should be taken into account. *First*, developing countries, as we have seen, suffer from what is known as 'structural unemployment' owing to a lack of capital equipment (see p. 5). This means that even during periods of economic upswing when all the available capital equipment is fully utilised, they possess a significant pool of unemployed labour. By far the largest part of this pool consists of unskilled and semi-skilled labour, although in many cases highly-trained and skilled personnel may at times find little demand for their services. In such conditions, the labour force which is actually in employment can be considered to be in a relatively privileged position (acquired by accident or through connection) and can properly be expected to make a contribution to government revenue. This constitutes a strong argument in favour of broadening the taxation base in a way that encompasses all wage and salary earners whose earnings exceed the amount required for subsistence level of consumption.

Secondly, in developing countries the public sector generally accounts for a bigger share of total employment than in industrial countries. This is partly because large-scale industrial, commercial and service enterprises in the private sector are more important in industrial than in developing countries. There is also an inherent bias towards overstaffing government departments in LDCs owing to the political exigency of limiting the volume of unemployment. The authorities in these countries are thus in a position to determine the volume of consumption of a relatively big section of population, which they can do through the determination of wage and salary scales and/or of taxation levied at the source.

It may be argued that in those developing countries which suffer from substantial structural unemployment, the government should take full advantage of its position to keep the net (take-home) wages and salaries to the minimum level compatible with maintaining an efficient administration. The take-home pay of the unskilled employees, who suffer most from structural unemployment, could thus be kept at a level that provides them with no more than a subsistence level of consumption. The other categories of employees could be allowed to enjoy a relatively higher standard of living depending on the degree of their skills and the supply of such skills in relation to the demand for them.

In determining the scale of net rewards paid to skilled personnel, it is important to bear in mind the risk of encouraging the migration of such people abroad if these rewards fall considerably short of those that can be earned in other countries. This is, however, more important in the case of the skilled technical personnel (doctors, engineers etc.) who enjoy a wider market abroad, than that of high-level executives and administrators. It might also be noted that the authorities are in a position to discourage the migration of skilled personnel who have enjoyed the benefit of a subsidised educational system by demanding reimbursement of at least part of the education and training outlay incurred by the state from the prospective migrants.

Taxation of business profits. In considering the techniques of taxation of business profits in LDCs it is important to distinguish between the big trading and industrial corporations, on the one hand, and small manufacturing establishments and retail traders, on the other. As far as large corporations are concerned, it is useful also to consider the domestic and foreign enterprises separately. These distinctions are made because of the differences in the ease and certainty of assessment of profits – and hence tax liability.

The taxation of *large national corporations* which are required to publish profit and loss accounts and balance sheets audited by authorised professional accountants, can follow the procedure used in industrial countries. In other words, published accounts can be used as the starting point for assessing the tax liability of such corporations. Under such a system a key role is played by accountants and auditors in authenticating the accuracy of the published accounts. The training of competent accountants and promotion of a reliable and reputable accounting profession, therefore, deserves top priority.

Foreign corporations operating in LDCs should in principle be taxed in the same way as domestic enterprises. In practice, however, most developing countries offer special incentives, which include tax exemptions, to foreign corporations to attract private direct investment from abroad. In assessing the tax liability of foreign enterprises, which are usually owned and controlled abroad, it is important to ensure that their declared profits are properly verified. The parent companies, commonly known as 'transnational', or 'multinational', corporations, with branches and subsidiaries operating in a number of countries, are often in a position to determine the exact level of profit that they wish to declare in each country. They do this simply by manipulating the prices of transactions within the family of branches and subsidiaries controlled by them; these are generally known as 'transfer prices'. The prices of inputs, including technical services, and of outputs supplied by the parent company or by one subsidiary or branch to others, can be fixed to ensure minimum overall tax liability for the transnational enterprise. To prevent tax evasion it is important to ensure, as far as possible, that 'transfer prices' correspond to open market prices.[22]

Small businesses, which consist primarily of retail traders, artisans and minor workshops, represent one of the two major sectors of the economy in which it is particularly difficult to impose and collect direct taxes; the other sector, examined below, is agriculture. It is important to note that these two sectors present special problems for the tax authorities even in industrial countries, which enjoy the services of more competent and reliable fiscal machinery and can resort to more sophisticated techniques of taxation. But the difficulty of taxing these sectors has considerably more serious implications for LDCs, in which they account for a far larger share of total economic activity and thus should provide an appreciably larger share of total tax revenue than in developed countries.

The chief problem of taxing small businesses is due to the difficulty of

22. For a detailed discussion of the problem of 'transfer pricing' by reference to the experience of a number of developing countries, see Sanjaya Lall 'Transfer Pricing by Multinational Manufacturing Firms', *BOUIES*, August 1973; and C. V. Vaitsos, *Intercountry Income Distribution and Transnational Enterprises*, Clarendon Press, Oxford (1974).

devising a practical and reliable means of estimating the revenue of the relatively large number of people engaged in them. It is almost impossible in practice to enforce a dependable system of bookkeeping on them which could be used as a basis for computing their net profits, as is done with large corporations. An alternative method of estimating such profits has therefore to be devised, but this is not easy.

Imposition of a 'fixed licence fee' per retail shop, or workshop, is probably preferable to taxation of profits derived from unreliable accounting records. This is despite the fact that, owing to significant differences in the size and profitability of individual businesses, the system of the fixed licence fee is likely to be highly inequitable. A system of 'variable licence fees' would obviously be more satisfactory provided it were possible to have clear and concrete criteria for determining such fees. If the determination of licence fees were left largely to the judgment of the tax assessors, the system would become open to arbitrariness and corruption. Such criteria as the 'location' of a business and its 'size', as determined, for example, by the area of the shop and the number of people working in it, can often serve as rough but concrete bases for determining the licence fee.

Direct agricultural taxes

Attempts to apply ordinary income tax to agricultural revenue have never been successful except in the case of large plantations. The reason for this is that there are practical difficulties of assessing the net income of individual farmers who, like small traders, are generally not in the habit of keeping adequate business records. This is not surprising since similar difficulties are often encountered in assessing the income of small farmers even in industrial countries. In a country like the UK, for example, with its highly efficient fiscal machinery and accounting profession, until 1950 many small farmers were taxed on the basis of the quinquennial valuation of the rentable value of their land rather than on their profits.

The two most common direct taxes applied to the agricultural sector are the so-called *personal taxes* and *land taxes*. The former are largely confined to African countries, south of the Sahara, where a large part of rural land is held communally without registered titles. *Personal taxes* in fact amount to 'poll' taxes of varying degrees of sophistication, although they are known by different names in different countries, such as 'hut tax', 'house tax', 'village tax', 'cattle tax', 'poll tax', 'minimum tax', etc. Although in some countries, such as Uganda, poll taxes have been related to incomes of the rural population, African 'personal taxes', by and large, remain regressive in character. This type of taxation does, however, offer the authorities an opportunity of mobilising rural unemployment by offering the villagers the option of paying the tax in cash or being liable to a number of days' labour on community development works, such as construction of roads, bridges, drainage and irrigation schemes.

'Personal taxes', which accounted for a significant proportion of government revenue under colonial administration, have declined in importance in recent years. The major exceptions are Niger where they continue to account for about one-third and Malawi where they bring in 10 to 15 per cent of the respective governments' tax revenues; in the remaining countries their share in taxation revenue has declined to about 2 to 5 per cent.[23]

Land taxes. Land tax is probably the oldest form of direct tax levied in organised societies. Surveys recording landholdings were carried out in ancient Babylonia in the 4th millenium BC and in China and Egypt around 3000 BC primarily for the purpose of establishing a base for taxation.

In theory, land taxes can be so framed as to serve the dual purpose of restraining the consumption of landholders and of stimulating agricultural production by encouraging a more intensive cultivation of land. It is thus possible through this fiscal instrument to ease the two major constraints on development, discussed earlier, by increasing the rate of growth of savings and of the supply of food (see pp. 55–6). Land taxes are for this reason, in principle, preferable to export and other indirect taxes which, as noted above, are not progressive and do not provide any incentives to production.

There are, in theory, two main criteria for assessing tax on land – its *rentable value* and its *capital value*. Where the capital value of land is used as a basis of tax assessment, a proportion of this value, corresponding, for example, to the average rate of interest prevailing in the country, can be considered as its notional rentable value. The two methods should generally yield broadly similar assessments, since the capitalised value of the rent of land should approximate to its market value; whenever possible, therefore, both methods should be used to cross check.

The choice between the two methods of assessment depends in practice on the availability of information. In the case of idle land with unknown productive potential, for example, it would generally be easier to use capital values as a basis of tax assessment. The difficulty

---

23. For further details see Bird, *Taxing Agricultural Land,* pp. 34–6 and 57–63.

here is that in certain areas with large landholdings there may be no land market for the valuation of land. One scheme for resolving this difficulty, which was adopted by the Chilean administration in the mid-1960s, is to ask the landlords themselves to value their land with a proviso that such valuation can be used as a basis for compensation in case of its acquisition under a land reform programme; the more seriously is the threat of land reform taken by landlords, the more likely is this scheme to succeed.

The two important points to note about land taxes are, *first*, 'rentable' values should, as far as possible, reflect the *potential* productivity as distinct from the *actual* yield of land. This would encourage more intensive cultivation and penalise those landowners who leave large tracts of their property uncultivated. It would also render land a less attractive proposition for speculation and for hedging against inflation.

Secondly, land tax should be levied on *current* and not on old and out-of-date rentable and capital values as is done in most developing countries. In other words, the tax assessment should reflect increases in these values due to inflation as well as to the growth in land yields. Otherwise, inflation alone can, as shown below, depress the purchasing power of land taxes to a derisively low level as it has done in most Latin American and Asian countries. This points to the need for periodic revision of tax assessments, whether based on rentable or on capital values of land; the higher is the rate of inflation, the more frequent should be such revisions.

In practice, a proper administration of land taxes along the above lines requires what few developing countries possess: reliable and up-to-date cadastral maps and a relatively efficient and honest body of tax assessors. Most countries would, therefore, be better advised to use a system of *taxation by area*, as a rough but simple way of subjecting agricultural land to direct taxation, instead of resorting to an elaborate system of land taxation: it is relatively easier to ascertain the area of land owned by landlords than its market or rentable value. The rate of tax per acre of land need not of course be uniform throughout the country, although the number of rates chosen should, in the interest of simplicity, be as small as is consistent with the known significant differences in such factors as topographical features, climatic conditions and soil fertility.

The tax rates, or assessments, should also be graduated according to the taxpayers' aggregate landholdings and should provide for exemptions for smallholders, in order to make the tax broadly progressive with respect to the potential income. Precautions would have to be taken, however, to ensure that large landholdings are not artificially divided among relatives to escape the burden of the progressive taxation. Moreover, in this case also it is important to link tax rates, in some way, to the prices of land and agricultural produce, in order to ensure that the real value of the revenue is not eroded by inflation.

Failure to exploit the potential of land tax. Although land tax can, in theory, serve as a powerful tool of development by both restraining consumption and stimulating agricultural production, in practice little use is made of it in developing countries. In a sample of 37 developing countries in Asia and Latin America, where land taxes are common, it was found that during the 1960s, in 20 countries the revenue received from this tax accounted for less than 5 per cent and in 34 for less than 10 per cent of total government tax revenue; only in 3 small countries (Ecuador, Nepal and Taiwan) did land tax amount to 10 per cent or more of tax revenue. In the larger countries, such as Argentina, Brazil, India, Indonesia and Pakistan, land tax accounted for 1 to 6 per cent of total tax revenue.[24] Moreover, in almost every single country included in the sample for which historic data are available, the contribution of land tax to government revenue has declined steadily and significantly in the course of the last few decades. In India and Pakistan, for example, the share of land tax in total tax revenue, which accounted for 36 per cent before the First World War, fell to 19 per cent before the Second World War, to 8 to 10 per cent immediately before independence and to 5 to 6 per cent in 1968-9.[25]

Statistically, the reason for the decline in the importance of land taxes in LDCs is to be found in the fact that out-of-date rental and land valuations are used as a basis of tax assessment in a period of steady rises in general price levels, including prices of land and agricultural produce. The *real explanation,* however, is more likely to lie in the social and political conditions of developing countries as reflected in the strong influence of big landlords on fiscal policies. It is true that the great majority of landholders in LDCs consist of poor peasants who live close to the subsistence level and who, according to our basic conditions of development, should bear little if any burden of taxation. But it is equally true, as we shall presently show, that in many developing countries a significant proportion, of the order of 50 per cent or more, of agricultural land is owned by rich landlords who

24. Derived from Bird, *Taxing Agricultural Land,* pp. 300-1.
25. *Ibid.,* pp. 34, 35 and 300.

account for a small fraction (1 to 2 per cent) of the rural population and who by and large escape direct taxation.

Table 3.4 shows a picture of the structure of land ownership in several Latin American countries between 1950 and 1961. Although the data represent very rough estimates, they do, nevertheless, indicate the order of magnitude of disparity in land ownership in much of Latin America. It can be seen that, on average, over 60 per cent of farmers occupied small plots of land which together covered less than 10 per cent of farm area,[26] whereas large farmers, who accounted for about 2 per cent of farm units, held more than 50 per cent of farm area; indications are that this picture of land distribution has not changed significantly to date (1981). This concentration of land ownership among a small number of families in Latin America originates in its colonial history.

Such information as is available for Asian countries suggests that in most of these countries also the big landlords own a disproportionately large share of agricultural land in relation to their number. Table 3.5 shows the distribution of landholding in India, for example, on the basis of a national sample survey in the mid-1950s. It can be seen that at the lower end of the scale over 60 per cent of households were either landless or had holdings of less than $2\frac{1}{2}$ acres, which accounted for only 6 per cent of land, whereas at the other end a mere 4 per cent of households owned over 40 per cent of the land. Indications are that, despite the many 'formal' attempts at land reform, the picture of landholding in India has not improved significantly since then. While redistribution of land on a small scale has taken place in a few states, the number of households has increased steadily in line with the growth of population. Because of this, subdivision of land has continued, so the proportion of households without land and with less than $2\frac{1}{2}$ acres combined must now be even higher than 60 per cent recorded over two decades ago.[27]

The tax potential of the agricultural sector in developing countries should, as noted above (p. 90), be estimated by reference to the wealth and income of the large and medium-size landowners, in particular the former, rather than by per capita wealth and income of the rural population, which are irrelevant to the issue. The size of the landholdings of the large and medium-size landlords provides a broad indication of their relative wealth as compared with the remainder of

26. Estimates of the 'weighted' arithmetic mean for the countries covered by the table show that small 'sub-family' farms accounted for only 2 per cent of land.
27. See Doreen Warriner, the 'source' in Table 3.5, Chapter vi, especially pp. 144 and 170–5.

Table 3.4: *Structure of landholding, by farm size, in selected Latin American countries*

(*Percentage of total*)

Countries	Sub-family[a]	Family[b]	Multi-family medium[c]	Multi-family large[d]
		Type of farm		
Argentina (1960)				
Number of farm units	43.2	48.7	7.3	0.8
Area in farms	3.4	44.7	15.0	36.9
Brazil (1950)				
Number of farm units	22.5	39.1	33.7	4.7
Area in farms	0.5	6.0	34.0	59.5
Chile (1955)				
Number of farm units	36.0	40.0	16.2	6.9
Area in farms	0.2	7.1	11.4	81.3
Colombia (1960)				
Number of farm units	64.0	30.2	4.5	1.3
Area in farms	4.9	22.3	23.3	49.5
Ecuador (1954)				
Number of farm units	89.9	8.0	1.7	0.4
Area in farms	16.6	19.0	19.3	45.1
Guatemala (1950)				
Number of farm units	88.4	9.5	2.0	0.1
Area in farms	14.3	13.4	31.5	40.8
Peru (1961)				
Number of farm units	88.0	8.5	2.4	1.1
Area in farms	7.4	4.5	5.7	82.4
Average[e]				
Number of farm units	62	26	10	2
Area in farms	7	17	20	56

Source: Inter-American Committee for Agricultural Development, as reported in Solon Barraclough, 'Agrarian Reform in Latin America: Actual Situation and Problems', FAO, *Land Reform, Land Settlement and Cooperatives*, 1969–No. 2, RU: MONO/69/7, reproduced in Bird, *Taxing Agricultural Land*, p. 80. (Misprints in FAO, reproduced in Bird, have been corrected.)

[a] Farms too small to provide employment for a single family (2 workers) with the typical incomes, markets and levels of technology and capital prevailing in each region.

[b] Farms large enough to provide employment for 2 to 3.9 persons, on the assumption that most of the farm work is being carried out by the members of the farm family.

[c] Farms large enough to provide employment for 4 to 12 persons.

[d] Farms large enough to provide employment for over 12 persons.

[e] Unweighted arithmetic mean.

Table 3.5:   *India: distribution of landholding, by size-level and number of households, in 1954–55*

Size-group (acres)	Percentage of Households	Area
0.00[a]	22	—
Under 1	25	1
1–2½	14	5
2½–5	14	10
5–10	13	19
10–15	5	13
15–20	3	10
20–25	1	7
25–50	2	19
Over 50	1	16
	100	100

Source: Doreen Warriner, *Land Reform in Principle and Practice*, Clarendon Press, Oxford (1969), p. 142; derived from National Sample Survey, 8th Round, as summarised in *Progress of Land Reform*, Planning Commission (1963), Appendix v.

[a] Households owning no land or less than 0.005 acres.

the rural population. It has not, unfortunately, been possible to obtain any concrete estimates of the income of the different groups of landholders apart from those for Latin America shown in Table 3.6. These are based on the studies of the Inter-American Committee for Agricultural Development (ICAD), ECLA and individual agricultural experts. Though very rough, the estimates give a broad idea of the taxation and savings potential of the agricultural sector of Latin America and, in a general way, also of other developing countries with a pronouncedly unequal distribution of land ownership, such as India.

The first three lines of Table 3.6 give a picture of land distribution for the Latin American continent as a whole in the mid-1960s, by size of farm units and number of families. The difference between the number of farm units and of families gives a rough indication of the number of landless rural families, which amount to just over one-third of total families. The next two lines show the contribution of each class of rural population to agricultural production and its share in agricultural income.

It can be seen that, at one end of the scale, the large landlords, who numbered about 1 per cent of the rural families, owned about 50 per cent of land, accounted for one-third of production and received about one-sixth of the total agricultural income. At the other end of the scale, about 90 per cent of the rural families owned just over 20 per cent of land and received about two-thirds of the income generated in the agricultural sector. The fact that the large landlords accounted for a smaller share of production in relation to their landholding is explained largely by a lower intensity of cultivation of their land as compared with medium – and especially small-size farm units. The lower share of income in relation to production in the case of both large and medium-size farms is, in turn, explained by wage and salary outlays incurred on hired labour. The wages so received must have accounted for almost one-half of the income of small farmers and landless peasants, since their share in agricultural income amounted to 64 per cent compared with a share of 38 per cent in agricultural production.

More direct and relevant indicators of taxation potential of the agricultural sector are provided by lines 11 and 12 of the table, which show the wide disparity in the net income and consumption per family of the different classes of rural population. It can be seen that in the mid-1960s the average net family income and consumption of large landholders amounted to about $15,000 and $12,000, respectively, and were about 15 times larger than the corresponding figures applicable to the 90 per cent of agricultural families included in the 'rest of rural sector' column. Measured in 1980 dollars the figures in question would be more than twice as large. In other words, the net income and consumption per family for large landholders would amount to over $30,000 and $24,000 per annum, respectively, and for medium-size landlords to over $6,000 and $5,500, respectively.

It is worth noting also that a large share of the consumption of big landlords is spent on luxury and semi-luxury goods and on imported luxuries; the same is no doubt true, though to a much smaller extent, also of medium-size landlords. One estimate made for Chile in the early 1960s, for example, suggests that big landlords devoted approximately 75 per cent of their consumption to what were considered to be inessential luxury goods and no less than 25 per cent to imported products, and that they paid only about 5 per cent tax on their personal income.[28]

28. See Sternberg, the 'source' in Table 3.6, p. 29.

	Unit	Latin America Total	Multi-family farm units Large[a]	Per cent[c]	Medium[b]	Per cent[c]	Rest of rural sector Small farms and landless peasants	Per cent[c]
1. Farm units	1000	10,000	180	2	1,060	11	8,760	88
2. Families	1000	16,000	180	1	1,080	7	14,740	92
3. Land area	mil. hectares	760	390	52	200	27	170	22
4. Production	$m	20,000	6,590	33	5,840	29	7,570	38
5. Gross agricultural income	$m	20,000	3,420	17	3,840	19	12,740	64
6. Gross personal income[d]	$m	19,600	3,180	16	3,680	19	12,740	65
7. Consumption[e]	$m	17,100	2,140	13	2,980	17	11,980	70
8. Gross agricultural investment	$m	2,500	1,040	42	700	28	760	30
9. Net agricultural investment	$m	900	400	44	290	32	210	23
10. Net agricultural income[f]	$m	18,400	2,780	15	3,420	19	12,200	66
11. Net agricultural income per family	$	1,150	15,110		3,180		830	
12. Consumption per family	$	1,070	11,900		2,770		810	

Source: Derived from M.J. Sternberg in FAO, *Land Reform, Land Settlement and Co-operatives*, 1970–No. 2, ESR/MONO/70/3.

[a] See footnote to Table 3·4.   [b] See footnote c to Table 3·4.   [c] Per cent of Latin America total.

[d] Income available for agricultural investment and consumption, as shown in lines 7 and 8. It is equal to gross agricultural income *plus* non-farm income, *less* net transfers, consisting of taxes and non-farm investment; it is assumed that net transfers for the 'rest of rural sector' are negligible.

[e] Consumption is obtained by deducting 'Gross agricultural investment' from 'Gross personal income'.

[f] Gross agricultural income *less* depreciation, which is obtained from lines 8 and 9.

Note: Because of rounding up of figures, components may not add to totals: absolute figures are rounded to the nearest 10 and percentages to the nearest whole number.

It can be seen from Table 3.6 (line 7) that any direct taxation, whether in the form of income or land tax, which had the effect of curtailing the consumption of big landlords by only one-third and of medium-size landlords by one-tenth, would increase the net savings of the Latin American continent by about $1 billion in 1965–7 dollars. This is equivalent to 40 per cent of gross investment and to over 100 per cent of net investment in agriculture (see lines 8 and 9 of the table). The failure to restrain the consumption of rich landowners through direct taxation is, in our view, explained largely by the political influence exercised by them in the formulation and administration of fiscal policy;[29] for example, in retaining low and out-of-date land and rental valuations for the assessment of land tax, noted above (p. 112).

Land reform and farm co-operatives

Governments that have the political will and power to tax the big landlords adequately, would also generally be willing and able to break up the big estates and distribute the land among landless peasants and small landholders by altering, or reforming, the system of land tenure. They might, in fact, generally find it politically easier to implement a land reform programme than a policy of taxing rich landlords because of the support they are likely to receive for the former policy from the great majority of the rural population who stand to benefit from it.

The success of a programme of land reform largely depends on effective government participation in the processes of production and marketing of agricultural produce through the organisation of farm co-operatives. The mere change in the land tenure system without the implementation of an integrated reform programme cannot ensure the success of the reform programme in terms of the growth in agricultural production and savings. This is, for example, confirmed by the experience of Iraq during the period 1958–63, when, partly because of the atmosphere of uncertainty caused by a delay in the distribution of requisitioned land, and partly because of the failure of the authorities to replace the big landlords' function as suppliers of capital, both the area under cultivation and the production of main crops declined.[30]

An example of a more successful land reform programme is provided by the experience of Egypt during 1953–70.[31] Here the agrarian

29. See also pp. 205–7 below.
30. See Doreen Warriner, *Land Reform in Principle and Practice*, Chap. iv, especially pp. 94–6.
31. See Éprime Eshag and M.A. Kamal, 'Agrarian Reform in the United Arab Republic (Egypt)', *BOUIES*, May 1968.

reform law involved the breaking up of large estates and the distribution of land among landless tenants and small farmers as well as regulation of the landlord–tenant relationships (see also pp. 208–9). These reforms were accompanied by the formal requirement that the beneficiaries of land redistribution should join co-operatives run under the direction of state-appointed supervisors – generally trained agronomists in government employment. The co-operative system was gradually extended to many farmers outside land reform areas.

The basic strategy adopted by the authorities was to combine the advantage of large-scale management through the co-operatives with that of providing the incentive of private gain to individual farmers. Although the latter were directly responsible for the cultivation of their plots, a number of important farming operations which are more efficiently performed on a large-scale basis were executed by the co-operatives or directly by the central government. Fixed investment in the construction of irrigation and drainage schemes and in land reclamation was undertaken by the central government itself. The operations covered by the co-operatives included mechanised plough-ing, pest control and maintenance of irrigation and drainage canals. In addition, the co-operatives were responsible for crop- and land-consolidation, for the introduction of a uniform crop-rotation scheme, for the provision of working capital in cash and kind, and for channelling cheap medium-term government loans to their members for the financing of private fixed investment.

The foregoing measures were aimed at and largely succeeded in raising the levels of land yields and agricultural production after a brief transitional period of 3–4 years. What was significant from a fiscal point of view, however, was the system of marketing the produce of co-operatives, which provided the authorities with a convenient means of taxing the agricultural sector. A central state organisation was entrusted with the task of collecting and selling the cash crops on behalf of the co-operatives. The farmers received the net proceeds of their crops through their co-operatives, after appropriate deductions for expenses incurred and for debts due for repayment. This marketing system enabled the authorities to tax the farmers by fixing the prices paid for their cash crops at a lower level than those actually received in the internal and foreign markets. According to one estimate made on the basis of official publications, during the years 1960–70 the Egyptian farmers received between 70 and 80 per cent of the world market price for their cotton crops; an even higher rate of taxation, amounting on average to over 40 per cent *ad valorem*, was levied on exported rice during the crop years 1965/66 to 1969/70.[32] The total exchequer revenue received from government profit margins in marketing agricultural produce and from export duties is estimated at £E330 million for the period 1965–70, which is equivalent to a tax of over 10 per cent on farm incomes.[33] This technique of taxation (through co-operatives) is similar to that used by the African commodity marketing boards mentioned earlier (see p. 104 above).

The chief drawbacks of the taxation system used in Egypt are that, like export taxes discussed earlier, the tax liability is proportionate to the volume of production of the individual farmers, and as such it provides no special incentive to production and, in addition, is not progressive. There are even indications that the Egyptian tax system is regressive in nature, since many agricultural products, such as livestock, dairy products, fruit and vegetables, which are produced primarily by rich farmers, are handled privately and largely escape taxation.[34] The small farmers have, of course, benefited from the public investment outlay and from the other land reform measures mentioned, which have increased land yields.

From a taxation point of view, the important point to note is that a land reform programme, such as the one implemented in Egypt, provides the authorities with sufficient cadastral information to implement a progressive system of direct land taxation assessed on the basis of the potential productivity of land. The fact that no advantage has been taken of this opportunity in Egypt can be partly explained by the fact that, since the death of President Nasser in 1970, the Government has tended to be somewhat more sympathetic to the richer landlords.[35] The value of direct land taxes in Egypt has in fact, in common with most developing countries, been allowed to be eroded almost to the point of insignificance by the process of inflation.[36]

Wealth, gift and inheritance taxes

The *wealth* of individuals can be regarded as a rough indicator of their income earning potential and as such be made subject to an

32. See Mahmoud Abdel-Fadil, *Development, Income Distribution and Social Change in Rural Egypt (1952–1970)*, CUP (1975), pp. 103–8.
33. *Ibid.*, p. 106.
34. *Ibid.*, p.107.
35. Since the death of Nasser in 1970, some of the land requisitioned from big landlords and distributed among poor farmers has been returned to the original owners.
36. See Mahmoud Abdel-Fadil, *Rural Egypt (1952–1970)*, p. 108.

annual tax, especially where serious difficulties are encountered in determining the actual income received. Moreover, the benefits derived by individuals from state expenditure on current and capital accounts bear a direct relationship to their wealth, and considerations of equity would require some contribution to the exchequer in proportion to the wealth of the taxpayers. The case for taxation of *gifts and legacies* on these grounds is less clear, but can be justified on the grounds of preventing the evasion of progressive wealth taxes.

Administratively, collection of revenue from these taxes in developing countries, except when applied to real estate, suffers from the same enforcement difficulties as those encountered in the collection of income tax discussed earlier. Evasion of tax is particularly easy in respect of movable property, such as jewellery and precious metals; securities generally account for a small share of wealth in LDCs. In practice, it is the wealth owned and transferred in the form of real estate that constitutes the primary source of revenue from such taxes.

The annual taxes on *real estate* (land and buildings) in urban areas should, as in the case of agricultural land tax discussed earlier, be assessed on the basis of the current potential rental valuation, or current market value, of individual properties. But this would, as in the case of land taxes, entail a large number of complicated assessments well beyond the administrative capacity of most developing countries. Pending the development of more efficient fiscal machinery in these countries, it would be preferable to resort to a more simple but rough technique of taxation of urban property similar to the 'area tax' proposed earlier for agricultural land (see p. 111). This would consist simply of dividing towns and cities into a small number of regions or districts, each carrying a different rate of assessment per acre of land and per square footage of building, according to a rough estimate of their potential rental valuation or market price. There is no reason why wealth tax should not be made progressive by varying the tax rates in accordance with the valuation of the total real estate owned by individuals or families and by providing exemptions for small properties; gift and inheritance taxes can also be made progressive in the same way. As in the case of agricultural land tax, it is important to vary the tax assessment of real estate in urban areas in line with changes in rental valuations or prices of the property in order to ensure that the purchasing power of tax revenue is not eroded by inflation.

It has at times been suggested that capital taxes, which include wealth, gift and inheritance taxes, have a particularly adverse effect on the accumulation of national capital because of their negative influence on private savings and investment.[37] The validity of this argument is, however, questionable, since there is in principle no difference between income and capital taxes as far as their impact on private savings and investment is concerned. All taxes inevitably result in a reduction of private incomes, as well as of private savings and consumption; whether they have a positive or negative effect on the overall accumulation of capital and on the process of development depends largely on how the authorities dispose of the tax revenue. What is significant from our point of view is that the taxation of wealth, like taxation of income, restricts private consumption, thereby increasing the volume of resources available for government consumption and investment.

CONCLUSION

The major conclusion to emerge from the analysis of the data presented in this chapter is that developing countries have failed to promote domestic savings and investment to anything like the maximum extent possible. This is due to their unwillingness, or inability, to take the necessary measures to restrain the growth of public and private consumption.

As far as the public sector is concerned, in the absence of complete data on the pattern of consumption, we have tried to examine governments' policies by comparing their outlay on defence with that on education and health. This comparison shows that most developing countries spend a relatively large proportion of their resources, comparable to and even exceeding that of industrial countries of the West, on defence, and that in many cases this type of consumption exceeds the combined expenditure on health and education. This is shown to be particularly true of Asia, which accounts for almost two-thirds of the population of developing countries. It is clear that in most LDCs a reduction in defence outlay would significantly augment the domestic resources available for development without necessarily reducing their security.

The available evidence indicates that developing countries have also failed to restrain private consumption of luxuries and semi-luxuries by the richer classes through taxation or other measures. This is broadly confirmed by the high level of luxury consumption observed in most developing countries as well as by the low share of direct

---

37. See, for example, Dino Jarach in *Fiscal Policy for Economic Development in Latin America*, Johns Hopkins Press, Baltimore, Maryland (1965), especially p. 212.

taxation in national income and in governments' tax revenue relative to the available tax potential. The failure to exploit the tax potential is particularly noticeable in the agricultural sector, where big landlords by and large escape the burden of direct taxation. The inability of most developing countries to increase the rate of growth of domestic savings and investment by curbing inessential private consumption is, in the view of many informed observers, to be explained largely by the influence of vested interests.

4

FINANCING ECONOMIC DEVELOPMENT (2) FOREIGN CAPITAL

This chapter, like the preceding one, is concerned with the problem of financing an accelerated rate of development without engendering inflation. Chapter 3 was devoted to a discussion of the problems encountered by developing countries in raising the volume of the first source of finance, namely voluntary savings; the present chapter is concerned with the second source of finance – external capital.[1] It is important to emphasise here that the topics of the two chapters are closely interrelated because of the likely interaction between savings and foreign capital. While on the one hand the availability of foreign capital can, as we shall see, be instrumental in increasing the rate of growth of voluntary savings, on the other it tends to reduce the pressure on the authorities to raise the share of savings in national income through fiscal and other measures. In this connection it is worth noting that the failure of many developing countries to raise the ratio of savings by restraining consumption, discussed in Chapter 3, goes some way to explain their growing reliance on foreign capital to finance domestic expenditure.

We shall first examine in somewhat greater detail than was done in Chapter 2 (pp. 60–2), the role that can be played by foreign capital in general in assisting economic development. We shall then present some data on the volume of different categories of external capital received from various sources by LDCs in recent years and examine the *potential* of each category of capital to promote economic development. The chapter concludes with a brief consideration of some of the problems encountered in the evaluation of the *actual* role played by foreign capital in development.

1. I am very grateful to the Secretariat of the Development Assistance Committee (DAC) of OECD, in particular to Mr Sigismund Niebel, as well as to the Secretariat of the Money, Finance and Development Division of UNCTAD, for supplying me with the bulk of the statistical data presented in this chapter.

THE DUAL FUNCTION OF FOREIGN CAPITAL
IN DEVELOPMENT[2]

In the last chapter, in considering the side-effects of fiscal measures on total production, it was assumed that the resources released by cutting down consumption can be readily utilised to promote investment, and that the rate of growth of aggregate effective demand and of national income can in this way be maintained at the desired level (see pp. 77–8). This assumption, which may at times legitimately be made for a closed economy, was introduced merely to focus attention on the problems of restraining consumption through fiscal measures with which alone Chapter 3 was concerned. In an open economy, policies designed to accelerate the rate of growth by switching resources from consumption to investment are, as we shall see, likely to have direct repercussions on the balance of payments, which have to be taken into account in setting the target rate of growth.

We shall attempt here to illustrate the dual role of foreign capital in development by way of a simple example. Take a typical developing country which has for a time been growing at a rate of, say, r_0, and which has some idle productive resources, in the form of land, labour and equipment, that can be brought into production by stepping up investment. Assume that investment, imports and exports have all been rising at the rate r_0 and that the country has been keeping its external account in balance. So that, in the *ex-post* picture for each period, as indicated by the identity

$$I_d = S + (M - X),$$

2. The dual role of international capital movements has been recognised by many economists at least since 1920, when Keynes wrote about what came to be known as 'the transfer problem' of extracting reparations from Germany after the First World War. See J. M. Keynes, *The Economic Consequences of the Peace*, Macmillan and Co. Ltd., London (1920), pp. 171–82; and *A Revision of the Treaty*, Macmillan and Co. Ltd., London (1922), Chapter III.

During the post-World War Two period, this subject has received considerable attention in the works concerned with the role of foreign capital in economic development by the United Nations and others. See, for example UNCTAD publications on the foreign capital needs of developing countries, such as the following: *Towards a New Trade Policy for Development*, Sales No.: 64.II.B.4 (1964); *Trade Prospects and Capital Needs of Developing Countries*, Sales No. E.68. II.D.13 (1968); *Trade Prospects and Capital Needs of Developing Countries During the Second United Nations Development Decade*, Sales No. E. 72. II.D.11 (1972); and *Trade Prospects and Capital Needs of Developing Countries, 1976–1980*, document TD/B/C.3/134 (15 April 1976). See also Michal Kalecki, *Essays on Developing Economies*, The Harvester Press (1976), Chapter 6, especially pp. 68–70; and H.P. Chenery and A.M. Strout, 'Foreign Assistance and Economic Development', *American Economic Review*, September, 1966.

$M - X = 0$ and $I_d = S$, which means that domestic investment has been financed entirely by national savings.[3]

Assume then that the government decides to step up the rate of growth for a period to r_1 by raising the ratio of investment in national income. Abstracting from the effect of any change in the pattern of investment, this will have the effect of accelerating the rates of growth of savings and of imports. On the assumption that marginal propensities to save and to import are equal to their respective average propensities, savings and imports will both rise at the rate r_1.[4] Barring, however, some favourable fortuitous factor, such as a bumper harvest or a rise in export prices, there is no reason why in the normal course of events exports should rise faster than at the rate r_0 experienced in preceding periods and, because of this, the country will incur a deficit on its external account. It should be noted that this would occur even if investment were concentrated in the foreign trade sector, at least during the gestation period of investment which may extend over several years.

This argument can be presented more precisely and pursued further with the help of the above identity. We use the suffix o to indicate the value of the variables in the period immediately preceding the acceleration of the rate of growth (Period o) and suffix 1 for the following period (Period 1) in which the rate of growth is accelerated from r_0 to r_1. The *ex-post* picture for the two periods can be presented in the form:

$$I_{d_0} = S_0 + (M_0 - X_0), \qquad (1)$$

$$I_{d_1} = S_1 + (M_1 - X_1) \qquad (2)$$

(corresponding to national incomes Y_0 and Y_1, respectively). Under the assumptions made, $M_0 = X_0$, $I_{d_0} = S_0$, and in Period 1, income, savings and imports all increase at a rate r_1, while exports grow at a rate r_0, suggesting a higher rate of growth than r_1 for investment. The deficit incurred on external account in Period 1, which has to be financed by foreign capital, is $(I_{d_1} - S_1)$ or $M_0(r_1 - r_0)$.[5]

What has happened in effect is that in Period 1 the

---

3. The identity is derived from equation (8) in Chapter 2 (see p. 37).
4. In practice the marginal propensities to save and especially to import are likely to be larger than their respective average propensities, so that savings and imports will tend to rise at a higher rate than r_1, but this will affect only the magnitude and not the nature of the problem under consideration (see p. 129 below).
5. This follows from the fact that $X_1 = X_0 r_0 = M_0 r_0$ and $M_1 = M_0 r_1$; external balance $(M_1 - X_1)$ in Period 1 is therefore equal to $M_0 r_1 - X_0 r_0$, or $M_0 r_1 - M_0 r_0 = M_0(r_1 - r_0)$.

acceleration in the rate of growth of investment, which has resulted in an external deficit, has generated a faster rate of growth of income and savings than that of Period 0. Measured in absolute terms, in Period 1, income and savings are higher by a factor of $(r_1 - r_0)$ and investment by a larger factor than they would have been in the absence of foreign capital to finance the deficit. The *additional* investment required to bring about the acceleration in the rate of growth is, in absolute terms, equal to $S_0(r_1 - r_0) + M_0 (r_1 - r_0)$, of which $S_0 (r_1 - r_0)$ is financed by the additional savings generated as a result of stepping up the rate of growth to r_1, and $M_0 (r_1 - r_0)$ by the inflow of foreign capital.[6]

It is clear from the above that foreign capital can perform two distinct functions in development: (a) it can increase resources available for investment by supplementing savings, and (b) it can augment foreign exchange resources by supplementing export earnings. The relative significance of these two functions in promoting the development of the individual countries will depend on whether the limit to their rate of growth is set by the availability of savings or by foreign exchange resources.

In the above example, if the country in question was unable to increase the rate of growth of voluntary savings above r_0, any attempt to raise the rate of growth of investment beyond that rate, without the requisite inflow of foreign capital, would, as explained earlier, have led to inflation and to a redistribution of income in favour of profits, resulting in 'forced savings' and 'lop-sided' development (see pp. 40 and 55–6). For such a country the acceleration in the pace of development, as defined by us, is constrained by savings, and foreign capital can be said to make such an acceleration possible by filling the *savings gap*. We need not be concerned here with the subject of what determines the rate of growth in voluntary savings, which was fully explored in Chapter 3. In practice, the 'savings constraint' on development is likely to play an important part in some of the poorest countries of Africa and Asia with a relatively small unexploited savings

---

6. The following simple algebra, illustrating the above propositions, may be helpful to some readers. Equation (2) can be rewritten in the form:

$$I_{d_1} = S_0 (1 + r_1) + M_0 (1 + r_1) - X_0 (1 + r_0) \tag{3}$$

or,

$$I_{d_1} = S_0 (1 + r_1) + M_0 (r_1 - r_0) \tag{4}$$

Had the rate of growth been maintained at r_0, investment in Period 1 would have amounted to $I_{d_0}(1 + r_0)$, or $S_0 (1 + r_0)$. It can be seen that the difference between the value of I_{d_1}, shown in equation (4), and $S_0 (1 + r_0)$ which represents *additional* investment required to make the acceleration to r_1 possible, is equal to $S_0 (r_1 - r_0) + M_0 (r_1 - r_0)$.

potential as well in some of the other LDCs where, as shown in Chapter 3, government policies fail to exploit this potential.

However, many developing countries with adequate savings potential to finance a higher ratio of investment may not be in a position to realise the requisite savings despite government efforts to do so. In the foregoing example, assume that the decision to accelerate the rate of growth to r_1 in Period 1, by raising the ratio of investment, is accompanied by measures which are calculated to curb the growth of consumption sufficiently to permit an equal rise in the ratio of savings in national income, so that at the level of income Y_1, savings would equal investment, keeping the external account in balance.

Assume first that imports will, as in the earlier case, rise at the same rate as income, namely r_1.[7] It is clear that success in realising a rate of growth of r_1 in exports requires: (a) that resources released by curbing consumption should become available for the production of export goods and (b) that demand for exports should actually grow at the same rate as imports. Obviously, in the absence of this degree of substitutability between consumption and *realised* exports, it will not be possible *simultaneously* to attain the target rate of growth of income and of exports: the attainment of the growth rate target will bring about a deficit on external account, whereas success in balancing this account can be attained only by slowing down the rate of growth of income. In such cases, the acceleration of the growth rate is constrained by the balance of payments considerations as represented by the shortfall in foreign exchange earnings. What the inflow of external capital does here in effect is to remove this constraint by filling the *foreign exchange gap*.

The question of the *substitutability* of exports for consumption deserves further consideration. Restriction on the consumption of *tradable export goods* of a country would clearly increase the supply *potential* of such goods for exports. As shown later, however, the bulk of the exports of LDCs consists of primary products of which only a small proportion is internally consumed, which means that their capacity to increase this supply potential is very limited. Moreover, whether any export potential is *realised* in practice will also depend on the availability of foreign markets which, for a large range of manufactured consumer goods exported by developing countries, is, in any case, largely determined by the quota restrictions imposed by developed countries (see pp. 195–6). The possibility of increasing exports by

7. We shall consider later the possibility of reducing the rate of growth of imports through selective measures (see pp. 237–9).

curbing the consumption of *non-tradable goods* will, in addition, depend on the mobility of resources which, as we have explained, is likely to be relatively low in developing economies (see pp. 11–12).

Abstracting from foreign demand for exports, it would be reasonable to assume that, generally, the smaller the share of domestic consumption in tradable export goods and the lower the mobility of resources in a country are, the smaller the *elasticity of substitution* between its consumption and exports and the more serious the foreign exchange constraint on its growth will be. This explains why the foreign exchange gap presents a more serious problem to LDCs than to developed economies.

To simplify the analysis, we have so far considered the difficulty of increasing export earnings sufficiently to match the growth of imports, having assumed that imports will rise at the same rate as income in Period 1. In practice, because the acceleration in the rate of growth is likely to result in the emergence of supply bottlenecks, the demand for imports will generally rise faster than income, thereby increasing the size of the foreign exchange gap.

One should note, however, that in many cases it should be possible to remove, or at least to ease, the external constraint on growth through government measures. One such case is where purchases of finished luxury goods and of inputs used for the domestic production of such goods account for a significant proportion of the import bill. Here selective curbs on the importation and consumption of such goods will tend to ease the balance of payments constraint by reducing the rate of growth of imports (see pp. 237–9). Similar results can be attained by a reduction in the purchase of armaments from abroad in some countries. In other words, the size of the 'foreign exchange gap', like that of the 'savings gap', is not an immutable datum, exogenously determined for all developing economies, but can for many of them be reduced by fiscal and other measures which succeed in cutting down private luxury and inessential public consumption outlays.

It is also worth noting that even developed economies may at times be faced with a balance of payments constraint on the growth of production because of an inadequate elasticity of substitution between their domestic expenditure and exports. This is partly explained by the fact that, despite their highly diversified structure of production, the resources of developed countries are not as mobile as most economics textbooks tend to suggest. The truth of this is demonstrated by the persistence of depressed regions in need of special government assistance in many industrial countries. Moreover, developed economies may also, like LDCs, be confronted by a stagnant demand for their products in foreign markets and, therefore, be unable to realise the export potential provided by the restriction of domestic expenditure. In such cases a country's success in promoting exports, through such measures as devaluation and export subsidies, can only be attained at the expense of its trading partners and competitors, and will involve practising what are commonly known as 'beggar my neighbour', or 'exporting unemployment', policies. A good example of the low degree of substitution between domestic expenditure and exports for industrial countries is provided by the inability of the UK during 1966–71 and again in 1974–8 to resolve its balance of payments problems through deflationary policies without engendering a significant increase in the level of unemployment.

But although the balance of payments problems can constrain the growth of both industrial and developing countries, this constraint is, as noted above, considerably more prevalent among the latter and has more serious economic implications for them. This subject, together with the problem of inflation, are discussed in greater detail later in the book, where it is argued that the relatively higher incidence of internal and external imbalances among developing countries can largely be traced to the structure of their trade and production (see pp. 218–27).

Absorptive capacity for foreign capital

A broad indication of how serious the foreign exchange gap is in restraining development in a country, is provided by the volume of idle productive resources, notably labour and equipment, which are not utilised because of the balance of payments constraint. It is clear that, other things being equal, the larger the volume of such unemployed resources in a country is, the greater the contribution of a given inflow of foreign capital to the growth of its national income, savings and investment is likely to be. In theory, the 'effectiveness' of foreign capital in promoting development should be measured by reference to the marginal ratio of the increment in national income, made possible by a given inflow of foreign capital, to the volume of such capital; the higher this ratio is, the more effective foreign capital can be said to be. The ratio in question also gives some indication of the capacity of a country to absorb foreign capital usefully in promoting economic development. A country can thus be said to be reaching its limit of absorptive capacity for foreign capital as this ratio approaches zero because of a gradual exhaustion of unemployed productive resources.[8]

8. See Kalecki, *Essays on Developing Economics*, pp. 71–2.

In practice, most developing countries are likely to reach the limit of their absorptive capacity for foreign capital long before the complete disappearance of all their idle productive resources. This is because of the emergence of important production bottlenecks, in the form of shortages of skilled and semi-skilled manpower as well as of economic infrastructure, notably transport and power. The more widespread these bottlenecks are, the smaller the increase in national income that can be generated by a given inflow of foreign capital is likely to be. In addition to production bottlenecks, the ability of a country to service its external debt may, as explained below, also set a limit to its capacity to import foreign capital (see Appendix 4B, especially pp. 170–1).

MAJOR TYPES OF CAPITAL FLOW

Foreign capital flowing into developing countries emanates from different sources and assumes a variety of forms each with its own potential for promoting economic development. Because of this, it is important to distinguish between the various categories of capital received. The classification used here is that generally followed by international organisations concerned with foreign aid, notably UNCTAD, the World Bank and the Development Assistance Committee (DAC) of the OECD.

The total capital flow is generally divided into two broad streams – *official* and *private*. The official capital flows are in turn subdivided into *bilateral* and *multilateral* flows. *Official bilateral flows* consist of capital provided by governments of donor to governments of recipient countries. *Official multilateral flows* consist of capital flows from multilateral organisations, such as the World Bank, the United Nations, the IMF and regional development banks.

Both types of the official flow mentioned can take the form of *grants*, *loans*, or *grant-like contributions*. 'Grants' consist of free gifts which may be made in cash or in kind. 'Loans' are sub-divided into two categories, *concessional* and *non-concessional*, depending on whether or not their terms of repayment are easier than those prevailing in money markets; as explained later, some concessional loans are classified by OECD as Official Development Assistance (ODA). 'Grant-like contributions' are generated largely by sales of commodities for the currencies of recipient countries; the proceeds are often designated as 'counterpart funds'. Part of these funds may be utilised to defray the expenses incurred by donors in recipient countries and the balance is generally placed at the disposal of the governments receiving aid. It is this balance that measures the unrequited transfer of resources from donor to recipient countries and thus represents the value of aid provided.

Private capital flows represent exports of capital by the private sector and take the form either of loans and credits or of direct investment. *Private loans and credits* may be advanced to the public or private sectors of the recipient countries, either in the form of simple loans and export credits or through the purchase of bonds issued by the borrowing countries. *Direct investment* in a country takes place through the acquisition of title to specific assets in it by non-residents – mostly foreign corporations. The assets in question consist largely of real estate, factories and other business establishments as well as of the right to exploit mineral resources.

The 'stock' of foreign direct investment at any given time measures the market value of the assets owned by non-residents. In the case of foreign-owned businesses, the 'net worth', i.e. the value of *all* assets (both tangible and intangible) less external liabilities, should be included in the 'stock' value of direct investment; for the sake of brevity we shall henceforth refer to this as the 'equity interest' or 'equity capital' of foreign corporations. In the case of joint ventures between foreign corporations and residents, only the share of the former in the equity capital is included in foreign direct investment. There are important statistical and conceptual difficulties in the valuation of the 'net worth' of foreign direct investment with which we need not be concerned here. The balance sheet valuations often used for this purpose can be highly unreliable. In the case of very profitable enterprises, for example, the value of 'goodwill' will account for a substantial proportion of total assets, although this may not be fully reflected in their balance sheets.

The 'flow' of direct investment during any given period represents the increment to equity interest of foreign owners. Such increments to foreign interest in an enterprise may result either from the introduction into it of new capital from abroad or from ploughing back a part of the profits earned.

Economic aid and its cost to donors

Of the various flows of foreign capital to developing countries mentioned, only 'grants', and the concessional element of 'grant-like contributions' and of 'concessional loans' represent an unrequited transfer of resources from donor to recipient countries and can, therefore, be considered as 'aid', broadly defined. A narrower definition of economic aid would, in addition, exclude all capital inflows which, for some of the reasons mentioned below, do not contribute to the economic development of the recipient countries.[9]

9. See also Kalecki, *Essays on Developing Economies*, pp. 64–5.

Because of the practical difficulties, discussed later in this chapter (pp. 159–62), of assessing the contribution made by foreign capital to economic development, we shall adopt the broader definition of economic aid in the classification of statistical data on the flows of external capital.

It is relatively easy to quantify the aid value of 'grants' received by developing countries in cash or kind; in the latter case, by estimating the market value of goods and services received as grant. But to calculate the value of aid provided through 'concessional loans' it is necessary to compute the difference between the actual cost of repayment of such loans and what it would have cost to borrow the same amounts on commercial terms. This is not, however, an easy task, because of the technical complications involved in estimating the notional cost of commercial loans. Apart from frequent changes in market rates of interest, the rates charged to individual borrowing countries are likely to vary from one recipient country to another and for the same country from one period to another, depending largely on the assessment made by lenders of the credit-worthiness of borrowers.

Despite these difficulties, it has generally been considered useful to have some estimate of the order of magnitude of the value of aid received by developing countries through concessional loans. To do this, the Secretariat of the Development Assistance Committee (DAC) of the OECD has devised a formula which assumes 10 per cent to be the average, or normal, rate of interest applicable to commerical loans raised by developing countries as a whole. The present cost of a concessional loan is then arrived at by discounting at an annual compound rate of 10 per cent all the payments made on it, in respect of interest and amortisation, until its final settlement. The difference between the cost of a concessional loan, so computed, and the nominal value of the loan is taken to be the value of the grant, or aid, provided by the lender; the ratio of the grant so provided to the nominal value of the loan is designated as its *grant element*.[10]

10. The exact formula used by DAC to compute the 'grant element' of concessional loans is as follows:

$$GE = 100 \times \left(1 - \frac{r/a}{d}\right) \left[1 - \frac{\dfrac{1}{(1+d)^{aG}} - \dfrac{1}{(1+d)^{aM}}}{d(aM - aG)} \right]$$

where GE = grant element as a percentage of the face value of a loan.
   r = annual interest rate.
   a = number of payments per year.
   d = discount rate per period, i.e. $(1+r)^{\frac{1}{a}} - 1$.
   G = grace period.
   M = maturity.
   Repayment is assumed to be in equal payments of principal.

It is clear that the 'grant element' will vary with three factors – the grace period,[11] the period of repayment of loan and the rate of interest: the longer the grace and repayment periods of a loan are and the lower the rate of interest charged on it, the larger its grant element will be. All loans to developing countries with a maturity of over one year which are advanced for the purpose of promoting development and have a grant element of at least 25 per cent are classified by DAC as *Official Development Assistance* (ODA).

The choice of the figure of 25 per cent as a demarcation line between ODA and other loans and credits is clearly arbitrary; the Trade and Development Board of UNCTAD has suggested that only those loans which have a grant element of at least 50 per cent should be classified as ODA.[12] A further difficulty arising from this methodology for computing the flow of aid is that some loans excluded from ODA may in fact provide a larger absolute amount of grant to the recipients than some of those included. For example, a loan of £10 million with a grant element of, say, 20 per cent, which provides a total grant of £2 million, will be excluded from ODA, whereas a loan of £1 million with a grant element of, say, 30 per cent, which provides a grant of only £0.3 million, will be included. We shall henceforth confine the term *concessional loans* to those loans which qualify for inclusion in ODA as defined by the DAC Secretariat; all other loans and credits will be designated as *commercial*, or *non-concessional loans*.

The DAC's methodology for the evaluation of the grant element of loans has, notwithstanding its theoretical imperfections, served two useful purposes in practice. *First*, it has provided a concrete statistical index for comparing the relative weight of concessionality, or aid, contained in the official loans of the individual donor countries. Publication of this information has undoubtedly exercised some moral pressure on certain countries to soften the terms of their loans, when these provided a relatively small grant element. *Secondly*, the DAC methodology has, as shown in Appendix 4A, enabled the United Nations and the DAC itself to formulate certain specific targets for the volume and the terms of ODA as well as to indicate how the target for terms can be reached by various combinations of the maturity, grace period and the interest rates of loans.

11. 'Grace period', as used here, is 'the interval to first repayment minus one payment period'. For example, if a loan is repayable annually and the first instalment is payable at the end of '*t*' years from the date of its disbursement, its grace period will be '*t* − 1'. (For a definition of the term 'disbursement' see p. 162 below).

12. See UNCTAD, *Report of the Group of Governmental Experts on the Concepts of the Present Aid and Flow Targets on its Third Session*, document TD/B/646, TD/B/C.3/135, TD/B/C.3/AC.7/10 (5 April 1977), p. 7.

The 'cost' of foreign economic aid to a donor country is the value of any resources sacrificed by it because of the provision of aid; this can be measured by the extent of contraction in its total internal expenditure i.e. consumption plus domestic investment. Abstracting for the time being from the balance of payments consideration, it is clear that only in conditions of full employment would the provision of aid by industrial countries entail a reduction in their internal expenditure and become an economic burden on them. In practice, these countries generally suffer from idle productive capacity, and the provision of foreign aid, by stimulating exports, is likely to raise the volume of their national income through the operation of the multiplier sufficiently to permit an actual increase in the level of their domestic expenditure. In such cases, foreign aid, far from entailing a positive cost, or being a burden on donors, actually enables them to increase their internal expenditure by stimulating economic activity. This would, for example, happen at the present time (in 1981) when most donor countries of the West are suffering from a severe economic recession.

As shown later (p. 223), LDCs purchase the bulk of their imports from industrial countries and, except for the rich members of OPEC, are generally not in a position to accumulate large foreign exchange reserves. Because of this, a rise in foreign aid by industrial countries will be reflected in a growth of their exports to LDCs and is unlikely to produce a deterioration in their combined balance of payments position *vis-à-vis* the aid-recipient countries. Individual donor countries may, however, feel reluctant to increase the level of foreign aid because of the fear that such an action will result in a worsening of their balance of payments position. Such fears will continue to inhibit foreign aid policies as long as developed countries do not succeed in finding a way of resolving their balance of payments problems without resorting to deflationary policies. But this cannot be the only explanation for the failure of many developed countries to reach the United Nations targets of aid discussed in Appendix 4A, because even the donor countries which have enjoyed persistent balance of payment surpluses have not done so (see p. 147 below). An important reason for the stagnation in the flow of foreign aid, discussed below, is the adoption by many donor countries of the traditional 'sound finance' approach to government expenditure. According to this approach, an increase in public expenditure must, irrespective of the prevailing level of unemployment, always result in an equivalent net reduction in resources available to the private sector.

VOLUME, COMPOSITION AND DISTRIBUTION OF CAPITAL FLOWS

In the next section we shall examine the development potential of the various categories of capital flow described above. But before doing so it will be useful to give the reader some indication of the magnitude of these flows as well as of the sources from which they emanate. The data presented here relate to selected years in the 1970s, but to enable interested readers to obtain more up-to-date information in the future, we first indicate the major publications from which this can readily be obtained.

The principal source of information on financial flows to LDCs and on their external debt (discussed in Appendix 4B) is the OECD, which receives directly from its DAC members detailed data on official and private capital flows and on contributions to multilateral institutions.[13] In addition, the DAC Secretariat collects data and publishes estimates on capital flows from members of OPEC and from socialist countries, but these estimates do not have the same degree of reliability as those published for DAC members. The DAC statistics on flow of capital exclude loans and credits with an original maturity of less than a year. The World Bank also collects, for a large number of developing countries, information on financial flows which give rise to 'public debt' and 'publicly-guaranteed' private sector debt, as well as, for some countries, data on non-guaranteed private sector debt.[14] The IMF, in assembling data on its members' balance of payments, collects information on international capital flows.[15] In recent years, the Bank for International Settlements (BIS) has become an increasingly important source for data on international bank loans.[16]

We have relied primarily on the OECD data, which are on the whole more comprehensive, for our estimates of capital flow to developing countries.[17] The attention of the reader should be drawn to two important qualifications concerning these data. *First*, the figures for capital flow from members of OPEC and from socialist countries represent estimates made by the DAC Secretariat rather than official data reported by the donor countries; in the case of socialist countries especially, the estimates amount to little more than intelligent guesses.

13. See OECD, *Development Co-operation, Efforts and Policies of the Members of the Development Assistance Co-operation*, annual *Reviews*.
14. See World Bank, *Annual Reports*, and *World Debt Tables*.
15. See IMF, *Balance of Payments Yearbooks*.
16. See BIS, *Annual Reports*.
17. Except where otherwise stated, the data presented in this section are derived from OECD, Statistical Annex to annual *Reviews* specified.

Secondly, the data on private capital flows – bilateral loans and credits, direct investment and bank loans – are likely to be less accurate than those on official flows. This is mainly because some of the private flows may not, for a variety of reasons, be publicised and are not, therefore, captured by the statistical network of reporters.

The countries which export capital to developing countries can be divided into three groups. *First*, those OECD countries which are members of the DAC, consisting of the industrial countries of Western Europe and North America together with Japan, Australia and New Zealand, 17 in all; these countries account for the bulk of capital exports as well as of the grants made by voluntary agencies to LDCs.[18] The *second* group is represented by members of OPEC; the capital provided by these countries has assumed significant proportions since the steep rise in oil prices that took place at the end of 1973. The *third* group, which plays a relatively minor role in the export of capital, consists of the socialist countries of Eastern Europe, namely the USSR and other members of the Council for Mutual Economic Assistance (CMEA).

Most of the concessional capital flowing from the three groups of countries takes the form of bilateral ODA, shown in section A of Table 4.1. However, the members of DAC and OPEC also channel a significant amount of resources through multilateral agencies engaged in the provision of development aid to LDCs, such as the World Bank, the United Nations and regional development banks.[19] In 1979, for example, the value of ODA provided by the members of DAC and OPEC to multilateral agencies amounted to over 40 and over 25 per cent, respectively, of their bilateral ODA shown in Table 4.1.[20] The contributions of OPEC members to these agencies, like their bilateral ODA, are designed to assist primarily the Arab and other Islamic countries through a number of agencies specially established for the purpose.[21] Members of CMEA make relatively small contributions to the United Nations aid agencies only.[22]

18. For a full list of DAC members see OECD, *1980 Review*, Table A.2.
19. We have excluded the IMF from these agencies. The bulk of IMF operations, which are reviewed in Chapter 6, consists of the provision of short-term credits in support of the balance of payments of its members. Only the loans advanced by the IMF Trust Fund (described in Appendix 6A), which qualify as ODA, are included in the flow of capital from multilateral agencies.
20. See OECD, *1980 Review*, Tables A.9. and G.4.
21. For details of the OPEC bilateral ODA flows during 1976–9 and of contributions to the various multilateral agencies in 1978–9, see *ibid.*, Tables G.5 to G.7.
22. In 1973 these countries established a special multilateral fund for economic and technical assistance to developing countries, but no information is available on the resources channelled to it.

Table 4.1   *Net external capital receipts of developing countries, 1970, 1975 and 1979[a]*

	In $ billion			Percentage of total		
	1970	1975	1979	1970	1975	1979
A. *Official development assistance* (ODA)	8.13	20.06	27.97	43	38	35
1. DAC, bilateral	5.67	9.81	15.91	30	18	20
2. OPEC, bilateral	0.35	4.95	4.02	2	9	5
3. Multilateral agencies[b]	1.07	3.84	6.10	6	7	8
4. CMEA countries[c]	1.04	1.46	1.94	5	3	2
B. *Non-concessional loans*	7.26	22.80	39.52	38	43	49
1. Bank sector and bond lending	3.30	12.42	19.67	17	23	24
2. Private export credits	2.16	4.22	9.42	11	8	12
3. Official export credits	0.55	1.39	1.50	3	3	2
4. OPEC, official bilateral	0.20	1.50	0.80	1	3	1
5. Multilateral agencies	0.69	2.58	4.20	4	5	5
6. Other	0.36	0.69	3.93	2	1	5
C. *Direct investment*	3.69	10.49	13.49	19	20	17
TOTAL (A + B + C)	19.08	53.35	80.98	100	100	100
Index, 1970 = 100 *At constant prices :[d]*						
ODA	100	130	130			
Total receipts	100	160	165			
Memorandum items :						
Private sector grants	0.86	1.34	1.95			
IMF purchases, net[e]	0.34	3.24	—			

Source: OECD, *1980 Review*, Table A.1, and DAC Secretariat.
[a] Excludes grants by private voluntary agencies.
[b] Includes IMF Trust Fund loans of $680 million in 1979.
[c] Includes small bilateral flows ($30 million in 1975 and $100 million in 1979) from other countries.
[d] Rounded to the nearest 5.
[e] Drawings less repayments; excludes loans by the IMF Trust Fund.
Note: Owing to rounding up, components may not add to totals.

The ODA contributions to multilateral agencies, which take the form of grants, concessional loans and capital subscriptions, account for the bulk of the resources of these institutions. Some agencies, however, notably the World Bank, raise additional funds by borrowing on non-concessional terms from private capital markets and from official sources. The method of funding the various agencies largely determines the relative share of ODA and non-concessional loans provided by them to developing countries.[23]

Apart from the official (bilateral and multilateral) flows mentioned, private capital exports have accounted for a large and growing share of the foreign resources provided to LDCs in the 1970s. As shown below a particularly important role in financing the external deficits of developing countries has been played by international bank loans, often described as 'Eurocurrency credits', many of which are syndicated. This market is in a sense stateless, or cosmopolitan, in character: most of its financial resources, used for advancing loans and credits to private as well as public sectors in industrial and developing countries (including centrally-planned economies), come from banks, business corporations and some governments which invest in it part of their foreign exchange reserves.

Table 4.1 gives a broad view of the flow of resources from the various sources mentioned to developing countries during 1970–9. The resources in question have been divided into three major streams–ODA, non-concessional loans, and direct investment. As explained later, there are significant differences between the development potential of the three streams of capital. In this connection one should also distinguish between 'official' and 'private' non-concessional loans since the former generally carry considerably easier terms than the latter (see p. 168 below).

It is important to note at this stage that almost all resources transferred to developing countries through ODA are tied to projects, as is the bulk of non-concessional flows provided by multilateral agencies. Bilateral ODA includes what are called 'programme loans' in the form of freely usable external credits. However, these account for only a very small fraction of the total ODA; by far the largest part of this flow is in the form of project loans.[24] Similarly, among multilateral agencies the World Bank and IDA provide some 'programme loans', but these too amount to a small fraction, estimated at about 5 per cent,

---

23. For details of ODA and non-concessional loans provided by various agencies during the 1970s, see OECD, *1980 Review*, Table C.2.
24. For further details see pp. 146–7 below.

of total loans advanced by them. Of the various types of capital export shown in Table 4.1 the principal flows which provide freely usable foreign credits, available for financing external deficits, are private loans, namely bank and bond lending, and export credits.[25]

It can be seen from Table 4.1 that the *nominal* value of the total net flow of capital, measured in US dollars, rose by about 180 per cent, from $19 billion to over $50 billion, between 1970 and 1975, and by a further 50 per cent, to about $80 billion, during the following four years. However, owing to a steep rise in prices during this period, the increase in the volume of *real* resources received by LDCs was considerably lower. Our estimates of the flow of real resources to LDCs shown in the table, suggest that the volume of total resources rose by only 60 per cent and that of ODA by 30 per cent between 1970 and 1975, and stagnated thereafter.

It is possible to obtain a rough indication of the importance of foreign capital to developing countries by relating its volume to the foreign trade and the national income of recipient countries. It is important to emphasise that what is aimed at here is simply a statistical measure of the proportions of imports and of total resources that have been financed by foreign capital, without any regard to the impact of this capital on the economy of recipient countries. Apart from the significant differences in the development potential of the various types of foreign capital, discussed below, the contribution of this capital to savings and investment and to economic development in general depends, as we shall explain, on the use made of it by recipient countries (see pp. 159–61).

According to our estimates, for the years 1973–5 total capital flow was equivalent, on average, to about 25 per cent of exports and 22 per cent of imports of oil-importing developing countries, the ODA accounting for just under two-fifths of the total.[26] As a share of the total resources of LDCs, estimates made by DAC show that, for developing countries as a whole, the ratio of ODA to GNP remained relatively constant between 1971 and 1978, amounting to about 1.5 per cent. Unlike ODA, the ratio of non-concessional flows to GNP rose steadily

25. As explained in Chapter 6, the credit facilities provided by IMF, which are excluded from the capital flows shown in the table, also provide balance of payments support to its members. However, unlike private loans and export credits, the bulk of these facilities is, as we shall see, subject to strict 'conditionality', generally requiring the adoption of restrictive fiscal and monetary measures by the countries utilising them (see pp. 257–63).

26. Because most of the transport and insurance charges in the foreign trade of developing countries accrue to industrial countries, exports are valued on a FOB and imports on a CIF basis.

during this period, from 1.7 per cent in 1971 to just under 4 per cent in 1978. Because of this, the ratio of total inflow of resources to GNP, for developing countries as a whole, increased from 3.2 in 1971 to about 5 per cent in 1978.[27]

The foregoing ratios do not, however, accurately reflect the magnitude of resources added to the national income and to the foreign exchange earnings of developing countries. *First*, the figures of 'net flow' of financial resources used to compute the ratios in question are, as explained in Appendix 4A, gross of interest payments on previously contracted external loans. These payments, which are estimated at $3.3 billion for 1971 and at about $20 billion for 1978, should be deducted from the figures of net flow in calculating 'net transfer' of resources;[28] this would reduce the ratios mentioned by about one-fifth for 1971 and by one-fourth for 1978.

Secondly, net private flows of capital include reinvested profits of foreign corporations under the heading of 'direct investment'. It is debatable whether such profits constitute a genuine transfer of resources to developing countries since they do not *add* to the foreign exchange resources of the host countries, although a repatriation of profits would increase their foreign exchange outlay. Estimates of reinvested profits for eight of the major capital exporting members of DAC, which include Canada, Germany, Italy, Japan and the US, indicate that such profits accounted for over one-third of direct investment in 1975–6.[29]

Composition and distribution of capital

Table 4.1 also shows a pronounced change in the composition of external capital between 1970 and 1979. It can be seen that the share of ODA, which, as will be explained later, has the highest development potential, in total capital flow, declined from 43 per cent in 1970 to 38 per cent in 1975 and to 35 per cent in 1979. All the major streams of non-concessional capital grew faster than ODA during the period under consideration. Particularly significant was the role played by bank and bond lending in the growth of total non-concessional flow. This stream of capital, which includes what have come to be known as 'syndicated Eurocurrency credits', rose almost

---

27. For details, see OECD, *1979 Review*, p. 71, Table *VI*-5.
28. See OECD, *1980 Review*, Table E.2.
29. See OECD, *1977 Review*, p. 69 and Table E.6.

fourfold between 1970 and 1975 and by about 60 per cent during the following four years.[30]

Apart from bank and bond lending, direct investment and export credits were the two most important sources of private non-concessional capital imported by LDCs. The flow of direct investment, while showing a clear upward trend, has been subject to relatively large year-to-year fluctuations, partly because of the 'lumpy' nature of this type of investment; major nationalisation programmes, which are treated as disinvestment, have also had the effect of disturbing the trend.

The chief reason for the rapid growth in the private non-concessional loans (in the form of bank and bond lending as well as export credits) was the severe deterioration in the external position of oil-importing developing countries during the 1970s. This was brought about largely by a pronounced deterioration in the terms of trade of these countries caused by the rise in the prices of petroleum and manufactured imports. A further contributory factor was the relatively slow growth in the exports of LDCs due to economic stagnation in industrial countries. Since, as noted above, the bulk of bilateral and multilateral official flows is tied to projects, many developing countries have been compelled to rely increasingly on the foreign private sources of credit mentioned for financing their external deficits. Foreign capital markets have thus served as a channel for 'recycling' a part of the export surpluses of the richer members of OPEC and of some industrial countries to those LDCs which have had access to these markets.

The distribution of external resources between the poorer 'low-income' and the relatively better off 'middle-income' developing countries has been highly uneven. The 'low-income' countries, which account for about 60 per cent of the population of LDCs, are defined by DAC as those whose annual per capita income in 1978 was less than $450; they include such densely populated countries as India, Indonesia, Bangladesh and Pakistan. All other developing countries are classified as 'middle-income'.[31]

DAC estimates suggest that the distribution of ODA between the low- and middle-income oil-importing countries in 1978 was roughly

---

30. Provisional data suggest that bank and bond lending reached a peak in 1978 and declined in the following two years, probably because of the fear of debt service difficulties on the part of some bankers and borrowing countries, discussed in Appendix 4B. See OECD, *1981 Review*, Table A.1.
31. See OECD, 1980 *review*, p. 75 and Table H.2.

proportional to their population.[32] Among the low-income countries, however, India, which accounts for just under 50 per cent of the population of the group, received a significantly smaller amount of ODA on a *per capita* basis than the average.[33] This implies that the share in ODA of most other low-income countries in relation to their population was somewhat larger than that of the middle-income group; the data suggest that this was particularly true of the 'least-developed' countries.[34]

Unlike the ODA, the distribution of non-concessional capital has been heavily weighted in favour of the middle-income countries. Owing to their relatively low credit rating and less promising economic prospects, the low-income countries, especially the least developed among them, have had little access to external private sources of capital. According to DAC less than 10 per cent of the total flow of non-concessional loans and direct investment went to low-income countries in 1978. The share of these countries in the flow of private loans and credits was even lower, amounting to about 6 per cent of the total.[35] Taking ODA and non-concessional flows together, less than one-fourth of the total external resources in 1978 went to low-income countries, which implies that, on a *per capita* basis, their share amounted to about one-fifth of that of the middle-income countries.[36]

The foregoing pattern of the distribution of external private finance has had important implications for the development of both low- and middle-income countries. On the one hand, the lack of balance of payments support in the form of foreign loans and credits to low-income countries has, as explained in Chapter 6 (p. 243), forced them, from time to time, to resolve their balance of payments difficulties by resorting to deflationary policies. There is little doubt that this goes some way to explain the relatively low rate of growth of these countries as compared with that of middle-income countries in the 1970s.[37] On the other hand, the middle-income countries which

32. *Ibid.*, p. 87 and Table H.2.
33. *Ibid.*
34. *Ibid.* For a description of 'least-developed' countries see Appendix 4A.
35. OECD, *1980 Review*, p. 88.
36. For information on the flow of total resources and of ODA to individual developing countries, see *ibid.*, Tables D.1 to D.4.
37. Estimates made by the World Bank suggest that, among the oil-importing developing countries, the annual per capita rate of growth in the GNP during the 1970s was only about 1 per cent for low-income countries as compared with 3 per cent for middle-income ones; the poor African countries, south of the Sahara, experienced little or no growth at all in per capita income. The World Bank has defined the 'low-income' countries as those whose per capita GNP was $360 or less in 1978; all other developing countries are classified as 'middle-income'. See World Bank, *World Development Report, 1980*, pp. viii and 11.

have had access to foreign capital markets and have made use of them to ease the balance of payments constraint on their growth, have, as explained in Appendix 4B, experienced a steady rise in their debt service burden. A number of them have already run into debt servicing problems, and many others, to avoid such problems, have been compelled to curb imports by restraining the growth of domestic demand and production.

It can be seen that, under the present system of development finance, the process of growth in LDCs is periodically interrupted by the need to resort to deflationary policies to resolve the balance of payments difficulties. Apart from hindering development, the present system has from time to time also tended to strengthen recessionary forces in developed economies by discouraging their exports to LDCs, as it has done since 1973. This, however, represents only one facet of the overall deflationary bias of the present international monetary system, discussed in Chapter 6 (see pp. 242 and 260–2).

It is clear that there is a serious gap in the system of development finance which could be filled through official 'programme loans' that provide balance of payments support to developing countries on terms and conditions that take fully into account their capacity to service them without the need to resort to deflationary measures. This means that in the case of many developing countries the loans in question would have to be provided on concessional terms. The Brandt Commission recommended the creation of a new institution, the World Development Fund, administered jointly by industrial and developing countries, one of whose major functions was to be the provision of such loans to LDCs.[38] However, bearing in mind the recent aid policies of the major industrial countries, which, as shown in Appendix 4A, have been largely responsible for the stagnation in the volume of ODA, it is unlikely that such proposals will be implemented in the near future. A further reason for this pessimistic prognosis is the marked preference shown by the major donor countries for channelling their aid bilaterally rather than through multilateral agencies of the type proposed by the Commission.

38. See *North-South: A Programme for Survival*, The Report of the Independent Commission on International Development Issues under the Chairmanship of Willy Brandt, Pan Books, London and Sydney (1980), pp. 232–4 and 252–4. See also United Nations, *World Development Fund, Report of the Secretary-General*, document A/36/572 (2 October 1981).

DEVELOPMENT POTENTIAL OF DIFFERENT CATEGORIES OF
EXTERNAL CAPITAL

The extent of the stimulus provided by foreign capital to development
depends not only on the volume of the capital inflow in relation to
national income and foreign trade of the recipient countries but also on
their 'absorptive capacity', discussed earlier, on government policies in
recipient countries and on the type of capital received. We shall here
approach the subject of assessing the role of foreign capital in economic
development in two stages. In this section we examine, in somewhat
greater detail than was done at the beginning of this chapter, the
potential of the different categories of external financial resources
received by LDCs to promote economic development. The next
section will be devoted to a discussion of the difficulties encountered in
any evaluation of the *actual* contribution of foreign capital to
development. We follow the classification adopted in Table 4.1 and
distinguish between the following three major categories of capital
flow: 'grants and concessional loans' (ODA); 'non-concessional
loans'; and 'direct investment'.

Grants and concessional loans (ODA)

It can be seen from Table 4.1 that grants and concessional loans, which
together constitute ODA, accounted for 35 per cent of net capital
receipts of LDCs in 1979. Prima facie, grants should be considered as
the most desirable type of foreign assistance, since they represent a net
addition to the resources available for development purposes and,
being free gifts, do not have to be repaid. For the same reason,
compared with commercial loans, concessional loans have also a larger
development potential; the larger the degree of their concessionality,
as indicated by their 'grant element', the greater this potential (see pp.
133–4). This explains the efforts of the United Nations, the World
Bank and the DAC to persuade the donor countries to increase the
volume of grants and ODA loans, as well as the grant element of the
latter, along the lines indicated by the 'aid targets' described in
Appendix 4A.

The development potential of ODA should not, however, be
evaluated solely by reference to its grant element. In practice a large
part of official bilateral foreign aid, with the exception of that made on
humanitarian grounds to assist countries affected by some natural
calamity, has associated with it some 'political strings', which may have
important economic implications for the recipient countries and which

should therefore be taken into account. These often take the form of a tacit understanding that the recipient countries will follow economic, political and defence policies favoured by donors. For example, the grants and concessional loans made by the free enterprise countries, in particular the larger members of DAC, are often made on the 'understanding' that the recipient countries will refrain from nationalising foreign property without 'full' compensation, from following radical socialist policies at home and from establishing close political and economic links with certain countries deemed to be 'unfriendly'.[39] Similarly, the aid given by members of OPEC and by socialist countries may have other kinds of 'political strings', not necessarily favourable to the development of recipient countries, attached to them. Because of the difficulty of measuring the economic effects of such obligations undertaken by recipient countries, it is not possible in many cases properly to evaluate the development value of economic aid provided in the form of grants and concessional loans.

Tied aid

Apart from 'political strings', the donor countries may attach other conditions to their aid, such as those which limit the recipients' choice of investment projects and of suppliers of goods and services financed by the aid. Such aid, whether provided in the form of grants or concessional loans, is known as 'tied aid'; it is called 'project-tied' or 'source-tied' depending on whether the recipient country's choice is limited in respect of the choice of projects or of the source of supply of goods and services, respectively. Untied aid, often designated as 'programme loans', 'cash contributions', or 'balance of payments contribution', on the other hand, provides the recipient countries with freely usable foreign credits on which they can draw to finance any development scheme and to purchase goods and services from countries of their choice. Source-tied aid may be tied *formally* by agreements concluded between the donor and recipient countries, or *informally* and indirectly in a number of other ways, such as through the influence exerted in recipient countries by business groups, advisers and civil servants with special connections in the donor countries.

The flow of aid and non-concessional loans from multilateral agencies is generally project-tied: it takes a variety of forms which include financing of specific investment projects, technical assistance

---

39. For further comments on the use of economic aid by some powers as an instrument of policy, see Kalecki, *Essays on Developing Economies*, pp. 92–3.

and provision of resources to local public institutions, such as industrial and agricultural development banks, discussed in Chapter 5. This aid is, however, rarely source-tied; goods and services financed by it are almost invariably procured through international tenders and recruitment agencies.

Bilateral ODA is often subject to both source- and project-tying. Figures published by DAC show that during 1978–9, about 50 per cent of the gross disbursements of bilateral ODA provided by its members was formally tied to procurements in donor countries and a further 10 per cent or more was subject to some form of restriction as to the source of procurement.[40] Although no information is published on project-tying, it is known that the bulk of the aid provided by DAC members is in fact tied in this way. The primary purpose of tying aid is to assist the exports of donor countries, although the available data indicate that even countries like Germany and Japan, which have enjoyed prolonged surpluses on the balance of payments account, continue to tie a significant proportion of their grants and concessional loans; this is particularly true of Japan.[41]

A large proportion of the aid provided by OPEC members is also project-tied, but only the aid given through subsidised oil exports is source-tied. In the case of socialist countries almost the entire aid is believed to be both source- and project-tied.

The bilateral aid provided under the heading of 'grant-like' contributions may also be tied through the imposition of conditions on the release of 'counterpart funds', described above (p.131). The recipient countries may, for example, be required to allocate the counterpart funds to financing specific projects, or to providing concessional loans to the private enterprise sector alone. The latter type of conditions were frequently attached to aid in kind given by the US Agency for International Development (AID) under PL 480 in the 1960s; the loans so advanced were known as 'Cooley loans'.[42]

It is clear that tied aid has a lower potential than untied aid for assisting the development of recipient countries. Project-tied aid usually has the effect of limiting the freedom of recipient countries to allocate investment resources to purposes and projects deemed to have highest priority in their development. Donor countries generally tend to prefer projects at which they enjoy a competitive advantage in international tenders and which can readily be identified with them. It

40. See, OECD, *1979 Review*, Table B.4. and *1981 Review*, Table B.3.
41. *Ibid.*
42. For specific examples, see Éprime Eshag, *Study of Tied Economic Aid Given to Tunisia in 1965*, UNCTAD, document TD/7/Supp. 8/Add. 3 (30 November 1967), pp. 3–4.

is, however, often argued that project-tied aid, which is supervised by donor countries, ensures that the resources provided by aid are used efficiently and exclusively for investment purposes. It is probably true that external supervision will in many cases result in a more efficient use of aid resources, but, as explained below, aid being 'fungible', its mere allocation to investment projects does not ensure an equivalent increment in total investment outlay (see p. 161).

Source-tied aid also suffers from a number of drawbacks which tend to reduce its efficacy. The goods and services available for procurement in a donor country may not, for example, be entirely suitable to the local conditions and requirements of a recipient country. This is likely to apply, in particular, to capital goods and to technology imported under a source-tied aid programme. There may also be excessive delays in the delivery of goods and of spare parts due to long distances and/or language barriers between the donor and recipient countries. Finally, the prices of goods and services imported under an aid programme may be higher in the donor country than those prevailing in some other countries.[43] This implies that the real value of aid is less than is indicated by the nominal value of grants and the grant element of concessional loans. As regards concessional loans, however, the real cost of such loans to recipient countries is equal to the present discounted value of total debt service charges on them. Developing countries may, therefore, at times prefer to receive some source-tied loans from countries with relatively higher prices, because of the significantly larger element of concessionality of such loans.[44] In such cases the governments of the donor countries, which offer easier terms, provide, in effect, an indirect subsidy to their export industries.

It is generally recognised that bilateral economic aid, especially the aid provided by the larger industrial countries, often does suffer from the drawback of having 'political strings' attached to it. This explains the pressure of many developing countries and of the United Nations agencies to have a larger proportion of economic assistance channelled through the United Nations and other multilateral institutions. But it would be wrong to assume that even the multilateral grants and concessional loans are always provided on an entirely impartial basis.

---

43. In some cases suppliers in donor countries are placed in a monopolistic position and enabled to raise prices on aid-financed exports.

44. For a more detailed illustration of the above points by reference to the experience of a number of developing countries, see UNCTAD, *The Costs of Aid-tying to Recipient Countries*, document TD/7/Supp. 8 (21 November 1967); Eshag, UNCTAD, document TD/7/Supp.8/Add.3, *op. cit.*; and *Study on the Excess Cost of Tied Aid Given to Iran in 1966/67*, UNCTAD, document TD/7/Supp.8/Add.2 (13 December 1967).

The reason for this is that the more important multilateral aid agencies, such as the World Bank Group which includes the IDA, and the United Nations Development Programme (UNDP), are, to a large extent, controlled by the major industrial countries of the West whose foreign policies are likely to influence the distribution of aid among LDCs.[45] It is, nevertheless, reasonable to assume that the presence of an international civil service in charge of administering the day-to-day affairs of multilateral agencies tends to mitigate to some extent the political influence of the major donor countries on aid policies.

It can be concluded from the above discussion that to increase the development potential of ODA, (a) a larger proportion of it should be channelled through multilateral agencies, notably the UNDP and the IDA in the World Bank Group, (b) the potential recipients of the aid should have a greater say than they have hitherto had in determining the policies of multinational aid agencies, including the allocation of their resources among developing countries, and (c) the proportion of tied aid in ODA should be progressively reduced. Although similar recommendations are to be found in the report of the Brandt Commission,[46] it would be somewhat unrealistic to anticipate a rapid progress along these lines in the foreseeable future. Experience has shown that the major donor countries are very reluctant to sacrifice the national economic and political advantages that can be derived from the provision of aid on a bilateral basis in the interest of increasing its efficacy in promoting development; this is broadly true of all the three groups of capital exporting countries mentioned.

Non-concessional loans

Non-concessional loans and credits accounted for about one-half of the total capital receipts of developing countries in 1979 (see Table 4.1). Although none of the components of this capital flow qualify for inclusion in the ODA, their relative desirability as sources of development finance varies significantly because of differences between their financial terms and conditions. Generally, 'official' loans, bilateral and multilateral, are granted on easier terms than 'private' loans: of the latter, private export credits often carry the hardest terms (see p. 168 below). This largely explains why official bilateral and multilateral loans are deemed by LDCs to be a relatively more

---

45. Socialist countries and the members of OPEC have often advanced this argument in support of their aid policies, mentioned earlier (see p. 137).
46. See *North-South: A Programme for Survival*, Chapters 14–15.

attractive source of finance than private loans. The principal sources of official multilateral loans are the World Bank, regional development banks and OPEC development funds and banks.

Non-concessional private loans are advanced both to governments and to the private sector in developing countries. On the whole, loans raised by governments have a greater potential value for promoting development than those borrowed by private firms. The reason for this is that the former can be used by the authorities to finance projects (private and public) which have a high social priority in their development plan, whereas private loans are used to expand the productive capacities of the borrowing firms, irrespective of the social priority of such investment. So, unless governments are willing to permit the market mechanism to determine the course of economic development and to take no active part in influencing the pattern of investment (a development strategy rejected in Chapter 1), they should strictly regulate the private sector's external borrowing by reference to the social priority of the investment financed by it. Alternatively, the authorities should themselves undertake the task of raising the bulk of non-concessional finance from abroad.

There is a further argument against allowing private firms in developing countries completely free access to foreign capital markets. It would be virtually impossible to plan the foreign exchange budget of a country if individual firms were permitted to contract external loans for such amounts and on such terms and conditions as they were able and willing to obtain. To reduce the risk of encountering periodic foreign exchange crises, due to excessive borrowing by private firms, it is, therefore, essential for the authorities to take action along the lines suggested above.

From the point of view of the burden of servicing foreign loans and the balance of payments constraint on development, the most desirable non-concessional loans are those linked to international trade in such a way that repayment is made in the form of goods exported to the creditor countries. Such loans can in some cases become completely 'self liquidating' when repayment takes place by shipment of a part of the output of a new plant which has been constructed through the loans in question.[47] It is clear, however, that this type of loan can be negotiated only with those capital exporting countries in which imports can to some extent be regulated by the authorities; they are, therefore, largely confined at present to some of the loans advanced to LDCs by the centrally-planned economies and Japan.

47. See Kalecki, *Essays on Developing Economies*, p.77.

Direct investment

In view of the great importance attached in traditional literature to direct investment as an engine of economic development, it is worth examining this flow of capital to LDCs in greater detail.

The available data on direct investment indicate a steep rise in the flow of this category of capital into developing countries since the mid-1960s. It is estimated that the annual average flow of direct investment by DAC countries to LDCs rose from about $2 billion in 1964–5 to $3.5 billion in 1970–1 and to over $10 billion in 1977–8, when it accounted for about 15 per cent of the total capital receipts of developing countries.[48] The bulk (over two-thirds) of direct investment is undertaken by large oligopolies, operating through subsidiaries and affiliates in a number of countries and known variously as 'multinational', 'transnational' and 'international' corporations.

Until the Great Depression of the 1930s the flow of capital from industrial countries to the less developed regions of the world, notably Africa, Asia, Latin America, Canada and Australia, was largely concentrated into the development of primary products (minerals and agricultural products) and the related economic infrastructure, such as ports and other transport facilities. These facilities were deemed essential for foreign trade, which consisted largely of the export of primary products and import of manufactured goods by LDCs.

The import restrictions imposed by primary producing countries after the steep fall in their foreign exchange earnings during the Great Depression encouraged the establishment and growth of manufacturing industries, largely of an import-substituting type, in many of them. The protection thus afforded to internal industries was an important element in attracting foreign capital into the manufacturing sector of developing countries, in particular into those with large domestic markets. Other factors which attracted foreign capital into manufacturing included proximity to raw materials and availability of cheap local labour as well as fiscal and monetary incentives, such as tax 'holidays' and cheap loans, offered to foreign corporations.

Transnational corporations have for some years been operating in such manufacturing industries of LDCs as those producing durable consumer goods (motor cars, refrigerators, washing machines, etc.), pharmaceuticals and other chemicals, food products, rubber and paper. Because the establishment of a manufacturing plant by one corporation in a foreign protected market presents a potential threat to the exports of its rivals to that market, there has been a tendency for

48. See OECD, *1970 Review*, p. 30, and *1979 Review*, Table A.1.

transnational corporations to follow one another into the same markets; this explains the proliferation of affiliates of rival corporations producing similar goods in the same country.

Since the end of the Second World War, there has also been a rapid growth in the supply by large corporations of such services as banking, insurance and even advertising. These corporations have also been active in promoting light, foot-loose industries, notably the assembly of electronic goods and office equipment in LDCs. These industries, which are export-oriented and use very few locally-produced raw materials, have concentrated in small areas, such as Hong Kong, Singapore, South Korea and Taiwan, offering a cheap supply of semi-skilled and skilled labour as well as attractive tax incentives.

Abstracting from the consideration of externalities discussed earlier (pp. 15–21), the impact of direct investment on development will depend largely on the type of goods and services it helps to produce. For example, direct investment in the production of luxury and semi-luxury goods for *domestic consumption* is more likely to hinder than to promote economic development as understood by us. This, as we have seen in Chapter 1, is true of any inessential investment whether undertaken by domestic or by foreign corporations. On the other hand, direct investment in luxury industries which cater primarily for *foreign markets* could contribute to development both by stimulating production and employment and by easing the foreign exchange constraint on growth.

Experience has shown that investment in heavily protected industries producing luxury consumer goods for internal consumption has had the effect of enabling the richer classes in developing countries to emulate the pattern of consumption of the middle and upper classes in industrial countries. As pointed out by some Latin American economists, the pattern of consumption followed by the rich in that continent has tended to aggravate the differences between their standard of living and that of the poorer classes of the community, and has increased the political and cultural alienation of the rich from the rest of the population.[49]

A large number of developing countries have attempted to direct foreign investment into specific sectors of the economy deemed important for the promotion of development. But despite these attempts, production of inessential goods for domestic consumption by foreign enterprises, consisting largely of transnational corporations, has continued to grow in most of them.

49. See, for example, Osvaldo Sunkel, 'National Development Policy and External Dependence in Latin America', *Journal of Development Studies*, Volume Six, Number One, October 1969.

Drawbacks, compared with loans

Leaving aside the pattern of direct investment, there are two important reasons for regarding direct investment as a generally less desirable source of development finance than non-concessional foreign loans.

First, the cost of foreign capital, measured in terms of profits remitted on direct investment and of interest paid on loans, will generally be higher for direct investment. One reason for this is that, considering the risk premium paid to entrepreneurs, the rate of profit earned on direct investment is likely, on average, to be higher than the interest rate paid on loans. A more important reason, however, is that profits are earned on the equity interest of a parent company in its foreign affiliates, only a part of which is accounted for by capital exported to the host country, the remainder having been acquired by reinvestment of profits.[50] In the case of loans, by contrast, interest is paid only on the capital received from abroad. As long as a parent company continues to plough back into its foreign affiliates some of their profits, the value of its equity in them and hence the amount of profits earned and remitted abroad will continue to grow. For this reason profits remitted on a given flow of direct investment from abroad are likely to exceed, over time, the interest element of servicing an equivalent amount of foreign loan capital.

The policy of ploughing back into a foreign affiliate a share of profits earned, practised by most parent companies, has also certain implications for the balance of payments of the host countries. The steady growth in the stream of investment income remitted abroad means that, unless the inflow of new investment from abroad also grows at least proportionately every year, eventually the amount of profits remitted abroad will exceed the inflow of new capital and the overall effect of direct investment on the balance of payments will become negative.[51] The size of this deficit on foreign account will continue to grow as long as the rate of profit on equity capital does not fall and the

---

50. We take no account here of profits earned on capital borrowed in host countries.
51. For a detailed illustration of this argument see Kalecki, *Essays on Developing Economies*, pp. 80–3 and p. 95. It can be shown by means of simple geometric progression formulae that, given a constant yearly inflow of capital, a rate of profits 'p' transferred abroad and a rate of profits 'q' reinvested, the net inflow of capital will become zero after 'n' years, where

$$n = \frac{\log \dfrac{p+q}{p}}{\log(1+q)}.$$

parent company maintains a policy of allocating fixed proportions of its annual profits to reinvestment and to remittances abroad.

According to a United Nations estimate, investment income remitted abroad by a sample of 61 developing countries during the three years 1971–3, was more than three times greater than the inflow of direct investment. This was largely because of the nine OPEC members included in the sample; but even for the remaining 52 countries, the outflow of investment income was of the same order of magnitude as the inflow of direct investment.[52]

It can thus be seen that whereas foreign loans give rise to clear and definite obligations on the part of the recipients, direct investments involve them in open-ended financial commitments of indefinite duration. The sole method of terminating such commitments is to acquire the ownership and control of the foreign enterprise through nationalisation or otherwise, but this may give rise to serious economic and political difficulties for the host country. In the case of investment which produces strategically important goods (for example minerals, such as petroleum), the government of the parent company may not be willing to relinquish the control of the enterprise at any price. But even in other cases, the price paid for acquiring the ownership of foreign enterprises must be acceptable to the parent company, if the host country wishes to avoid the risk of being subjected to economic and political sanctions, and even to military intervention, by the parent company and its government.[53]

It is, in addition, worth noting that in some instances the mere

---

52. See United Nations, *Transnational Corporations in World Development: A Re-examination*, document E/C.10/38 (1978), p. 251.
53. There have been a number of cases of such sanctions and military interventions, prompted by actual or feared nationalisation of foreign property, in the post-War period of which one need mention only a few well documented ones: the British blockade of oil exports from Iran and subsequent overthrow of Dr Mosaddeq through a US-backed *coup d'état*, following the nationalisation of the petroleum industry in 1951; the invasion of Guatemala and the overthrow of President Arbenz with the help of the US Government and the United Fruit Company in 1954, following the introduction of an agrarian reform programme; the Anglo-French invasion of Egypt in 1956, following the nationalisation of the Suez Canal; the US termination of trade and diplomatic relations with Cuba after the Castro revolution of 1959 and the CIA-organised Bay of Pigs invasion of that country in 1961; the support given by the Union Minière to the Katanga rebellion against the central government of Lumumba in the Congo Republic (now Zaire) in 1960; and the interference by the International Telephone and Telegraph Corporation (IT and T) in the presidential elections of Chile in 1970 against the left wing parties led by Salvatore Allende, followed by the relentless opposition of the US Government and transnational corporations to the government of Allende, which ended in his overthrow and assassination in the military *coup d'état* of 1973.

acquisition of the ownership of a foreign enterprise does not pass on to the host ·country complete control over all the operations of the enterprise. This is true in most cases where the transport and/or marketing of the product of the enterprise is primarily in the hands of a small number of large foreign corporations operating in collusion, as was the case in the petroleum industry until about the mid-1970s.

The *second* important reason for regarding direct investment as less desirable than loans is that the operations of foreign enterprises, notably their investment, production and sales activities, are determined by these enterprises rather than by host countries. A foreign corporation may, for economic or political reasons, decide to curtail its operations in some countries and to expand them in others, without regard to the interests of the countries concerned. Moreover, since it is generally known that one reason for cutting down its activities in a country may be the corporation's dislike of the policies followed by that country, the host countries are inevitably compelled to take account of this in formulating their economic and social policies.

The above amounts, in effect, to a loss of political and economic autonomy on the part of the host countries; the larger the volume of foreign direct investment in relation to the size of the economy is, the greater the loss in question is likely to be. It is clear that every country, depending on its size and on the resilience of its social and political institutions, must have what could be termed a 'social absorptive capacity' for the inflow of foreign capital in the form of direct investment which, if exceeded, will undermine its political and economic independence and change its cultural characteristics. It was no doubt largely because of this consideration that even a large industrial country like France, introduced, under General de Gaulle, measures to restrict the inflow of direct investment by the US corporations.

It is now generally recognised that the operation of transnational corporations can give rise to serious political and economic problems in the host countries. In 1974, the United Nations established the Commission on Transnational Corporations as the forum for the comprehensive and in-depth consideration of issues relating to transnational corporations, and charged it, *inter alia*, with the task of formulating a 'code of conduct' dealing with transnational corporations. Some two years later, the Commission gave a mandate to an intergovernmental group, known as the Intergovernmental Working Group on a Code of Conduct, to formulate a draft code. Although the group had by the end of 1980 met in twelve sessions, it had not succeeded in drafting a code of conduct acceptable to both industrial and developing countries.[54] The need for regulating the conduct of transnationals was also emphasised in the report of the Brandt Commission mentioned earlier.[55] It is very likely that some code of conduct for transnational corporations will eventually be formulated, although it is not certain how effective it will be in practice.

Special advantages

Compared with the foregoing drawbacks, such benefits as may be conferred by transnational corporations on host countries are, in our view, less important in most cases and do not negate the proposition that direct investment is generally a less attractive source of development finance than foreign loans. The advantages often attributed to direct investment largely relate to their production and marketing efficiency and can be summarised under three broad headings: advanced technology, experienced management and marketing facilities.

Advanced technology: It is known that in mining and manufacturing as well as in some service industries, transnationals are generally in possession of the most up-to-date production technology and that, with the large resources devoted by them to 'R and D', they are in the forefront of modern technological innovations. This often enables them to produce the desired commodities more efficiently i.e. at lower market costs, than could be done by other forms of production. It is also true that by training the local labour force to operate their equipment these corporations help to spread modern technology in the host countries. The significance of the benefits so conferred on host countries will, however, vary with a number of considerations of which we mention only two.

First, it is necessary to consider the suitability to host countries of the technology introduced by transnationals. It has been argued, for example, that the technology in question, having been developed to meet the production needs of industrial countries in which these corporations primarily operate, may be too capital intensive to suit the present needs of many developing countries, which suffer from a shortage of capital in relation to labour force.[56] In practice, this

---

54. Differences have arisen as to the scope of regulations, as to whether the code should be legally binding or voluntary and as to whether host countries should undertake certain obligations on the treatment of transnationals, especially as regards their nationalisation.

55. See *North South: A Programme for Survival*, Chapter 12.

56. For a brief summary of some of the discussions on the question of choice of technology in LDCs, see Frances Stewart 'Choice of Techniques in Developing Countries', *Journal of Development Studies*, October 1972.

argument is likely to apply to the production of such goods as textiles, clothing, footwear and furniture, which can be manufactured through different technologies with varying degrees of capital intensity.

Secondly, it is important to examine the possibility of acquiring the most suitable technology available to a country by producing the required goods under licence and by hiring technicians from abroad. Such a choice is, however, more likely to be available to semi-industrialised rather than to other developing countries, which generally lack the requisite organisational and technical capacity to produce under licence. Moreover, there are cases in which corporations are not willing to issue licences for the production of their patented goods abroad. Where the production of essential goods under licence proves to be impossible, developing countries are faced with the choice of permitting direct investment by foreign corporations, or continuing to import the goods in question.

Experienced management: Transnationals have at their disposal the services of trained managers experienced in organising production and trading activities as well as in the administration of personnel. Like advanced technology, this would contribute to efficiency and also provide an opportunity for training local staff in management skills. Some developing countries, notably the semi-industrialised ones, are, however, in a position to acquire such services by the recruitment of trained personnel from abroad. This can be done in respect of some industrial skills, but more widely for such service industries as banking and insurance. There must, for example, be very few developing countries which would not be able to set up and manage their own banking system with the aid of some technical assistance and hired personnel from abroad; in fact most of them have done so. It is, therefore, somewhat surprising to see many of them, including some of those which already have national banks, encouraging the establishment of branches and affiliates of foreign banks within their territories. This is especially so since the resources used by banks in general consist predominantly of customers' deposits and retained profits, and so the capital introduced by them from abroad is unlikely to account for more than a small fraction of the total.

Marketing facilities: In addition to possessing worldwide networks of distribution channels and marketing outlets, transnationals are experienced in oligopolistic techniques of competition, such as advertising, product differentiation, etc., which enable them to break into new markets. This is clearly an important consideration which should be borne in mind when it is intended to export a significant proportion of the product of a new enterprise. It is particularly relevant to certain mineral industries, such as petroleum, in which a large proportion of the world distribution channels and marketing facilities are controlled by a small number of corporations. Developing countries should, of course, aim at creating their own independent marketing channels, but this is a long and costly process. In the short run, therefore, many of them may have no alternative but to invite direct investment for the exploitation of their mineral resources and for the establishment of other export-oriented industries. A further reason for this as regards minerals is the heavy outlay often involved in exploration and other initial investment, which many developing countries may not be in a position to finance through their own and borrowed resources.

The conclusion emerging from the foregoing discussion can briefly be summarised under two broad headings. *First*, the volume and the pattern of the inflow of foreign direct investment should be strictly regulated by the host country through a system of licensing. This is to ensure: (a) that direct investment is confined to those investment projects which developing countries are, for some reason or other, unable to undertake with their own and borrowed capital resources supplemented by hired management and technology; (b) that the total amount of foreign direct investment is kept well below the threshold of what was termed the 'social absorptive capacity' of the recipient country in terms of its capacity to maintain its economic and political autonomy; and (c) that investment is directed to the localities and sectors which conform to the development needs of the recipient country. This should preclude unbalanced regional development of the economy as well as investment in the production of luxuries and semi-luxuries catering primarily to the domestic market. It is clear that this would require an overall development plan which indicates the pattern and location of investment, a requirement which is equally necessary for a rational and proper utilisation of all the other categories of external capital discussed earlier as well as of domestic resources (see p. 173).

Secondly, developing countries have to exercise maximum care and caution in negotiating the various terms and conditions concerning the operations of foreign enterprises. It is, in particular, important to have clear and precise understanding on: the volume of the initial and subsequent capital inflows; employment and wage policies; training of the local technical and managerial personnel; borrowing facilities in the host country; taxation liability of the affiliate; repatriation of profits and capital; inspection and audit of the accounts of the enterprise; and terms and conditions for acquiring part of, or the entire, equity interest of the parent company in its affiliate.

The above and many other issues involved in direct investment give rise to complicated economic, financial and legal questions, which many developing countries would find too difficult to handle without external professional advice such as that provided by the United Nations' Centre on Transnational Corporations. Especially difficult problems are likely to be encountered in devising a system of auditing the books and accounts of the foreign enterprise to ensure that the host country does not suffer from what has come to be known as 'transfer pricing', discussed in Chapter 3 (see p.108).

EVALUATION OF THE ACTUAL CONTRIBUTION OF FOREIGN CAPITAL TO DEVELOPMENT[57]

The problem of evaluating the *actual* contribution of foreign capital to the economic development of recipient countries is considerably more complex than that of assessing its *potential* development value, considered in the preceding section. Conceptually, the impact of foreign capital on development should be measured by reference to its influence on the 'warranted' rate of investment and of growth which, as explained in Chapter 2, is subject to two distinct constraints, namely, availability of 'voluntary' savings and the supply of necessities (see pp. 55–6). A positive contribution to development would thus be reflected in a rise in the ratio of 'essential' investment in GNP made possible by the inflow of foreign capital.[58]

Given the development potential of foreign capital, the most important single factor determining its actual contribution to development consists of government policies in the recipient countries. Foreign capital cannot, for example, be considered to have made a positive contribution to development if, as happens at times, by augmenting the resources available to the authorities, it encourages them to step up useless public expenditure, or to forgo the taxation of high income groups and thereby stimulate the consumption of luxuries. Because of this, it can be highly misleading to use the ratio of the inflow of foreign capital to domestic investment as an indicator of the actual contribution made by it to the formation of domestic capital.

Nor does foreign capital, whether received in the form of loans or direct investment, make a positive contribution to development if it is allowed to promote primarily inessential investment designed to produce luxury goods for domestic consumption. Such investment, to quote Kalecki, 'adds to the lop-sidedness of the economy and leads

---

57. This section owes much to a paper published jointly by Michal Kalecki and Ignacy Sachs in *Social Science Information*, 1966 (1), and reproduced in an abridged form in Kalecki, *Essays on Developing Economies*, Essay no. 6.
58. For a definition of 'essential' investment, see p. 8 above.

to "perverse growth": in the short run it promotes growth' by increasing employment and wage income, 'but in the long run it adversely affects the growth prospects of the economy'.[59] This is because it ties up resources which could otherwise have been used to expand productive capacity and employment in the sectors of the economy which produce essential goods and services.

Foreign capital, especially when received in the form of aid, may also be used to delay important economic and social reforms, such as land reform and the improvement of the quality of administration, which play a key role in determining the long-term development prospects of the recipient countries. What happens in such cases is that resources provided by foreign aid are in effect used by governments to cover up the deficiencies of the archaic social and economic institutions, by keeping the political opposition to their régimes below 'boiling point'. It is worth noting that relatively large mineral royalties, such as those received by some countries from petroleum exports, like foreign aid, make it possible for the authorities to postpone institutional reforms required for economic development (see pp. 97–100). Although we are not here concerned with the motivation of donor countries, it should nevertheless be noted that the direction of the flow of economic aid in the post-War period does show a positive correlation between the flow of aid to various developing countries, on the one hand, and the potential threat posed by the structural reforms in them to the economic and political interests of the donor countries, on the other.

In any evaluation of the contribution of foreign capital to development, it is also important to recognise that such evaluation cannot be based on the commodity composition of imports financed by foreign capital. It would, for example, be wrong to consider the contribution of capital goods financed by foreign capital as invariably being larger than that of consumer goods similarly financed. The reason for this is that the commodity pattern of imports provides no information on the final destination, or utilisation, of imports. Additional imports of capital goods financed by foreign capital may, for example, be used for inessential investment in industries producing luxury goods which, as noted above, would harm the long-term development prospects of the economy. On the other hand, additional imports of necessities, such as food, may assist development by enabling the authorities to step up the rate of essential investment.[60]

59. See Kalecki, *Essays on Developing Economies*, p. 69.
60. For further explanation, see Kalecki, *ibid.*, pp. 70–1. See also pp. 56 and 60–1 above.

The relation between the contribution of external capital to development and imports financed by it is, however, even more complex than is indicated above. For even if it were known that the imports in question were used exclusively to promote essential investment, it could still not be inferred that foreign capital had made an equivalent contribution to the growth of such investment. This is because foreign capital is 'fungible'; it releases an equivalent amount of domestic resources for financing other outlays which may have a high or low social priority. To evaluate the real net contribution of a given inflow of foreign capital to development, therefore, it is essential to ascertain how the resources released by it have been utilised.

To illustrate the above point, Kalecki mentions the example of a developing country with a motor-car factory capable of producing both lorries and passenger cars for its domestic market, the former having for it a high social priority and the latter a very low one. Assume that in the absence of foreign aid the factory would have been used to produce only lorries, but because foreign aid for the import of lorries becomes available, it is made to specialise in the production of passenger cars. In such circumstances, it would be true to say that aid received in the form of lorries is, in reality, used to finance the production of passenger cars.[61]

It should have become clear even from the foregoing brief consideration of some of the difficulties encountered in the evaluation of the role of external capital in development, that this problem is too complex to be resolved by means of the time series statistical analysis between the inflow of foreign capital, on the one hand, and some such variables as imports, national income, savings and investment, on the other. Even more unsatisfactory are the attempts to deal with this problem through inter-country regression analyses.[62] A meaningful evaluation of the role of foreign capital can only take place, to quote Kalecki, 'in the context of a comprehensive analysis of the development problems of the recipient country seen as a whole'.[63] Such an analysis requires the framing of a hypothetical plan for the recipient country, which indicates the broad outlines of its course of development

61. See Kalecki, *Essays on Developing Economies*, p. 71.
62. See, for example, A.I. MacBean, *Export Instability and Economic Development*, George Allen and Unwin, London (1966), and A. Maizel's review of the book, *American Economic Review*, June 1968. See also K. Griffin, 'Foreign Capital, Domestic Savings and Economic Development', *BOUIES*, May 1970; and comments on Griffen, by C. Kennedy and A.P. Thirlwall, Frances Stewart, Éprime Eshag, and reply of Griffin, *BOUIES*, May 1971.
63. Kalecki, *Essays on Developing Economies*, p. 69.

and the nature of the problems likely to be encountered, thereby providing a framework within which the role of foreign capital can be examined.

It is clear that a study conducted along the above lines will not be an easy one. The work of framing a plan, no matter how sketchy, would alone require a survey of the economic, political and social structure and institutions of the recipient country and of its natural and human resources. But the study would, in addition, require an analysis of developments in government policies and in the volume and pattern of production, investment and private and public consumption in a way which would throw some light on the role played by foreign capital in shaping the course of these developments. An examination of the influence so exercised by foreign capital in the light of the development needs of the country, as indicated by the plan, should then permit a broad assessment of the contribution (positive or negative) made by the inflow of foreign capital to economic development.

APPENDIX 4A: INTERNATIONAL AID AND CAPITAL FLOW TARGETS

We describe here some of the important targets of capital flow and of economic aid recommended by international organisations in the course of the 1970s and indicate the degree of compliance of the donor countries with these recommendations. But before doing so, the reader should be made familiar with the meaning of some of the headings under which the relevant data are generally published; these are 'commitments', 'disbursements', 'flows', 'debt service' and 'net transfers'.

A *commitment* is a firm obligation by a donor to make resources, in the form of grants or concessional loans, available to a recipient country. A *disbursement* occurs when resources, in the form of grants, loans etc. are placed at the disposal of a recipient country and generate a debit entry in the donor country's balance of payments, irrespective of the date at which they are actually utilised; in the case of foreign credits, this is likely to occur later. Because of this, disbursements during any period are unlikely to correspond exactly to the volume of resources received during the same period. Disbursements, as defined above, should be and are generally designated as *gross disbursements*, or *gross flows*. *Net disbursements*, or *net flows*, during a period are equal to gross flows *minus* amortisation payments on loans during the period. *Debt service* is the payment made by debtor to creditor countries in respect of both interest and amortisation of loans. *Net transfers* are equal to gross flows *less* debt service, or to net flows *less* interest payments.

Recommendations

The United Nations proclaimed the 1970s as its Second Development Decade, the 1960s being its First Development Decade. The development strategy for the Second Development Decade set a target of an average annual rate of growth of 6 per cent in the gross national product of the developing countries taken as a whole. It recommended two targets, one for total capital flow and the other for ODA, that would be required to attain the proposed rate of growth. These targets were subsequently embodied in a resolution of the General Assembly in October 1970.[64]

The *first* target required that 'each economically advanced country should endeavour to provide annually to developing countries resource transfers of a minimum net amount of 1 per cent of its GNP at market prices in terms of actual disbursements'.[65] This target includes both public and private grants and loans as well as private direct investment.[66] The *second* target specified that 'each economically advanced country will progressively increase its ODA to developing countries and will exert its best efforts to reach a minimum net amount of 0.7 per cent of its GNP at market prices by the middle of the decade'.

The first target was accepted by all the 17 DAC members, but the second by only 13 countries, many with a reservation as to the date by which they propose to reach it. The US, which is the largest provider of ODA, was among the four countries that did not accept this target in principle.[67]

Another United Nations aid target was proposed by the third session of UNCTAD in Resolution 60 (III) adopted in May 1972. This resolution invited the developed countries to take into consideration the view that, '(a) on average, interest rates of official development loans should not exceed 2 per cent per annum; (b) maturity periods of such loans should be at least 25 to 40 years and grace periods should be

---

64. General Assembly Resolution 2626 (xxv).
65. See UNCTAD, *Debt Problems of Developing Countries*, document TD/B/545/Rev. 1, Sales No. E. 75. II. D. 14 (1975), p. 3.
66. In the last two sections of this chapter we have questioned the validity of the assumption underlying this part of the UN resolution, which suggests that *all* capital transfers to LDCs are likely to make a positive contribution to development.
67. For details see OECD, *1975 Review*, p. 129, and UNCTAD, *Debt Problems of Developing Countries*, p. 3.

not less than 7 to 10 years; (c) the proportion of grants in total assistance of *each* developed country should be progressively increased' and, not later than 1975, reach the average of 63 per cent recorded in 1970 by DAC members as a group.[68]

The aid and capital flow targets proposed by the foregoing two resolutions reflect largely the views of developing countries – the potential beneficiaries of aid – which command a majority of votes in the United Nations Assembly and in UNCTAD, with some support from a number of smaller industrial countries, such as Canada, the Netherlands and the Scandinavian countries. But since the bulk of development assistance is provided by the members of DAC (see pp. 137–9), the targets for aid proposed by the DAC have a greater significance in terms of the economic aid that is likely to be forthcoming in practice.

In October 1972, the DAC recommended two targets concerning the terms and conditions of the ODA commitments made by its members on or after 1st January 1973. *The first* recommendation, which covers ODA in general, states 'In order to achieve a further softening of overall financial terms of ODA, Members should use their best efforts to reach and maintain an average grant element in their ODA commitments of at least 84 per cent'; this target was raised to 86 per cent in February 1978.[69] The recommendation adds, 'Countries whose ODA commitments as a percentage of GNP are significantly below the DAC average will not be considered as having met the terms target.'[70]

The second recommendation sets a special target of aid to 25 countries which had, a year earlier, been identified by the United Nations as *least-developed*.[71] Four other countries, including Bangladesh, were added to the list in 1975 and another two in 1977.[72] The 31 least-developed countries consist primarily of the small Afro-Asian countries which have gained independence since 1960 and which, in the view of the United Nations, represent the 'hard core' of underdevelopment because of their low per capita income and literacy rate, lack of

68. See UNCTAD, *Third Session, Santiago de Chile*, Vol., 1, Sales No. E. 73. II. D.4 (1973), p. 91; and UNCTAD|IV, *International Financial Co-operation for Development*, document TD/188/Supp. 1/Add. 1 (May 1976), p. 7/8; emphasis added.
69. See OECD, *1972 Review*, p. 208, and *1978 Review*, p. 172.
70. *Ibid.*
71. The list was proposed by ECOSOC and approved by the UN General Assembly in November 1971 in Resolution 2768 (XXVI).
72. For a list of the original 25 countries, see OECD, *1972 Review*, p. 210. For a list of the 31 least-developed countries, see OECD, *1978 Review*, p. 181.

infrastructure and narrow range of export commodities.[73] The DAC recommendation specifies that ODA to least-developed countries 'should preferably be in the form of grants and the average grant element of all commitments from a given donor should either be at least 86 per cent to each least-developed country over a period of three years, or at least 90 per cent annually for the least-developed countries as a group'.[74]

Compliance with recommendations[75]

Of the three groups of donor countries mentioned (see p. 137 above) only members of OPEC have, as a group, reached and surpassed the target of 0.7 per cent of GNP set by the United Nations for the 1970s.[76] DAC estimates indicate that the ratio of ODA to GNP for these countries amounted on average to about 1.5 per cent of GNP in 1979; particularly large was the flow of ODA from the Arab members of OPEC for which the ratio in question was as high as 2.8 per cent.[77] It is also estimated that the average grant element of the total ODA commitments of OPEC members during 1978–9 amounted to about 85 per cent.[78]

Unlike OPEC, the members of DAC as a group have failed to reach the United Nations target by a large margin although they continue to account for the bulk of the development assistance. The average ratio of ODA to GNP for these countries remained almost unchanged at a figure of about 0.35 per cent in the 1970s and was somewhat lower than it had been in the late 1960s.[79] The chief reason for this has been the relatively slow rate of growth of grants and concessional loans from the larger industrial members of DAC, in particular the US, which has

73. The three basic criteria used in identifying least-developed countries were: per capita GDP; share of manufacturing production in total GDP; and literacy rate. In 1968, in the great majority of these countries, per capita GDP was estimated at less than $100, share of manufacturing production in GDP at less than 10 per cent and literacy rate at less than 20 per cent. For the details of the criteria used in identifying least-developed countries see *Official Records of the ECOSOC*, 51st Session, Supplement 7, document E/4990, New York (1971), pp. 16–19.
74. See OECD, *1972 Review*, p. 209, and *1978 Review*, p. 172.
75. The discussion which follows is largely confined to the performance of the various 'groups' of donor countries. Readers interested in the performance of the individual donor countries should consult the references mentioned in the footnotes.
76. The GNP estimates for these countries are the conventional ones and include the oild revenue, which strictly should have been excluded (see p. 95).
77. See OECD, *1981 Review*, Table G.2.
78. See OECD, *1980 Review*, p. 126.
79. See OECD, *1979* and *1981 Reviews*, Tables A.3.

been the major contributor of ODA.[80] The flow of ODA from some of the smaller members, namely Denmark, the Netherlands, Norway and Sweden, has, on the other hand, increased rapidly enough to surpass the United Nations target.

Most DAC members had, however, no difficulty in complying with the United Nations recommendation on the flow of total resources to developing countries; the average ratio of this flow to GNP for the group rose from 0.78 per cent in 1970 to 1.17 per cent in 1979.[81] With the exception of Japan, all DAC members had by 1979 also complied with DAC's own recommendations on softening the terms of the ODA loans and on economic aid to least-developed countries.[82] The average grant element of the total ODA commitments of DAC members in 1978–9 is estimated at about 90 per cent.[83]

As noted earlier (p. 136) there is no reliable information, comparable to that available for the members of DAC or even OPEC, for the flow of development assistance to LDCs from socialist countries of Eastern Europe – members of CMEA. The figures of net disbursements of ODA, shown in Table 4.1, as well as the information on terms and conditions of loans granted, are largely derived from press reports and cannot be considered as being either comprehensive or accurate. Estimates made by the Secretariat of DAC suggest that the average ratio of ODA to GNP for this group of countries was of the order of 0.1 per cent in 1978–9.[84] These estimates also indicate that the average grant element of the ODA commitments by the members of CMEA in 1978–9 was about 75 per cent.[85]

Although the financial terms of the concessional loans of the socialist countries of Eastern Europe are believed to be somewhat harder than those of the members of DAC and OPEC, their loans have in one important respect a special attraction, mentioned earlier, for recipient countries (see p. 150). The loans advanced by these countries are frequently coupled with trade agreements which provide for the repayment of loans in kind rather than in foreign exchange. This is likely to reduce the burden of repayment of loans, discussed in

---

80. Between 1970 and 1980 the ratio of ODA to GNP for the US declined from 0.31 to 0.27 per cent and its share in total flow of ODA from DAC fell from 45 to just over 25 per cent; see *ibid.*
81. *Ibid.*, Tables A.2.
82. See OECD, *1981 Review*, Table B.2.
83. *Ibid.*, and *1980 Review*, p. 126.
84. See OECD, *1980 Review*, p. 125. Owing to the well-known statistical difficulties of estimating the GNP of socialist countries, the estimate of this ratio is likely to be even less reliable than those of the absolute figures of ODA shown in Table 4.1.
85. See OECD, *1980 Review*, p. 126.

Appendix 4B, by providing the debtor countries with an assured market for their exports.

APPENDIX 4B: GROWTH IN EXTERNAL DEBT OF DEVELOPING COUNTRIES

There is a clear trend of growth in the foreign indebtedness of developing countries since the early 1950s due to persistent deficits on their current balance of payments account. In the early post-War years most developing countries were able to finance their deficits by drawing on foreign exchange reserves accumulated during the War. But after exhausting these reserves they have been compelled to rely increasingly on the finance provided by foreign loans and credits. From a long-term point of view, an important reason for the growing external deficit of developing countries has been their failure to implement a strategy of balanced development aimed at a gradual reduction of their dependence on foreign capital. This is particularly true of many semi-industrialised countries, notably Brazil and Mexico, which, as shown below, have relied heavily on the inflow of foreign capital to finance their domestic expenditure and have ended as the largest debtors among LDCs.[86]

A broad indication of the rate of growth of foreign indebtedness of developing countries during the period 1955–65 is provided by the estimates of their external 'public' debt made by the World Bank. According to these estimates the outstanding external public debt (including undisbursed) of a sample of 71 countries, which amounted to $8 billion in 1955, rose to $16 billion by 1960 and to over $34 billion by 1965; in other words it more than quadrupled in the course of ten years.[87] The World Bank data for later years show that this rate of growth in public debt, which was more or less maintained until 1970, sharply accelerated thereafter. The outstanding public debt (including undisbursed) for a sample of 86 developing countries rose from $38 billion at the end of 1965 to about $73 billion by the end of 1970 and, for a larger sample of 96 countries, from $88 billion to $285 billion during the six years from the end of 1971 to the end of 1977.[88]

The OECD data, which cover both public and private debt, provide a better indication of the size and the rate of growth of the external

86. See OECD, *1981 Review*, Table E.6.
87. See World Bank, *The External Debt of Developing Countries*, Report No. 1595 (May 1977), Annex Table 1.
88. See World Bank, *Annual Reports*, 1974 and 1979, Statistical Annex, Tables 4A and 3–4, respectively.

debt of LDCs during the 1970s, although even these exclude short-term loans with original maturities of less than one year as well as the debt to the IMF and military debt.[89] Table 4.2 shows the OECD estimates of the growth in external debt (disbursed only) by category of debt since the end of 1970. It can be seen that according to these estimates the total outstanding debt of developing countries rose by about 430 per cent in the course of nine years between the end of 1970 and the end of 1979, reaching $400 billion by the latter date.

There was a significant acceleration in the rate of growth of this debt after 1972, the annual rate of growth rising from about 14 per cent in the three years 1970–2 to well over 20 per cent during 1973–9.[90] The primary reason for this was the adverse effect on the balance of payments of oil-importing countries of the steep rise in petroleum prices. Another important factor was the slow growth in their exports and the rise in the prices of imported manufactures due to conditions of 'stagflation' in developed countries mentioned earlier.

Table 4.2 also gives a broad indication of the change that took place in the composition of external debt due to the shift in the pattern of capital flow discussed in the text (see pp. 142–3). It shows that, whereas the volume of outstanding concessional ODA debt increased by about 220 per cent, that of non-concessional debt rose by 570 per cent between 1970 and 1979; because of this, the proportion of the former in total outstanding debt fell from 40 to 24 per cent and that of private debt borrowed from international capital markets alone rose from 17 to 40 per cent. Debt due in respect of private export credits accounted for a further 20 per cent or more of the total.[91] This means that at the end of 1979 about 60 per cent of the total foreign debt of LDCs consisted of private loans in the form of bank loans, bonds and private export credits.

The growth in the proportion of private loans in the total external debt of LDCs has produced a significant shortening in the average maturity period of their outstanding debt, resulting in a more rapid rise in the annual debt service than in the debt itself. This is because private loans, which are borrowed on commercial terms, carry appreciably harder terms, not only than ODA, but also than non-concessional official loans received bilaterally and through multilateral agencies.[92] It can be seen from Table 4.2 that between 1970 and

89. See OECD, *1979 Review*, p. 261.
90. OECD, *1978 Review* Table E.5. and *1981 Review*, Table E.1.
91. In 1979 about four-fifths of the debt due in respect of export credits was private; see OECD, *1980 Review*, p. 157.
92. According to DAC, private bank loans in 1979 had, on average, a maturity of 10

Table 4.2: *Outstanding debt (disbursed only) and debt service of developing countries, 1970, 1975 and 1979*

	Amount (in $ billion)			Per cent of total		
	1970	1975	1979	1970	1975	1979
Outstanding debt[a]						
1. ODA, bilateral and multilateral	29.8	52.2	94.8	40	29	24
2. Non-concessional	44.9	126.9	302.5	60	71	76
a) Multilateral agencies	6.1	13.8	28.3	8	8	7
b) Export credits	26.2	54.1	114.3	35	30	29
c) Capital markets[b]	12.6	59.0	159.9	17	33	40
TOTAL	74.7	179.1	397.3	100	100	100
TOTAL, *Index*, 1970 = 100	100	240	532			
Debt service						
1. ODA, bilateral and multilateral	1.4	2.8	4.4	15	11	6
2. Non-concessional	8.0	23.4	69.2	85	89	94
a) Multilateral agencies	0.8	1.2	3.0	9	5	4
b) Export credits	5.2	12.0	28.1	55	46	38
c) Capital markets[b]	2.0	10.2	38.1	21	39	52
TOTAL	9.4	26.2	73.6	100	100	100
TOTAL, *Index*, 1970 = 100	100	279	783			

Source: OECD, *1979 Review*, Table E.7. and *1981 Review*, Table E.3.
[a] At the end of the year.
[b] Bank loans (other than export credits), bonds and other private lending.
Note: Owing to rounding up, components may not add to totals.

1979 the amount of debt service rose about 50 per cent more than the volume of outstanding debt.

The pattern of distribution of external debt and of debt service among developing countries inevitably corresponds to that of the flow of capital discussed in the text. The bulk of debt is owed by a small number of 'middle-income' countries which have made use of their relatively easy access to foreign capital markets to finance external deficits.[93] Leaving aside the members of OPEC, it is estimated that the middle-income countries, which account for less than 40 per cent of the population of the remaining LDCs, were in 1980 responsible for about 80 per cent of the external debt and for 90 per cent of the debt service of these countries.[94] Among the middle-income countries, eleven, classified by DAC as 'newly industrialising countries', which account for about 20 per cent of the population of LDCs, owed about 50 per cent of the total debt and were responsible for 65 per cent of the debt service of non-OPEC developing countries.[95] Three of these countries – Brazil, Mexico and South Korea – alone accounted for over 30 per cent of the external debt and for about 45 per cent of the debt service in question.[96]

It is possible to obtain a rough indication of the burden of external debt, in terms of the drain on the foreign exchange and domestic resources of debtor countries, by examining the proportion of export earnings and of national income devoted to servicing it; the ratio of debt service (amortisation and interest) to export earnings is generally designated as 'debt service ratio'. The DAC estimates suggest that the ratio of debt service to export of goods and services for non-OPEC developing countries rose from about 22 per cent in 1973 to 34 per cent in 1981.[97] Our own estimates, based on OECD data, show that, as a proportion of GNP, the debt service doubled, from 1.7 per cent to 3.5 per cent, between 1973 and 1979.[98]

years, a grace period of 2 years and carried 13 per cent interest charge, compared with a maturity of 18 years, a grace period of 5 years and interest charge of 9 per cent for loans advanced by official multilateral development institutions. The maturity and grace periods of the other two major types of private credit, namely bond lending and export credits, were even shorter than those of bank loans, although they carried somewhat lower interest charges. See OECD, *1980 Review*, p. 157.

93. For a definition of 'low-income' and 'middle-income' countries see p. 142 above.
94. See OECD, *1981 Review*, Table E.5.
95. *Ibid.* DAC has classified the following as 'newly industrialising countries' (NICs): Argentina, Brazil, Greece, Hong Kong, South Korea, Mexico, Portugal, Singapore, Spain, Taiwan and Yugoslavia (see *ibid.*, Table H.2).
96. See OECD, *1981 Review*, Tables E.4. and E.6.
97. See OECD, *1979 Review*, Table E.6., and *1981 Review*, Table E.2. and p. 72.
98. See OECD, *1979 Review*, p. 95 and *1981 Review*, Tables E.4. and H.2.

For a number of middle-income developing countries which have, as noted earlier, borrowed heavily from international capital markets, both the rate of growth in and the absolute levels of debt service ratios are significantly higher than the global figures mentioned. Our estimates show that in the case of the two largest debtors, Brazil and Mexico, for example, the debt service, computed as a ratio of the export of goods and services, rose from 40 to 60 per cent and from about 35 to 70 per cent, respectively, between 1975 and 1979; as a proportion of GNP it amounted to over 5 per cent for Brazil and to almost 10 per cent for Mexico in 1979.[99]

It is important to note at this stage that debt service ratios by themselves do not provide an adequate indication of countries' ability to service their external debt. This is largely because of the significant differences between the capacity of individual countries to increase exports, which affects their credit rating and hence their ability to 'roll-over' amortisation payments through new borrowing. This is illustrated by the example of Brazil and Mexico, the two largest debtors, which had not until 1981 encountered any difficulty in servicing their debt. A number of other countries, such as Argentina, Chile and Peru, on the other hand, with lower debt service ratios, have had continuous difficulties in meeting their external debt obligations.[100]

The balance of payments and debt servicing difficulties of many non-OPEC countries were seriously aggravated during 1979–80 by a slow growth in their exports, due to economic recession in industrial countries, and by the deterioration in their terms of trade explained earlier (see p. 142). There are in 1981 clear signs of a steady deterioration in the external position of these countries, which goes a long way to explain the steep rise in their applications for the IMF 'conditional' credits entailing the adoption of restrictive fiscal and monetary policies.[101] The mounting pressure on the balance of payments of LDCs is likely to lead to an increase in the incidence of debt servicing difficulties among them. This is partly because some commercial banks find themselves (in 1981) in an exposed position and have become more cautious in their lending policies, thereby rendering the practice of 'rolling-over' amortisation payments more difficult than in the past.

---

99. See OECD, *1977 Review*, Table E.1; *1981 Review*, Tables E.6, and H.2; and IMF, *International Financial Statistics*, December 1981.
100. See R. Thorp and L. Whitehead (eds.), *Inflation and Stabilization in Latin America*, Macmillan (1979).
101. See *IMF Survey, Supplement*, May 1981. See also p. 242 below.

THE PATTERN OF INVESTMENT

The preceding two chapters were devoted to an analysis of the first of the two major roles that fiscal and monetary policies can play to stimulate development. This is to provide adequate resources for financing a target *volume* of investment without engendering price inflation. Chapter 3 was concerned with the problems of augmenting investment resources through domestic savings and Chapter 4 with those related to the importation of such resources from abroad. This chapter is devoted to the analysis of the second role of fiscal and monetary policies, namely their use to influence the *pattern* of investment i.e. its sectoral and geographical allocation (see pp. 53–4. and 63–4).

It will be recalled that, in the context of Kalecki's simple model of development of mixed economies, there are two basic reasons for the authorities to play an active role in determining the pattern of investment. *The first* is simply to prevent, or discourage, investment in the production of inessential luxury goods in order to avoid a 'lop-sided' development. *The second* reason is to ensure that adequate resources are devoted to the production of necessities, or wage goods, to ease the constraint imposed by the supply of such goods on the rate of investment and growth (see pp. 56–9). But since, apart from the supply of necessities, other bottlenecks, such as those in the economic infrastructure and in skilled labour, can also seriously retard the pace of development, the second purpose of regulating the pattern of investment can be expressed (in wider terms) as being the attainment of a 'balanced' growth of the major sectors of the economy.

It is important to note two points at the outset. *First*, the larger the share of public investment in total investment is, the more effective government policy will be in determining the overall pattern of investment in the economy. The reason for this is simply that investment in the public sector is determined directly by the authorities themselves, whereas the pattern of private investment can only be regulated indirectly through fiscal, monetary and, at times, other measures, whose efficacy can, as shown later, rarely be predicted with any degree of precision. The total investment of the public sector is, of course, equal to its savings plus its net internal and foreign borrowing.

Second, the formulation of a meaningful and coherent policy for the allocation of investment resources can only take place within the framework of a development plan. Such a plan should give at least a broad indication of the projected movements in the volume and pattern of production and demand, as well as of the requirement for productive capacities, including raw materials and labour. The plan should thus provide a general outline of the requisite pattern of investment and should, in addition, indicate the order of priority of the various investment projects in terms of the attainment of its basic objectives.[1]

INVESTMENT IN THE PUBLIC SECTOR

Although the pattern of investment in the public sector is determined by the authorities themselves and does not require the use of fiscal and monetary measures, some categories of public investment, notably investment in public enterprises, do raise important fiscal issues which deserve consideration. Partly because of this, and partly because there is often some interaction between public and private sector investments, it will be useful first to consider briefly the question of investment policies in the public sector. The discussion will be confined to an examination of the general guidelines for the choice of investment projects and to the fiscal questions related to the pricing policies of the public enterprises.

Guidelines on the choice of public investment projects

The choice of investment projects by the public sector should of course be made within the framework of the overall pattern of investment as indicated by a country's development plan. In a mixed economy, the crucial question posed to the authorities is simply which of the various investment projects required by the plan should be undertaken by the public sector and which should be left to private entrepreneurs. The answer to this question will depend on a large number of factors which

1. The subject of the choice of investment projects and their ranking in order of social priority, which was briefly considered in Chapter 1 (see pp. 8–10 and 20–3), falls outside the scope of this book.

will differ from one country to another and for the same country from one period to another. All that we can do here is to consider some of the more important factors which should be borne in mind in dealing with this question.

First, priority should be given to those projects which play a strategically important role in the fulfilment of the development plan as a whole. These will generally include investment projects that are planned to provide inputs to a large number of economic sectors, or to play a major role in the expansion of the productive capacities of the essential consumer goods. A failure to execute such projects according to the plan is likely to generate widespread production bottlenecks and supply shortages, giving rise to inflationary pressures and balance of payments difficulties. It would, therefore, be somewhat imprudent to leave their fate to the uncertain decisions of private entrepreneurs who, despite financial incentives, may fail to implement them on the scale and in accordance with the timetable envisaged in the development plan.

Because of the key role played in economic development by the supply of food and by the foreign exchange earned on the export of primary agricultural products, public investment in the agricultural sector, e.g. in irrigation, drainage, flood control, fertiliser plants, etc., should generally be ranked among those with the highest order of priority. Such outlays, by increasing the rate of growth in the production of food and of industrial primary products available for exports and for domestic industry, would, as we have seen, ease the constraints imposed by the supply of necessities and by the balance of payments on the warranted rates of investment and growth (see pp. 55–6 and 125–30). As shown later, the failure of most developing countries to devote adequate resources to the promotion of agricultural production has been an important factor in generating internal and external imbalances; this is as true of developing socialist countries as it is of mixed economies.

Investment by the public sector in the economic and social infrastructure also falls under this heading and should be given a high priority. The economic infrastructure includes power and water, sewage, transport and communication; the social infrastructure covers such facilities as housing, health and education (including technical training). Apart from supplying essential consumer goods and services, the infrastructure also provides a variety of inputs required by almost all the other sectors of the economy.

Secondly, consideration should be given to divergences between net private and social benefits likely to be derived from different projects (see pp. 15–20). Generally, the larger the estimate of social return relative to private return of a project is, the more essential it is to ensure that it is undertaken and, for this reason, greater preference should be given to its adoption by the public sector.

Thirdly, the authorities should consider taking over, or initiating, projects which lend themselves to a monopolistic system of production. Such projects, which generally enjoy relatively large economies of scale, often cater to the production of essential inputs, such as steel, petroleum products and fertilisers. There are, in addition, some service and financial industries, like railways, insurance and banking, which again, if left to the private sector, would be operated under conditions of monopoly, or oligopoly, and would earn abnormally high profits. Because of the difficulties of levying direct taxes in most LDCs discussed in Chapter 3, the government may be better advised to establish state monopolies in such industries and place itself in a position to exploit, where it is deemed desirable, their profit-earning potential as a source of revenue.

Fourthly, account must be taken of the availability of the administrative and managerial personnel for the efficient operation of investment projects. Generally, preference should be given to large-scale projects producing standardised goods whose investment and production activities lend themselves to long- or at least medium-term planning. Investment in industries composed of small-scale manufacturing, trading and service enterprises are on the whole better left to private entrepreneurs.

Finally, in some cases the authorities may be compelled to undertake, by themselves or in co-operation with foreign and local entrepreneurs, certain large-scale projects with a relatively long gestation period, such as iron and steel plants and mineral explorations, when it is clear that their proper implementation is beyond the financial, technical and managerial capacity of the domestic private sector.

Pricing policies in the public sector

Investment projects in the public sector may be operated directly by government, or through autonomous bodies, generally known as parastatals, public corporations, or government enterprises; we shall not here distinguish between different categories of these institutions. The operations of the social infrastructure, such as health, education and housing, are usually administered directly by the central or local government departments, whereas those of the economic infrastructure and of industrial plants are often run by autonomous public corporations under government control. As a rule governments appoint the board of directors of these corporations and confer upon them varying degrees of autonomy in respect of investment, production and pricing policies.

Most current economic writings on the pricing policies of public enterprises, like those on the choice of investment projects, view this problem as being one of optimising welfare, a problem which has to be solved along the general lines followed by Pareto's optimality analysis. The conclusions emerging from this type of analysis generally require that prices of goods and services produced by the public sector should be equal, or at least be related, to their marginal, or average, cost of production; the costs in question being 'private' or 'social', depending on the moral philosophy of the writers.[2]

Where estimates are based on 'social' costs, resort has to be made to shadow pricing, which suffers from the drawbacks noted earlier (see pp. 20–3). The case for setting prices charged by public corporations at average 'private' costs and thus avoiding losses is argued at times on the grounds that such a policy would promote efficiency on the part of the management of the corporations. But this is far from being a valid argument, since the primary precondition for efficiency is *accountability*, i.e. the requirement that the managers of public enterprises adhere to a certain standard of performance set for them by governments. This may require that they break even, or aim at a given surplus target, or hold a deficit within certain limits. There appears no logical reason to suppose that, given the prices charged by public corporations, the requirement to break even is any more conducive to efficiency than, for example, that of maintaining the deficit below a specified level. It is also clear that the pricing policies of public corporations, which inevitably affect their profitability, do not in themselves provide a rational criterion for judging the efficiency of their operations.

Consumer goods: One way of relating public sector pricing policy for consumer goods to economic development is to examine the effect of such policies on total private consumption and savings as well as on the pattern of consumption; a somewhat different approach will be suggested for the sale of inputs to producers. The relation of prices to production costs determines the amount of profits earned, or losses

2. See, for example, Ralph Turvey, *Optimum Pricing and Investment in Electricity Supply*, George Allen and Unwin (1968), Chapters 4 and 8, and *Economic Analysis and Public Enterprises*, George Allen and Unwin (1971), Chapters 6–7; M.G. Webb, *The Economics of Nationalised Industries*, Thomas Nelson and Sons (1973), Chapters 7–8; and Ray Rees, *Public Enterprise Economics*, Weidenfeld and Nicolson (1976), Chapters 4–6.

incurred. Profits, which have the same effect on private expenditure as indirect taxes, would tend to discourage consumption and to augment the volume of savings, whereas losses would have the reverse effect of providing consumer subsidies and thus stimulating private consumption. Prices for individual goods and services would, in addition, have an effect on the pattern of private consumption expenditure. Looking at the problem in this way, it becomes possible to provide a number of broad guidelines for pricing policy which we briefly consider here.

In the first instance, a distinction must be made between essential and non-essential consumer goods, or 'necessities' and 'luxury goods', as defined earlier (p. 8). The important necessities generally supplied by the public sector include basic health, education, housing and power requirements as well as cheap transport.[3] In addition, the authorities in some cases take charge of, or participate in, the purchase and sale of staple food, such as wheat and rice.

Goods and services classified as necessities should, in some cases, like health and education, be offered free of charge and in others be sold at prices which are within the reach of low income groups even when this entails provision of subsidy by the authorities. Given the rates of subsidies, the amount of goods and services supplied by the public sector will determine the amount of resources devoted to the support of private consumption. The primary factors determining the scale of such subsidies must obviously be the volume of total resources available to governments and the relative urgency of the competing claims on such resources by current consumption of necessities and by the expansion of productive capacities through investment.

In many cases, because of a shortage of resources available for the provision of subsidies on necessities, the supply of such goods may fall short of the need for them. In these cases, rationing provides the only equitable means of distributing the subsidised goods.[4] But in practice, effective administration of a rationing scheme requires a reasonably efficient and honest administrative machinery which, as noted earlier, most developing countries lack (see pp. 24–6).

Sri Lanka is one of the few countries which has had considerable success in administering a rationing system of subsidised food, notably

3. As noted earlier, expenditure on health and education, although usually classified as 'consumption', can legitimately be regarded as 'investment' in human resources (see p. 80).
4. It would, in theory, be possible to introduce a means test for the provision of subsidised goods, disqualifying the higher income groups. But this is likely to complicate the administration of the rationing schemes.

of rice. Although the ration per person has varied from time to time, it has generally included a certain quantity per person per week supplied free of charge and a further amount at subsidised prices. In recent years a ration of sugar at heavily subsidised prices has also been distributed on a monthly basis.[5] The average annual amount of consumer food subsidy during the years 1975–7, accounted for over 15 per cent of the government's current expenditure and was equivalent to about 3.5 per cent of GNP.[6]

Because the rate of investment expenditure in Sri Lanka, in common with many other developing countries, is subject to the balance of payments constraint, the country has, from time to time, been charged with devoting an excessive proportion of its foreign exchange resources to consumption, through its policy of subsidising food. It is argued that a reduction in the level of subsidies and consumption would enable the authorities to step up the rate of investment and to attain a higher rate of growth. In one sense, this is a valid argument, since a large proportion of the food is imported from abroad and any decline in food consumption would result in an equivalent saving of foreign exchange. There are, however, some reasons for believing that a reduction in the amount of food subsidies will not necessarily speed economic development as defined in Chapter 1.

First, the purpose of food subsidies has been to ensure a minimum level of consumption by the poorer sections of the population, and it is not clear that a higher rate of growth in the volume of *unweighted* GNP, attained at the expense of the standard of living of these classes, can be regarded as an improvement in the rate of economic development.

Secondly, unlike many other developing countries, Sri Lanka has, since its independence, succeeded in maintaining a reasonably stable democratic régime, a success that owes much to the government's policy of providing a rapidly growing population with a tolerable standard of living. Compared with autocratic régimes and military dictatorships, Sri Lanka's political system has thus had important social welfare advantages which deserve consideration in their own right. But even from a purely economic point of view, the absence of strong mass opposition to the régime has, as we have seen, enabled the country to keep its defence expenditure at a very low level compared with most of the other developing countries of Asia (see Table 3.1). In other words, the expenditure incurred on subsidies has been largely, if not entirely, offset by a significant economy in defence and internal security outlays.

5. For details, see Central Bank of Ceylon, *Review of the Economy, 1977*, pp. 191–2.
6. *Ibid.*, Appendix II, Tables 6 and 40.

At least part of the subsidies provided on the supply of necessities should be recouped by profits earned on the sale of non-essential services, such as first class travel by air and train, supplied by the public sector. Additional resources could be raised through profits on the operation of such services as telephone, cable, banking and insurance. As noted earlier, there are strong reasons for governments to establish state monopolies for the supply of such services and to exploit to the full their potential for earning profits.

Producer goods: As regards the inputs supplied by the public sector to private business, it would generally be advisable, in the interest of simplicity, to charge a uniform price to all buyers. In the trading and manufacturing sectors the price charged could be set at a level that covers not only the average cost of production but also a margin of profit to finance at least a proportion of desired expansion in productive capacity. Such incentives as the authorities might wish to provide to certain industries could then be given through the selective fiscal and monetary measures discussed below rather than through input subsidisation.

In the case of agriculture, on the other hand, it may be administratively preferable for the authorities to bear the full cost of providing irrigation, drainage and technical assistance services. They should, in addition, consider subsidising essential inputs, such as fertilisers and pesticides, since such inputs increase land yields and farmers should be encouraged to use them (see also pp. 197, 206 and 208). The outlay so incurred could, where it is deemed desirable, be recouped, in whole or in part, by increasing agricultural taxes correspondingly.

PRIVATE INVESTMENT

The share of the public sector in total domestic investment of mixed economies depends primarily on the economic philosophy of the authorities concerning the respective roles of private and public sectors in economic development; the more involved in promoting development the government is, the larger this share will tend to be. There are in this regard significant differences between developing countries. The available data suggest that in the early 1970s the share of fixed investment outlay of the public sector, including state enterprises, in total domestic fixed investment ranged from about 30 per cent for countries like the Dominican Republic and Thailand to around 40 per cent for Argentina, Mexico and Nigeria and to as much as 50 per cent for Brazil, Iran, Pakistan and Turkey. It is thus safe to assume that in most developing countries the volume of private investment outlay in industry, agriculture, residential construction and commerce equals, or is larger than, public investment. We shall, however, confine our discussion to industrial and agricultural components of private investment.

Private investment decisions are on the whole motivated by profits and need have no regard to development priorities. There is, as we have seen, little reason to expect that the pattern of private investment for a country, left entirely to individual entrepreneurs, would correspond to that needed for its development (see pp. 15–20). The realisation of this fact has prompted almost all developing countries to take a variety of measures to influence the allocation of investment resources by the private sector. We are here concerned exclusively with the fiscal and monetary measures used for this purpose, making little more than passing reference to other measures that can be taken on occasion to influence the pattern of private investment.

Fiscal measures[7]

Tariffs and quotas

Historically, import tariffs have been the most popular fiscal measure used to direct investment into the industrial sector. As noted in Chapter 1, this instrument of policy was employed by the countries of Western Europe and by the United States in the early stages of their industrialisation to protect their domestic industries against foreign, primarily British, competition. Since the Great Depression of the 1930s, it has also been widely used by developing countries to stimulate industrialisation by discouraging imports from developed countries.

The protection afforded by a specific rate of tariff to domestic industry depends partly on the price elasticity of demand for imported goods, which may be very low and which cannot, in any case, be estimated with any degree of accuracy. To ensure that the inflow of certain imports is limited to the levels desired by the authorities, tariffs have, therefore, often been reinforced by import quotas administered through an import licensing system. For brevity, we shall use the term 'import restrictions' to cover tariffs, quotas and other measures used to discourage imports.

There can be little doubt that the policies of import restriction have

7. These measures are also discussed later in connection with the problem of 'imbalances' (see pp. 237–9).

played a major role in encouraging the growth of import-substituting industries in many LDCs since the early 1930s. But the pattern of industrialisation induced by these policies in most of them can hardly be regarded as being entirely suitable to their economic development as defined by us in Chapter 1. The chief reason for this is that restrictions on the imports of luxuries, which have made the domestic production of such goods more profitable, have not been accompanied by the appropriate internal investment measures required to direct resources into industries with a high social priority. Instead, the determination of the pattern of domestic investment has been left largely to market forces, which have inevitably pulled a significant proportion of resources into the production of luxury goods to meet the relatively strong demand of the richer classes of the community. As noted earlier, this type of protection has also encouraged the flow of foreign capital, in the form of direct investment, into non-essential industries (pp. 151–2).

It is in principle possible to combine import restrictions with a system of *investment licensing* to ensure that the benefit of protection accrues primarily, if not exclusively, to essential industries. Apart from the prohibition of luxury imports, this would entail the imposition of high tariffs and strict quotas on the finished products of those industries which the government plans to encourage, while allowing easy importation of inputs for such industries. It would, in addition, require a refusal to issue licences for the establishment of non-essential industries. But although most developing countries have some form or other of investment regulations or licensing schemes in operation, hardly any of these have in practice proved to be effective in preventing investment in many projects with low social priority. The reason for this is to be sought in the general inefficiency and corruption of their administrative machinery, as well as in the political influence exercised in the formulation and implementation of investment regulations by the richer classes; most goods regarded as 'luxuries' by the majority of the population are considered 'necessities' by the rich.

Import restrictions naturally have the effect of raising the prices of importable goods above their world prices. The difference between the two sets of prices will depend on the stringency of the restrictions, namely on the tariff rates and on the size of the import quotas. Such price differences give rise to two major problems that need to be tackled. *First*, the greater the difference between the internal and the world prices of imported goods is, the larger the temptation to import them illicitly by smuggling and by bribery of customs and other officials will be. *Second*, when the difference in price is due to the stringency of the import quotas, the recipients of import licences stand to reap abnormally high profits, and this is also likely to tempt some importers to resort to political pressure and bribery to acquire such licences. This problem can, however, be resolved either by auctioning the import licences among potential importers, or by establishing a state monopoly for the importation and marketing of the goods through wholesale channels.

Tax concessions

Most developing countries employ fiscal incentives, in the form of tax 'holidays' and tax rebates, to encourage certain types of investment. Although tax concessions vary from country to country and are subject to periodic revisions, the following examples illustrate the type of measures that have been employed by some developing countries in the post-War years.[8] In India, the profits of all new industrial undertakings, up to 6 per cent of the capital employed, have been exempted from income tax for five years, and, in addition, tax rebates have been made on profits earned in industries designated as 'priority industries'. In Malaysia, 'pioneer industries', defined as new industries which the government wishes to encourage, have been exempted from taxation for periods ranging from 2 to 5 years, depending on the scale of their investment outlay. Tax 'holidays' ranging from 5 to 15 years have been granted to new industries by Ethiopia, Madagascar, Somalia and Zambia, and to the shipping industry in the Philippines. The Philippines has also provided tariff concessions on the importation of inputs used in the textile, chemical, ship building and cottage industries. Similarly, Colombia and the East African countries have exempted all capital goods and industrial raw materials from import duties. To encourage exports of manufactures, a variety of tax reliefs as well as subsidies, discussed below, has been given on such exports by Brazil, Colombia, India and the Philippines.[9]

Like tariffs and quotas mentioned earlier, the type of tax incentives

8. The dates of the publications mentioned in the following footnote give a rough indication of the years in question.
9. For details of tax incentives given by Asian countries, see *Asian Taxation 1965*, Japan Tax Association (1966). For similar information on the East African countries, see United Nations, *Economic Bulletin for Africa*, Vol. VII, Nos. 1 and 2, Sales No.: 67. II.K.6 (1967), pp. 11–34; for Brazil and Colombia, see United Nations, *Economic Survey of Latin America, 1974*, Sales No.: E.76.II.G.1 (1976), pp. 59 and 88–9.

For more up-to-date information, see the country studies prepared in connection with *UNDP/UNCTAD Report*, mentioned later (see p. 217, fn. 8). See also p. 238.

described have in practice helped primarily to foster industrialisation in general rather than to direct resources into essential projects. This is quite obvious where the exemptions from import duties cover all capital goods and industrial raw materials. Regarding tax 'holidays', it can in fact be argued that, unless granted very selectively, they will tend, on the whole, to favour non-essential industries more than the essential ones. The degree of inducement given by this measure to promote investment will vary directly with the expected rate of profit which in developing countries is likely to be relatively high in the production of those luxury and semi-luxury goods whose importation is restricted and for which there is a relatively strong demand from the richer classes of the community.

Tax 'holidays' also provide a further explanation of the heavy concentration of foreign manufacturing investment in the production of durable consumer and other non-essential goods, noted earlier (p. 151). In addition, developing countries frequently compete with one another in offering tax 'holidays' to foreign investors, often to the point where the benefits offered exceed the inducement required to attract the investment. The effect of this has been to whittle away the gain of host countries from foreign investment and to increase the profits of foreign corporations correspondingly.

Subsidies[10]

This instrument of policy can be used more selectively than import restriction and tax concessions to influence the pattern of private investment. Apart from credit subsidies, discussed later, subsidies have been used in industry primarily to promote the export of manufactured goods, already mentioned. They have, however, been more widely used to stimulate agriculture.

There are two common methods for the provision of subsidies to agriculture, the first of which is the supply by the authorities of agricultural inputs at subsidised prices. The other method is the setting of guaranteed prices for farmers at levels that often exceed the world prices of their crops. A large number of developing countries have, from time to time, employed these two techniques to stimulate agricultural production.[11] Sri Lanka, which has for the last three

10. This section excludes 'credit subsidies', which are examined below under the heading of 'Monetary Instruments'.
11. For details of the subsidies granted by a number of Asian countries in the late 1960s, for example, see United Nations, *Economic Survey of Asia and the Far East, 1969*, Sales Number: E. 70.II.F.1 (1970), pp. 22–30.

decades continuously used these techniques to promote domestic rice production with some success, provides a good illustration of them.[12]

The general policy followed in Sri Lanka to promote domestic rice production has been to extend the area of paddy cultivation by landless farmers. This has involved the development of large stretches of previously uncultivated land, construction of the necessary irrigation schemes and provision of guaranteed prices and subsidised inputs. The present Guaranteed Price Scheme for rice was initiated early in 1948. It replaced the Internal Purchase Scheme which had been introduced by the British Government in 1942 to stimulate the production of rice in the colony during the second World War when it became difficult to import food from abroad. The purpose of the Guaranteed Price Scheme has been to encourage the production of rice, which constitutes the staple diet of the population and accounts for a significant proportion of the country's imports, by providing farmers with a ready market at prices that assure them of a livelihood.

In the early years of the Guaranteed Price Scheme, the prices paid to cultivators were only marginally higher than the import prices of rice, but since 1952 there has in most years been a significant difference between the two sets of prices. During 1976–7, for example, the price paid for local rice was about 40 per cent higher than the CIF price of imported rice. The value of 'producer subsidies', defined as the excess of the total payments made for the purchase of paddy and for milling and distribution over the CIF value of rice, amounted to about 8 per cent of the Government's current expenditure.[13] Additional stimulus to the production of paddy has been provided through the supply of fertilisers to farmers at sabsidised prices and through paddy cultivation loans advanced by rural banks, most of which are guaranteed by the Central Bank up to 75 per cent of defaults.[14]

Multiple exchange rates

Although variations in foreign exchange rates are generally classified as a monetary rather than a fiscal instrument, the system of

12   In more recent years, Sri Lanka has also tried to promote the production of its major export crops, namely tea, rubber and coconut, by giving replanting subsidies to the cultivators of the first two crops, and by distributing coconut seedlings at subsidised prices to those of the third. See *ibid.*, p. 29, and Central Bank of Ceylon, *Review of the Economy 1977*, pp. 16–18.

13. See Central Bank of Ceylon, *op. cit.*, p. 169, and Appendix II, Table 40.

14. *Ibid.*, pp. 15 and 27–33, and United Nations, *Economic Survey of Asia and Far East 1969*, p. 29.

multiple exchange rates has very similar effects to those produced by tariffs and subsidies and is, for this reason, included among fiscal measures. This system, which was more widely used in Latin America during the post-War period, consists of the application of differential exchange rates to various categories of imports and exports and entails at least partial governmental control of foreign exchange transactions.[15] In principle, the use of multiple exchange rates in LDCs can, as explained later, be justified on the ground of significant differences prevailing between the productivity and the relative costs of the different sectors of their fragmented economies (see pp. 264–5).

Regarding imports, the rates charged on the sale of foreign exchange for the purchase of goods deemed to be essential, generally consisting of staple food, capital goods and raw materials, are usually kept lower than those charged on other types of goods. Where foreign exchange transactions are only partially controlled and the authorities permit the operation of a free exchange market, the importers of some low priority goods may be required to buy the requisite foreign exchange in the free market where the price of foreign exchange is higher. Similarly, to encourage the export of some products, often consisting of manufactured or semi-manufactured goods, a more favourable rate is applied to the surrender of the foreign exchange earned on the exportation of such goods than that applicable to traditional exports of primary products.[16] Alternatively, the exporters of manufactures may be permitted to retain a proportion of their foreign exchange earnings for sale in the free exchange market, or to purchase imports that are subject to restrictions. In practice, this instrument of policy, like tariffs, quotas and tax concessions, discussed earlier, has been used primarily to encourage industrialisation as a whole rather than to direct resources to high priority industries alone.

It is clear that the four categories of fiscal instrument outlined here are not mutually exclusive and are often used together, in various combinations, to reinforce one another. As explained later, the IMF authorities tend to be particularly critical of import quotas and multiple exchange rates because of their general disapproval of governmental interference in foreign trade and exchange transactions (see p. 263). Countries seeking loans from the Fund are often

---

15. For references to multiple exchange rate schemes used in the post-War years, see IMF, *The International Monetary Fund, 1945–1965*, Vol. II, p. 125.
16. For details of the differential rates of exchange applied to the exports of coffee and manufactured goods in Colombia, for example, see United Nations, *Economic Survey of Latin America 1974*, p. 88. For other and more recent examples see p. 238 below.

expected to take steps towards the gradual abolition of quotas and the unification of foreign exchange rates.

Monetary instruments

It will have been noted that, in examining the problems and policies related to increasing the *volume* of domestic savings and investment in Chapter 3, no mention was made of the possibility of using monetary instruments for this purpose. The reason for this is simply that, as explained earlier, we believe that monetary measures, apart from those concerned with hire purchase, or consumer credit, do not exercise a significant *direct* influence on propensities to save and to consume (see pp. 44–6). These measures can, however, be employed to influence the *pattern* of investment by channelling resources into specific sectors of the economy, and are, in practice, widely used for this purpose. In addition, some monetary institutions can, as we shall see, serve the purpose of augmenting the resources available to a country by encouraging the inflow of capital, official and private, from abroad.

Before examining the use of monetary instruments to regulate the pattern of investment, it should be pointed out that their influence is generally confined to a relatively small proportion of total domestic investment. There are two reasons for this. *First*, investment financed by retained profits, which generally accounts for a substantial proportion of total investment undertaken by large industrial and commercial enterprises as well as by big landlords, falls largely outside the range of influence of these instruments. *Second*, not all investment financed by outside credit can be selectively regulated by the authorities through normal financial channels. Private commercial banks and credit institutions, which finance a large proportion of such investment, can at the most be subjected to general directives, requiring them, for example, to restrict loans to certain specified sectors of the economy. It would clearly be somewhat unreasonable to expect such institutions to abandon the normal criterion of 'profitability' in their individual investment decisions in favour of some other criteria specified by the authorities.

Because of the latter consideration, most governments have, in one way or other, encouraged the formation of special banks and credit institutions whose method of funding permits them to give some weight to developmental considerations. The scope of influence of monetary instruments on the allocation of resources is effectively confined to that part of investment which is financed by these institutions; for brevity, they will be referred to simply as 'development banks', or 'public credit institutions'.

There has been a spectacular increase in the number of development banks in LDCs during the post-war period. A study conducted for the Development Centre of OECD in the mid-1960s identified as many as 340 such banks operating in some 80 developing countries.[17] About 40 per cent of these banks were in Latin America, 33 per cent in Asia and the Middle East, 20 per cent in Africa, and the remainder in the less developed countries in Europe. The indications are that the number of development banks has continued to increase in all these regions since that date.[18]

To facilitate its own task of lending to the private sector, the World Bank has actively encouraged the establishment of development banks. The Bank has used them as vehicles for advancing loans to private enterprises many of which could not obtain the government guarantee required by the Bank's charter for loans advanced to non-governmental borrowers. Development banks, which can readily obtain such guarantees, borrow from the Bank and re-lend the proceeds to their private clients.

The OECD study defined a development bank as 'an institution providing general medium- and long-term financial assistance to a developing economy'. The definition excludes central and commercial banks as well as the institutions which provide short-term credit and some of those that are very specialised, such as marketing boards and mortgage banks.[19]

The finance provided by development banks takes the form of loans and participation in the equity capital of enterprises, the former being more important; for short, we shall use the term 'investment' to cover both types of finance. Although the majority of these banks are required by their charters to confine their investments to financing private enterprises, a few are permitted to invest in mixed and in publicly owned businesses; this is the case, for example, with the *Banque Nationale pour le Développement Économique* in Morocco and with some Colombian development banks.[20]

---

17. See J.D. Nyhart and Edmond F. Janssens, *A Global Directory of Development Finance Institutions in Developing Countries*, The Development Centre of the OECD, Paris (1967).
18. See J.A. Kane, *Development Banking*, Lexington Books (1975), p. 3.
19. See Nyhart and Janssens, *Global Directory*, p. v.
20. See Kane, *Development Banking*, pp. 115–16. For a discussion of the differences in the charters of the various development banks, see *ibid.*, and Shirley Boskey, *Problems and Practices of Development Banks*, published for the World Bank by The Johns Hopkins Press, Baltimore (1959), pp. 13–15.

The sphere of operation of development banks extends over all the important sectors of the economy – industry, mining, agriculture, the infrastructure and some services, like tourism. We are here concerned solely with investment in the private sector and shall, in addition, confine our analysis to industrial and agricultural development banks which together account for the bulk of the credit provided by these institutions.

Industrial development banks

Because of the great emphasis placed on industrialisation in the development policies of most LDCs, development banks tend to be heavily concentrated in industry. Although the primary function of industrial development banks is the supply of finance to selected private industrial enterprises, many of them also provide their clients with a number of other services, such as technical assistance in engineering, management and accounting. In addition, some development banks play an active role in the promotion of new industrial ventures, directly or in partnership with existing enterprises, as well as in fostering the development of capital markets.[21]

Industrial development banks can, in theory, play an important role in directing the resources entrusted to them into certain projects with high social priority. They can do this by providing finance on concessional terms to those entrepreneurs who, in the absence of such finance, would not be willing or able to undertake the projects in question. If essential projects have relatively uncertain or low profit prospects, businessmen would be reluctant to undertake them without some external assistance and would, in any case, find it difficult to raise adequate finance through normal commercial channels for the purpose. It is clear, however, that to exercise a positive influence on the pattern of investment in terms of promoting economic development, these banks would have to use the criterion of 'social priority' as defined earlier, rather than 'profitability', of investment, in the selection of projects.[22] Whether in practice they do so depends, as explained below, largely on the methods used for funding them and on the development strategy and policies followed by the authorities.

21. For a discussion of these functions, see Boskey, *Development Banks*, pp. 5–6, and Kane, *Development Banking*, pp. 42–8.
22. See p..8 above. For a discussion of the conflict between the two sets of criteria, see Kane, *Development Banking*, pp. 17–24.

Sources of funds

Of the 340 development banks listed in the OECD study, it was possible to identify the ownership of just over 200. Of these about 55 per cent were state-owned, or public, 30 per cent had mixed ownership and the remaining 15 per cent were private.

State-owned and some mixed banks receive funds from annual budgetary appropriations, exchequer loans, or a lump sum allocation of funds, sometimes in the form of a subscription to their share capital. In some cases the authorities require certain private companies and institutions to make contributions, in the form of capital subscriptions, to the financial resources of these banks. In Mexico, for example, financial, investment as well as insurance companies were required to subscribe to the share capital of the Nacional Financiera, a mixed development bank, in amounts proportional to their capital and reserves.[23]

Most private and mixed development banks have to be given some governmental subsidies, usually in the form of interest-free or cheap loans, at the start of their operation. In the absence of such assistance, it would be difficult for these banks to attract private capital subscribers, who would expect a normal rate of return on their investment. This is partly because the interest rates charged by development banks tend to be lower than the prevailing market rates, and partly because some of the operations of the banks, such as technical assistance and the promotion of pioneering enterprises, may yield relatively low returns in the short run. Government contributions to the initial capital of private development banks were, for example, made to the Industrial and Mining Development Bank of Iran (INMIDEL) and to the Pakistan Industrial Credit and Investment Corporation.[24] Concessional loans of similar character have been advanced to a number of other private and mixed development banks including the Development and Finance Corporation of Sri Lanka and the Industrial Credit and Investment Corporation of India.[25]

The potential earning power of private equity in mixed banks is at times further enhanced by the government's agreement that its shares in the bank would carry no dividend rights, as in the case of the Industrial Bank of Peru, or that they would be classified as deferred

23. See Boskey, *Development Banks*, p. 25.
24. See Nyhart and Janssens, *Global Directory*, pp. 170 and 292; and INMIDEL, *Eighteenth Annual Report for the Year 1977/78*, p. 97.
25. For details see Nyhart and Janssens, *Global Directory*, pp. 50 and 142.

shares not eligible for dividend until the private investors have been paid a specific minimum rate of dividend.[26]

To ensure financial viability, private and mixed development banks are generally required by their charters not to exceed a specified debt-equity ratio. The higher this ratio, the larger the proportion of fixed charges that have to be met out of revenue is, and the more vulnerable the bank will become to insolvency, or even liquidation, due to losses incurred on bad debts or on the promotion of pioneering enterprises. There is no single 'safe' debt-equity ratio applicable to all development banks. Generally, the less conservative a bank is in its investment policies, the less it can afford to rely on external borrowing. The World Bank had suggested a debt-equity ratio of 3 to 1 for the development banks it had helped to establish in India, Iran, Pakistan and Turkey.[27]

In addition to the limitations placed on external borrowing, the charters of some private and mixed development banks contain other provisions aimed at increasing their financial strength. These include the requirement to transfer to reserves a specified percentage of profits until the reserves equal a stated proportion of paid up capital or of external debt, to establish a separate reserve for bad debts and to limit dividends paid to shareholders.[28]

Given government subsidies and their financial soundness, many private and mixed development banks are able to present the prospect of earning a reasonable rate of profit on their investments, and to attract subscribers to their share capital from private domestic firms and from foreign institutions operating within the country, as well as from individual investors. Commercial banks and insurance companies were, for example, the initial subscribers to the capital of the development banks of Sri Lanka, India and Pakistan mentioned above. At times, however, special inducements, in the form of tax concessions and government-guaranteed dividends, have to be offered to private investors to ensure subscriptions to the capital of development banks. The initial share capital of the Industrial Development Bank of Turkey was, for example, taken up by industrial firms, commercial banks and trade associations after the Government had guaranteed a minimum dividend on the bank's share capital.[29]

Because of the risk of losses through foreign exchange fluctuations, non-resident foreign investors are generally unlikely to subscribe to the

26. See Boskey, *Development Banks*, p. 30.
27. *Ibid.*, p. 24.
28. For details of such requirements, see *ibid.*, pp. 16–17; for the legal reserve requirement of INMIDEL (Iran), see INMIDEL, *Annual Report, 1977/78*, p. 97.
29. See Boskey, *Development Banks*, p. 26.

share capital of development banks unless they anticipate that such action will place them in an advantageous position for obtaining future business in the country. Non-resident subscribers, therefore, tend to be banks, finance companies and other corporations with business connections in the country.[30]

Loan capital. The bulk of the funds of private and mixed development banks are, however, raised through borrowing at home and abroad rather than through subscriptions to their equity capital. As far as internal sources of loans are concerned, mention has already been made of the interest-free and concessional loans granted to them by governments, directly or through central banks. Additional funds have been raised by some banks through the issue of bonds, generally sold to local institutions, although these account for a relatively small fraction of their total resources. To make such obligations more attractive, the bonds have, on occasion, been guaranteed by the government and made eligible for rediscounting with the central bank. Such action was, for example, taken in respect of the obligations sold by the Industrial Finance Corporation of India – a mixed development bank.[31] State-owned banks, like the Government Development Bank for Puerto Rico, have, on the other hand, been able to sell their bonds against their own security.[32]

External loans, from official bilateral and multilateral institutions as well as foreign private sources, account for an appreciably larger proportion of the loan capital of development banks than domestic loans. The most important bilateral official sources of foreign loans have been the US aid agencies, notably the Agency for International Development (AID) and its predecessor agencies; 'counterpart funds', described earlier,[33] are often utilised to advance such loans. In addition, many development banks receive substantial funds in the form of loans from multilateral institutions, such as the World Bank and regional development banks. The World Bank, which plays an important part in funding development banks, had adhered until recently to the policy of dealing only with privately owned banks, but

---

30. *Ibid.*, p. 29, and Kane, *Development Banking*, p. 28. For a list of foreign subscribers in development banks of India, Iran and Pakistan, see Boskey, *Development Banks*, p. 29, fn. 6.
31. See Boskey, *Development Banks*, pp. 31–2.
32. *Ibid.*
33. See p. 131. For details of bilateral official loans, see Boskey, *Development Banks*, pp. 32–5, and Kane, *Development Banking*, pp. 101–4.

since 1970 it has extended its lending and technical assistance operations to mixed and publicly owned banks.[34]

Apart from the official external sources of finance, foreign commercial banks, investment corporations and capital markets have in recent years played a progressively growing role in providing loan funds to industrial development banks. In the case of the INMIDEL (Iran), for example, loans obtained directly from foreign commercial banks, together with the outstanding value of bonds issued abroad, amounted to over one-third of the bank's total liabilities at the end of its 1977/8 financial year.[35]

The following table shows in summary form the various sources of funds of a sample of 31 development banks established primarily to stimulate industrial development; all the banks, chosen from 26 countries on the basis of the availability of data, had received funds from the World Bank.[36]

Sources of Funds of 31 Sample Banks[a]
(Weighted Percentage Averages)

Domestic	48
Public	31
Private	17
External	52
Official	47
Private	5
TOTAL	100

Source: Derived from Kane, *Development Banking* Table 4.2, p. 98.
[a] Except for Venezuela, single year in the period 1970–2; Venezuela, 1967. For details of the years covered see the source, Table 3.3, p. 58.

34. See Kane, *Development Banking*, pp. 106–7.
35. See INMIDEL, *Annual Report, 1977/78*, pp. 92 and 98.
36. See Kane, *Development Banking*, pp. 55–6. For a list of the sample banks see *ibid.*, p. xv.

It can be seen that the external funds, most of which consisted of official bilateral and multilateral loans, accounted for just over one-half of the total resources raised through equity capital and loans by the sample banks in the early 1970s and that the public sector accounted for the bulk of the domestic funds. The data on individual banks suggest that just under two-thirds of the banks raised 50 per cent or more of their total funds from external sources. In the case of the development banks of the Philippines and Turkey included in the sample, official external institutions alone accounted for over 80 per cent of their total resources.[37]

In addition to the funds raised through capital subscription and through borrowing, some development banks acquire supplementary resources from governments and other public bodies through agency agreements. Under these agreements the banks act as agents for the investment of public funds, on a fee basis. The Industrial Development Bank of Turkey and INMIDEL (Iran), both private banks, have, for example, such arrangements with the authorities.[38] Apart from increasing the investment funds placed at the disposal of the banks, agency arrangements also provide them with a source of assured income, since any loss incurred on the investment of the managed funds is borne by governments.

Investment policies

The role of industrial development banks in promoting development should be evaluated primarily by reference to their policies determining the allocation of their resources between different enterprises. In other words, such e aluation requires an examination of the criteria used by the banks in their day-to-day investment decisions; their contribution to development will vary directly with the relative weight they are willing and able to attach to 'social priority', as compared with the 'profitability', criterion. In this connection, it should be emphasised that the mere fact that the presence of development banks encourages the inflow of foreign capital should not by itself be regarded as a positive contribution to development on their part; what matters is the pattern of investment of such capital by the banks.

37. For full details of the sources of funds of the 31 sample banks, see Kane, *Development Banking*, Table 4.1, pp. 94–7.
38. For details see Boskey, *Development Banks*, pp. 33–4, and INMIDEL, *Annual Report, 1977/78*, p. 99.

In practice, all development banks, whether public or private, are, as banks, concerned with the financial results of their investment and attach some weight to the profitability of their operations. They apply, therefore, the conventional business tests to appraise the risk and expected returns on their investment. These tests include: the technical and financial soundness of new projects, the profit history of the enterprises seeking finance, the structure of their assets and liabilities and the value of security offered for loans.[39] At the same time, as development banks, they cannot rely exclusively on these criteria of 'creditworthiness', or 'profitability'; they have to take into account the wider developmental implications of their investment decisions. The relative weight given to these two considerations varies from one development bank to another, partly because of differences in the objectives and functions prescribed for them by the authorities and partly because of different methods used for funding them.

The investment policies of *state-owned and mixed banks* in which governments have a majority shareholding are formulated by the authorities themselves. These banks, which rely on government funds and on official dividend and loan guarantees, can absorb losses and accept relatively low returns on their investment. They are, therefore, in principle in a position entirely to ignore the 'profitability' criterion of the projects financed by them. In practice, although they do tend to give a larger weight than private banks to the development impact of their investment, they nevertheless generally require that the projects should be financially sound. For example, even a bank like the Industrial Finance Corporation of India, which is required by the terms of its charter to assist those enterprises that are unable to obtain the requisite finance from the normal commercial sources, 'insists on rigorous financial tests and requires that the projects be self-liquidating'.[40]

Most development banks can be said to base their investment policy on the general hypothesis advanced by Shirley Boskey, a specialist in this field, in the following passage:

the fact is that, in the less-developed countries, almost any soundly conceived productive enterprise likely to be profitable without undue tariff protection will have a sufficiently high economic priority to warrant financing by the development bank.[41]

39. See Boskey, *Development Banks*, p. 49.
40. *Ibid.*, pp. 53–4.
41. *Ibid.*, p. 52. As noted earlier (p. 187, fn. 20) this book was published for the World Bank.

This interpretation of 'economic priority' clearly differs from that presented earlier in this book (see pp. 8–10).

The criterion of 'profitability' is, however, of particular importance to *private development banks* and to those mixed banks which do not enjoy official dividend and loan guarantees. These banks have to earn sufficient profits to build up reserves in accordance with the requirements of their charter. In addition, the profitability of such banks has a direct bearing on their credit rating and hence on their ability to attract loan capital from private sources at home and abroad. Because of these considerations, according to Shirley Boskey, only 'in the unlikely situation that two applications with comparable and satisfactory profit prospects were presented at a time when funds were insufficient to permit acceptance of both, the bank would probably consciously apply the economic priority criterion to help it in deciding between the two'.[42]

Bearing in mind the investment policies of the various categories of industrial development bank, it would be safe to conclude that these banks have not to date adequately exploited their potential for directing resources to projects with high social priority. Their primary function, like that of fiscal instruments discussed earlier, has been to encourage industrialisation in general, without significant discrimination between high and low priority industries.

It is worth noting at this stage that these efforts to diversify the structure of production and exports through industrialisation are partially frustrated by the protectionist policies of industrial countries, which have become more pronounced during the post-1973 periods of economic recession. The most important recent example of these policies is the Multi-Fibre Arrangement concluded in 1974 and extended four years later. This expands the scope of discriminatory measures, first introduced in 1962, on the shipment of textiles from developing to industrial countries. The earlier restraints, which were introduced in 1962 as a 'temporary' measure to permit adjustments in the textile industry under international supervision and applied only to cotton textiles, have now been extended to woollen and synthetic fibre goods. Moreover, they affect supplies not only from major exporters of textiles, but also from poorer countries such as Bangladesh and Indonesia.[43]

Industrial countries have also introduced quota restrictions against

42. See Boskey, *Development Banks*, pp. 52–3.
43. See Sidney Dell and Roger Lawrence, *The Balance of Payments Adjustment Process in Developing Countries*, Pergamon Press (1980) p. 128, and World Bank, *World Development Report, 1978*, Washington, DC (1978), pp. 15 and 18.

the importation from LDCs of a variety of other manufactured goods, such as footwear, petrochemicals and bicycle tyres and tubes. These are in addition to the barriers imposed against the traditional exports of developing countries, notably, vegetables, tobacco, grains and beef.[44] Such protectionist measures, which reflect the influence of domestic pressure groups in industrial countries, cannot easily be reconciled with the declared aims of foreign aid policies of these countries.

Agricultural credit institutions

Agricultural credit institutions take a variety of forms which include agricultural development banks, farmers' co-operative societies, credit unions and commercial banks operating in rural areas. The primary function of these institutions is to advance credit to the agricultural sector, in particular to small farmers, although many of them also provide a number of other complementary services mentioned below.[45] There is no precise definition of 'small farmers', but they can broadly be described as those landowners and farm tenants who generally cultivate relatively small plots of land with little fixed capital and with backward technology, and earn no more, and often less, than a subsistence level of income. The exact size of their plots would clearly vary with the quality and location of land as well as with its access to irrigation facilities.[46]

Most of the agricultural credit institutions are publicly-owned and governments' capital subscription and loans constitute the main domestic source of their funds; the contribution of the private sector to their resources is confined to relatively small amounts of deposits held with them. The credit institutions are thus in a position to operate on a semi-commercial basis by subsidising credit.

As in the case of industrial development banks, in addition to domestic resources, external funds are channelled to some of these institutions by foreign official sources, notably the AID, the World

44. For further details see Dell and Lawrence, *op. cit.*, pp. 38–9.
45. For a detailed list of public and private agricultural credit institutions and a description of their functions see FAO, *Monthly Bulletin of Agricultural Economics and Statistics*, December 1973, pp. 8–9 for the *Near East* (Middle East and North Africa); *ibid.*, October/November 1974, pp. 8–11 for *Africa*; and *ibid.*, June 1975, pp. 9–10, for *Asia*, and pp. 14–18 for *Latin America*. This publication is henceforth referred to simply as *Monthly Bulletin.*
46. See also the description of 'small farmers' in need of credit in: FAO, *Monthly Bulletin*, June 1975, p. 12; and Gordon Donald, *Credit for small Farmers in Developing Countries.* Westview Press, Boulder, Colorado (1976), pp. 15–17.

Bank Group (IBRD and IDA) and regional development banks. There has been a particularly rapid growth in the volume of credit channelled by the World Bank Group through credit institutions for the purpose of re-lending, or 'on-lending', to local farmers.[47] The available data indicate a steady increase in the resources of and in the volume of credit advanced by the agricultural credit institutions in developing countries.

There has been a growing volume of literature on agricultural credit, including the operations of agricultural credit institutions, in various developing countries in recent years which cannot adequately be examined within the scope of this book.[48] The most that we can do here is to analyse briefly the development 'potential' of these institutions and to indicate some of the important factors which, in the opinion of many experts, have been responsible for their failure to realise this potential.

Development potential

Agricultural credit institutions have a great potential for promoting economic development by channelling a larger proportion of the available resources to the agricultural sector. More specifically, the instrument of agricultural credit can perform two positive functions in development. It can be used: (a) to improve the lot of small farmers by reducing the cost of their borrowing and (b) to stimulate the growth of agricultural production by financing the cost of modernising cultivation techniques. Of the two functions, it is the second that is more important, because, as explained elsewhere in the book (pp. 56 and 218–21), agricultural production plays a key role in determining the pace of development.

In a traditional setting, small farmers use credit largely for consumption purposes since their methods of cultivation, being based on a stagnant technology, require little investment. Some poor farmers borrow regularly to finance their consumption in the months preceding the harvest. But most farmers borrow only when they have had a poor harvest or when they have to pay for an unusual family event, such as a wedding or a funeral. The loans are usually contracted for

47. See, World Bank *Agricultural Credit, Sector Policy Paper* (May 1975), Annex 14, for the period up to mid-1973; and World Bank, *Annual Reports*, for subsequent years.
48. Readers interested in this subject should refer to a survey article by Michael Lipton, 'Agricultural Finance and Rural Credit in Poor Countries', *World Development*, July 1976. A vast quantity of primary research material on agricultural credit in a number of developing countries is to be found in the US Agency for International Development (AID), *Spring Review of Small Farmer Credit, 1972/73*, Washington DC (1973), published in 17 volumes.

short periods of a few months and are repaid after the harvest. A succession of bad harvests, or a prolonged decline in the price of crops, can, however, result in a steady accumulation of debt and, on occasions, to a foreclosure of land mortgages securing the debts.

Part of the borrowing of small farmers is from 'private non-commercial' sources – relatives, friends and neighbours – to whom little or no interest is paid. A significant proportion of their credit is, however, provided by 'private commercial' lenders, notably professional moneylenders, landlords and middlemen.[49]

Table 5.1 gives a very rough indication of the interest rates charged by credit institutions and by private commercial lenders in a selected number of developing countries around the year 1970. The rates for institutions represent the average interest rates charged for different types of loans by various public and private credit institutions, the rates charged by public institutions being generally about 3 percentage points lower than those charged by private ones.

The World Bank estimates that, to cover the opportunity cost of capital together with the cost of administering credit and losses incurred through defaults, the 'real' rate of interest on institutional credit should be between 15 and 22 per cent, which is not unreasonable.[50] It would, therefore, appear that, with the exception of Malaysia, all the countries listed in the table subsidise their institutional credit heavily; this is by and large true of almost all developing countries.

The figures for private commercial lenders, being based, at best, on sample surveys and in some cases on hearsay evidence, merely indicate the order of magnitude of the annual rates of interest charged. These figures are obtained by multiplying the monthly rates of interest by twelve and therefore exaggerate the scale of the actual cost borne by the borrowers and of the income of the lenders per year. On the other hand, the same figures take no account of such 'hidden charges' as the requirement that the borrower should provide free labour services to lenders, or that repayment should be made in kind by delivering crops at prices which are usually lower than those prevailing in the market.[51]

Notwithstanding the above qualifications concerning the quality of the data, there can be little doubt that the information presented in Table 5.1 fully confirms the observations of many students of

49. For the sake of brevity, we have used the term 'moneylenders' to cover all 'private commercial' lenders.
50. See World Bank, *Agricultural Credit*, p. 10.
51. For examples of other 'hidden charges' made by moneylenders, see Donald, *Credit for Small Farmers*, p. 83.

Table 5.1 : *Interest rates charged to farmers, by source of loans*[a]
(*Percentage per year*)

Country	Nominal rates		Real rates[b]	
	Institutions	Commercial lenders[c]	Institutions	Commercial lenders[c]
Africa				
Ethiopia	12	70	8	66
Ghana	6	70	—	64
Ivory Coast	10	150	6	144
Nigeria	6	200	− 2	192
Sudan	7	120	7	120
Asia				
India	10	25	—	15
Indonesia	14	40	3	28
Jordan	7	20	2	15
Korea, Republic of	16	60	5	49
Malaysia	18	60	16	58
Pakistan	7	30	4	27
Philippines	12	30	6	22
Sri Lanka	12	50	6	44
Thailand	11	30	9	28
Vietnam, Republic of	30	48	2	20
Latin America				
Bolivia	9	100	5	96
Brazil	15	60	− 7	39
Chile	14	82	− 16	52
Colombia	12	41	4	33
Costa Rica	8	24	4	20
El Salvador	10	25	8	23
Honduras	9	40	6	37
Mexico	10	60	7	57

Source: World Bank, *Agricultural Credit, Sector Policy Paper* (May 1975) Annex 9.
[a] The data are derived largely from US Agency for International Development, *Spring Review of Small Farmer Credit, 1972/73*, Department of State, Washington DC (1973), and relate to different years around 1970.
[b] In most cases nominal rates were converted to real rates by deducting the average rate of inflation between 1967 and 1970 from the nominal rates. The true differences between 'real rates' are, therefore, exaggerated in the Table (author).
[c] Consisting of professional moneylenders, landlords, retail traders and middlemen merchants.

agricultural economics regarding the wide differentials between the interest rates charged by 'moneylenders' and formal credit institutions.[52] As explained below, however, interest is often not the only charge associated with institutional loans and, because of this, small farmers may at times prefer to borrow from private commercial sources rather than from institutions.

There are a number of reasons which explain why private commercial loans to small farmers should usually carry appreciably higher rates of interest than those prevailing in the money market in general. These include the high cost of administering small farm loans, the seasonal demand for loans and the relatively big risk of lending; the last is due partly to the fact that a large number of borrowers from individual 'moneylenders' tend to be located in the same village and all of them may simultaneously be affected by such factors as adverse weather conditions.[53] In addition, private commercial lenders at times enjoy a monopoly position and are able to charge relatively high rates of interest on their loans. Credit institutions, by providing small farmers with an alternative source of borrowing, can in such cases contribute to a lowering of interest rates.[54]

Considerably more important than lowering interest rates is the potential of rural credit institutions for accelerating the growth of agricultural production, by stimulating the modernisation of techniques of cultivation used by farmers in general and by small farmers in particular. Modernising agriculture involves the introduction of various kinds of cultivation techniques, such as the adoption of practices which prevent soil erosion and conserve moisture, the use of fertilisers, pesticides and new varieties of seeds and crop strains, as well as new irrigation methods.

Some technological innovations, such as new seeds, may require little or no additional finance, but many do. Such finance is unlikely to be forthcoming from private commercial lenders whose limited supply of funds is used primarily for short-term consumption credits. Agricultural credit institutions are in a position to provide the additional capital required by small farmers for the adoption of

52. See, for example, the IMF survey by U. Tun Wai, *IMF Staff Papers*, Vol. 6, No. 1, November 1957, reviewed in Donald, *op. cit.*, pp. 88–90; Eprime Eshag and M.A. Kamal, 'A Note on the Reform of Rural Credit System in U.A.R. (Egypt)', *BOUIES*, May 1967, pp. 97–8; A. Bhaduri 'Agricultural Backwardness under Semi-Feudalism', *Economic Journal*, March 1973, p. 123; and FAO, *Monthly Bulletin*, December 1973, p. 2.

53. See Michael Lipton in J.A. Roumasset *et al.* (eds.), *Risk, Uncertainty and Agricultural Development*, Searca, Manila (1979).

54. See World Bank, *Agricultural Credit*, pp. 7 and 27–9.

modern technology. It is generally recognised that medium farmers who, unlike the large farmers, often lack adequate savings to finance desired innovations, can also make effective use of institutional credit to promote agricultural productivity. But from the point of view of promoting economic development, as defined by us, it is the poorer small farmers that have the highest claim to it.

Credit is, however, only one element in the package of inputs and services required for raising the productivity of small farmers through modernisation. It is particularly important for the farmers to recognise and accept the profitability of new technology and to have the opportunity of learning the necessary skills; pilot schemes may prove useful for this purpose. Equally important is the provision of marketing outlets for farm produce, as well as of delivery systems which ensure that the required inputs, e.g. seeds, fertilisers and pesticides, are readily available at the time they are needed. These complementary inputs and services can be provided by the credit institutions themselves, or by specialised agencies entrusted with the supply of 'extension services' as well as the sale of inputs and marketing of produce.

There would, of course, be a strong, understandable temptation to the poor farmers to use the loans received from credit institutions, in the first instance, for consumption rather than cultivation purposes; even loans in kind may be used to finance consumption outlays. It is, for example, reported that some Indonesian peasants resold the fertilisers bought on credit from the authorities at two-thirds of their price in the village.[55] Moreover, credit being 'fungible', even the provision of loans in kind which are properly used in cultivation under outside supervision cannot prevent increases in consumption. The volume of credit granted to small farmers should, therefore, in principle, be related to both their seasonal consumption and cultivation requirements.

Distribution of institutional credit

The available evidence suggests that few developing countries have in practice succeeded in exploiting to any significant extent the development potential of institutional credit in agriculture; this is clearly indicated by the relatively low proportion of credit utilised by small farmers. Table 5.2 shows a broad picture of the distribution, between small farmers and medium and large farmers combined, of credit advanced by the institutions established primarily to assist small farmers in a selected number of developing countries around the year

55. See United Nations, *Economic Survey of Asia and the Far East, 1969*, p. 27.

Table 5.2: *Distribution of institutional loans, by size of farms*[a]

(*Percentage share in the value of loans*)

Country	Small farmers[b]	Medium and large farmers
Africa		
Kenya	41	59
Asia		
Bangladesh	18	82
India	16	84
Malaysia	18	82
Pakistan	23	77
Taiwan	26	74
Latin America		
Brazil	1	99
Bolivia	6	94
Costa Rica	10	90
Ecuador	24	75
El Salvador	7	93
Honduras	19	81
Nicaragua	10	90
Peru	21	79

Source: Gordon Donald, *Credit for Small Farmers in Developing Countries*, Westview Press (1976), p. 80. Derived from reports presented to the AID *Spring Review of Small Farmer Credit, 1972/73*, Department of State, Washington DC (1973).
[a] Colombia is excluded from this table because the data shown in the 'source' covered only credit provided by the land reform agency (see the 'source', p. 79).
[b] For details of the maximum size of land holding of the farmers classified as 'small farmers' in each country see the 'source'.
Note: Because of rounding up, components may not add to 100.

1970. The data shown in the table are obtained from the papers presented to the AID conference, *Spring Review of Small Farmer Credit, 1972/73*, mentioned in the 'source'; some of the figures come from sample surveys and others directly from credit institutions.

It can be seen that in 12 out of 14 countries included in the table the share of small farmers in total institutional loans is estimated at less than 25 per cent, and that in 5 of them (all in Latin America) it is 10 per cent or less. The figures derived from sample surveys are unlikely to be very accurate and must be treated with due care and caution. But despite this qualification, it would be safe to conclude from the table that in the large majority of developing countries well over 70 per cent of institutional credit is granted to medium- and large-size farmers; this ratio would appear to be particularly high in Latin America.

Moreover, despite the rapid growth in the volume of institutional credit, the number of small farmers benefiting from it remains relatively small. The majority of these farmers either do not borrow or continue to depend on the private commercial and non-commercial sources described above. According to the World Bank, 'it is common to find 70 or 80 per cent of small farmers in a given country with virtually no access' to institutional credit.[56] On a continental basis, only about 5 per cent of farmers in Africa and about 15 per cent in Latin America and Asia (excluding Taiwan) benefit from institutional credit.[57] The broad conclusion of the World Bank, confirmed by FAO and other independent studies of agricultural economists, is that the main beneficiaries of institutional credit have been large farmers.[58]

There is some evidence to suggest that this pattern of distribution of credit has in some cases actually hindered development by aggravating the disparity between the income and wealth of small and large landholders.[59] *First*, the greater access of larger farmers to subsidised institutional credit has enabled them to adopt innovations at a relatively low cost, and more readily than small farmers, as a result of which their production has tended to rise faster than that of small farmers. *Second*, the availability of cheap credit to large farmers, by encouraging the introduction of capital intensive mechanised technology, has in some cases resulted in a fall of demand for labour, thereby making agricultural labourers and the small farmers who derive some of their income from part-time employment absolutely worse off.[60] *Third*, cheap credit has increased opportunities for the realisation of economies of scale through mechanisation, at times 'resulting in eviction of tenants by owner-cultivators' and to 'the

56. See World Bank, *Agricultural Credit*, p. 5.
57. *Ibid.*, p. 23; for details by country see Annex 3. In Taiwan, which has few large landholders, nearly all farmers have access to institutional credit.
58. For illustrations, see, for example, FAO, *Monthly Bulletin*, October/November 1974, p. 14, and June 1975, p. 11; Lipton, *World Development*, July 1976, pp. 546–7; Dale W. Adams and J.L. Tommy, *Agricultural Finance Review*, October 1974, catalogued in AID, *Agricultural Credit and Rural Savings : III*, July 1977, p. 1; and Uma J. Lele, in Nurul Islam (ed), *Agricultural Policy in Developing Countries*, Macmillan (1974), p. 418.
59. See Donald, *Credit for Small Farmers*, p. 82; and Lele, ed. Nural Islam, pp. 418–19.
60. See Lele, ed. Nural Islam, p. 419.

purchases of small farmers' land by large farmers'.[61] *Finally*, because of
the 'fungibility' of credit, large landlords have, on occasion, been able
to use institutional credit for purposes other than agricultural
investment. The cash resources freed by such credit have been used to
finance purchases of land and to invest in commerce and industry, as
well as to lend to small farmers at appreciably higher rates of interest
than those paid to institutions.[62] In these ways, subsidised institutional
credit in some developing countries, has, according to some writers,
served 'to reinforce traditional rural power structures', rather than to
help small farmers.[63]

    Explanatory factors. A number of reasons have been advanced
to explain the very limited access of small farmers to institutional
credit. On the demand side, small farmers may, for a variety of reasons,
find institutional credit in some cases less attractive than that provided
by private commercial lenders, despite the lower interest rates charged
by the former. The reasons include long delays in processing loan
applications by credit institutions, because of the need to establish the
creditworthiness of the borrowers. A number of complex forms have
generally to be filled by small farmers who are often illiterate and,
before a loan is granted, officials usually have to inspect the farmer's
holding and operations. The risk of not receiving credit in time to
purchase the required inputs would by itself deter many farmers from
applying for it. The absence of flexibility in the repayment terms of
institutions also tends to add to the risk of borrowing from them.

    Apart from the interest charge, borrowing from institutions often
entails additional costs, some 'open' and others 'informal' or 'hidden',
which may deter the small farmers from borrowing. The former
include application fees, travel expenses and time lost in travelling to
and from the nearest branch of the institution. The 'hidden' costs
consist of the need to 'entertain', or less euphemistically, to bribe, the
officials concerned with the processing of loan applications.[64] Studies of

61. *Ibid.*, pp. 419–20; see also World Bank, *Agricultural Credit*, p. 22, which reports that,
    in Colombia, Ethiopia and Pakistan, the new technology financed by loans has
    contributed to the displacement of tenants.
62. See World Bank, *Agricultural Credit*, pp. 12 and 47; Dale W. Adams, 'External
    Credit Policy for Latin America', *American Journal of Agricultural Economics*, May
    1971, p. 167; Lipton, *World Development*, July 1976, p. 547; and Gordon Donald,
    Credit for Small Farmers, p. 106.
63. See Solon Barraclough, *World Development*, July 1976, p. 557; see also Lipton,
    World Development, July 1976, pp. 546–9.
64. The prevalence of bribery in LDCs is a generally known fact. The World Bank
    mentions Bangladesh, Brazil and 'various countries in the Middle East' as
    examples, and adds that 'significant "informal" charges on public credit are not
    confined to these areas'. See World Bank, *Agricultural Credit*, p. 46.

institutional credit in Bangladesh, Brazil and Colombia have shown that small borrowers incurred substantially higher costs on their borrowing than larger borrowers and that, for the former, interest payments accounted for only a relatively small proportion of total borrowing costs.[65]

But even when small farmers are willing to borrow from credit institutions, it is difficult for them to compete with large farmers for the institutions' limited resources. One reason for this is the reluctance of the institutions to undertake the relatively high costs of administering small loans to widely dispersed farmers. Another reason is the inability of many small farmers to provide a collateral acceptable to the institutions to secure their loans. In most countries, however, a more important reason is the political and social influence of large farmers with the credit agents. By using this influence they are usually able to appropriate the bulk of government-provided subsidised credit; this is a widely recognised fact among agricultural economists.[66]

According to the FAO, apart from large farmers, there is also 'a tendency for politicians to interfere in the day-to-day work of credit institutions to promote personal career objectives. Managers are pressed to give loans in politicians' constituencies at the cost of other regions'.[67] This is confirmed by the World Bank, which notes that in many countries, 'politicisation' of the credit delivery mechanism has invaded not only the tactical but also the operational level of credit mechanism. 'The choice of directors for the credit institutions, and sometimes even of the staff, may be made on grounds of political loyalties rather than qualifications'.[68]

There is some evidence to suggest that large farmers at times use their political influence also to delay or even to avoid the repayment of their loans. Failure to repay loans is common to small and larger farmers alike. In the case of the former, the reason for delinquency is usually financial difficulties due to such factors as a poor harvest and the need to defray some unusual expenses. The delinquencies of large farmers, however, are often deliberate as 'they use their political power to protect themselves against penalties'.[69] The World Bank has found

65. See D.W. Adams and G.I. Nehman, 'Borrowing Costs and the Demand for Rural Credit', *Journal of Development Studies*, January 1979.
66. See, for example, Lipton, *World Development*, July 1976, pp. 546 and 550. See also FAO, *Monthly Bulletin*, December 1973, p. 10; October/November 1974, p. 15, and June 1975, p. 8; World Bank, *Agricultural Credit*, pp. 36, 42 and 52.
67. FAO, *Monthly Bulletin*, December 1973, p. 10.
68. World Bank, *Agricultural Credit*, p. 52.
69. See World Bank, *Agricultural Credit*, p. 42, and FAO, *Monthly Bulletin*, December 1973, p. 10.

that in several countries, including Bangladesh, Bolivia, Colombia, Costa Rica and Ethiopia, large farmers actually have a poorer repayment record than small farmers.[70]

In *theory*, the basic institutional requirement for the realisation of the development potential of agricultural credit is the presence of *local* organisations at village-level, such as farmers' co-operatives, or informal groups, through which credit is channelled.[71] These organisations, being familiar with the conditions and requirements of local farmers, can, with the help of technical and administrative personnel assigned to them by the authorities, allocate credit on the basis of the seasonal consumption and cultivation needs of farmers rather than their credit-rating as is done by most institutions. They can, in addition, provide technical services and supervise the use made of loans in kind, such as fertilisers, seeds etc. In order to reduce the incidence of defaults and the role of middlemen merchants, the institutions in question could also be assigned the task of collecting the major cash crops of their members for sale through official marketing organisations.

In *practice*, however, few local co-operatives have succeeded in performing these functions effectively. There is general agreement among economists who have studied this subject in depth, including some staff members of FAO and the World Bank, that the chief reason for this has been the unfavourable socio-political climate in which they have had to operate.[72] As in the case of other agricultural credit organisations, discussed earlier, two factors in particular have played an important role in subverting the work of the local credit institutions. *First*, the social and political influence wielded in the locality by large landlords in countries with archaic, or semi-feudal, land tenure, enabling them both to appropriate a relatively large proportion of the available funds of the institutions and to ignore the conditions set for the settlement of their loans. There is some evidence to suggest that co-operatives have been more successful in areas where large landholdings did not exist, usually after a land reform programme.[73] *Second*, the lack of integrity in the political system and in the administration of the credit institutions of many developing countries. These two factors are generally closely linked together. As explained earlier in the book, the

70. *Ibid.* For further illustrations, see references in Lipton, *World Development*, July 1976, p. 546.
71. See World Bank, *Agricultural credit*, pp. 16 and 56; and FAO, *Monthly Bulletin*, June 1975, p. 8.
72. See, for example, FAO, *Monthly Bulletin*, June 1975, p. 8; World Bank, *Agricultural Credit*, pp. 16 and 42; Lipton, *World Development*, July 1976, p. 550.
73. See World Bank, *op. cit.*, pp. 56–7; Lipton, p. 550; and Eshag and Kamal, *BOUIES*, May 1967, pp. 98–105, and *BOUIES*, May 1968, pp. 85–98.

social and economic structure of a country plays an important role in shaping the character and policies of its government as well as the quality of its administrative machinery (see pp. 24–6).

Subsidised credit

The fact that large farmers are the primary beneficiaries of subsidised loans, is, in our view, the single most important argument for discontinuing subsidies on the credit provided by public institutions and for charging appreciably higher rates of interest on their loans. Bearing in mind the small proportion of credit allocated to small farmers, such a policy would have only a marginal effect on them; it might, in any case, be better to provide small farmers with subsidised inputs rather than cheap credit.[74] Higher rates of interest would, however, have the effect of reducing the waste of national resources, which have been used to enrich large landlords and influential politicians as well as to promote a lop-sided development in agricultural sector.

Mention should also be made of three other popular arguments which are frequently advanced for charging higher rates of interest on institutional loans, although we have some doubts about their theoretical validity and practical importance.[75] *First*, it is argued that higher rates of interest charged by public credit institutions would permit them to raise the interest paid on customers' deposits and that this would somehow stimulate, or 'mobilise', rural savings. This is, however, a dubious proposition, since, as explained earlier, there is no evidence to suggest that savings propensities are closely and positively correlated to interest rates (see p. 46). The only important effects of raising the rate of interest paid to depositors would be a transfer of funds from other banks and from cash hoards into agricultural banks as well as a rise in the element of 'rent' in the income accruing to depositors, the bulk of which is likely to go to the richer classes of the community.

A *second* argument advanced against subsidised credit is that agricultural borrowers should be charged the full opportunity cost of credit, as indicated by market rates of interest, in order to avoid a 'misallocation' of resources. As explained earlier, however, the assumption that market prices provide a satisfactory criterion for the

---

74. See World Bank, *Agricultural Credit*, p. 49.
75. For references to these arguments see: FAO, *Monthly Bulletin*, December 1973, p. 10; October/November 1974, p. 15, and June 1975, p. 8; Adams, *American Journal of Agricultural Economics*, May 1971, pp. 168–9; World Bank, *Agricultural Credit*, pp. 12–13 and 47–50; and Donald, *Credit for Small Farmers*, pp. 81–2 and 103–6.

allocation of investment resources in LDCs is of doubtful validity (see pp. 11–20). It is not the credit subsidies as such, but the pattern of allocation of the subsidised loans, that has been the cause of the misallocation of resources in this case.

Finally, it is claimed that low rates of interest have the effect of reducing the revenue and hence the resources available to credit institutions. The effect of this, combined with that of price inflation and debt delinquencies, has been to erode the resources, or the real value of the loan portfolio, of credit institutions. This is no doubt true, but there seems to be no logical reason for expecting public credit institutions to be self-financing as long as their resources are used effectively to promote agricultural development. In terms of the administration of agricultural subsidies, however, it may as noted above, be more efficient to subsidise the inputs required for the introduction of modern technology by small farmers rather than credit.

Land Reform: Experience has shown that the obstacles presented by socio-political factors to the development of the agricultural sector in general and to the implementation of a rational agricultural credit policy in particular cannot entirely be removed by mere procedural and administrative changes in rural credit institutions. To resolve difficulties of this type, it is essential, in the first instance, to introduce fundamental changes in the economic and political structure of the countries facing them; land reform constitutes an important in-gredient of such changes. But although land reform is usually a *necessary* condition for bringing about a significant improvement in the performance of the agricultural sector, including that of the rural credit system, it is not a *sufficient* condition. To ensure such improve-ments, it is also necessary to have in power governments that are willing and able to organise a reasonably efficient and reliable administrative machinery for the implementation of their agricultural policies.

The above argument can be illustrated by the experience of Egypt where two attempts (in 1902 and 1931) at channelling institutional credit to small farmers failed to produce a significant result largely because of the constraints imposed on reform policies by the semi-feudal system of land tenure. The government that came into power after the revolution of 1952, was, however, bent on eliminating the political influence of the big landlords, who had formed the power base of the previous régime. It therefore implemented a land reform programme which transformed the semi-feudal land tenure system into one of small- and medium-size farmers (see also pp. 118–19).

At the same time, the authorities created the institutions that came to be known as 'supervised co-operatives', staffed with expert agronomists and administrative personnel. These co-operatives, apart from organising cultivation and providing technical services, were charged with the task of distributing loans in kind and in cash among farmers, and of collecting the cash crops of their members for delivery to an official marketing organisation. The farmers received the proceeds of the sale of their crops less the debts due to co-operatives; in this way the problem of debt defaults was largely resolved. The available data for the decade that followed the initiation of the land reform programme indicate that the share and volume of subsidised credit allocated to small farmers increased significantly as did their production and income.[76]

CONCLUSION

Governments of developing countries can promote economic development, not only by increasing the *volume* of investment resources, but also by directing the flow of such resources to projects which have a high social priority. Apart from determining the allocation of their own investment resources, the authorities are also in a position to exercise a significant influence on the *pattern* of private investment. Fiscal measures, combined with an appropriate investment licensing scheme, provide a powerful instrument for discriminating between essential and inessential investment. This instrument of policy can be reinforced by monetary policies, implemented through industrial and agricultural credit institutions, to promote essential investment.

In practice, few developing countries have adequately exploited the potential of fiscal and monetary instruments for stimulating the flow of resources to high priority projects and for discouraging inessential investment. Outside agriculture, these instruments have been used to promote industrialisation in general, largely through the encouragement of import-substituting activities, without adequate discrimination between different types of industries. Because of this, a relatively high proportion of resources have been devoted to the domestic production of luxury and inessential consumer goods. Countries like Brazil and Mexico, for example, which have recorded relatively fast progress in industrialisation in recent years, have also shown pronounced signs of 'lop-sidedness' in their growth, as indicated by their

76. For details see Eshag and Kamal, *BOUIES*, May 1967, pp. 98–105 and *BOUIES*, May 1968, pp. 85–98.

pattern of investment and of distribution of income. The same was true of Iran under the Shah's régime and is by and large true of many other LDCs with less spectacular growth records.

Economic development has been even more seriously hampered by the failure of developing countries to make adequate use of fiscal and monetary instruments to stimulate agricultural production and to improve the lot of poor peasants. The available evidence suggests that this failure is to be attributed largely to the institutional, or socio-political, factors, notably the land tenure system.

6

INTERNAL AND EXTERNAL EQUILIBRIUM

Fiscal and monetary measures are frequently used in both industrial and developing countries to resolve the problems of internal and external disequilibrium, or imbalance; henceforth the words 'equilibrium' and 'balance' are used indifferently, as are 'disequilibrium' and 'imbalance'. The main purpose of this chapter is to analyse the *efficacy* and *relevance* of these instruments for attaining the objectives in question especially when used in developing countries. We first examine the meaning of and significance for LDCs of internal and external equilibrium. We then analyse the nature of imbalances commonly experienced in LDCs and indicate the main categories of remedial measures available to them. In the light of this analysis, we examine the monetary approach to imbalances, concentrating on the approach of the IMF (the Fund) – a leading advocate of the monetary approach. To give a concrete impression of the scope and method of operation of the Fund, we also present some factual data on its organisation, resources and credit facilities.

THE MEANING AND SIGNIFICANCE OF EQUILIBRIUM

Strictly, the word *equilibrium*, borrowed from the mechanical sciences, describes a condition in which there is no endogenous tendency to change. In Economics, however, the word often carries a normative connotation, signifying a 'satisfactory' or 'desirable' state of affairs. It is in this normative sense that we shall examine the meaning and significance of internal and external equilibrium.

Internal equilibrium

A country can be said to be in a condition of *internal equilibrium* when (a) the volume of its aggregate effective demand is adequate to ensure the full utilisation of its productive capacity,[1] and (b) its general index of domestic prices of goods and services is stable. Conversely, a country should be considered to be in a state of 'internal disequilibrium', if it is experiencing *either* a deficiency in its aggregate effective demand in relation to its productive capacity, *or* price instability, *or* both. The extent, or intensity, of internal disequilibrium should thus be measured by reference to two separate indices: *first*, the ratio of the idle productive capacity, which could be brought into employment through the expansion of effective demand, to total available productive capacity, and *second*, the rate of price inflation. For developed economies, movements in the ratio of unemployed workers to total labour force provide a good indicator of the changes in magnitude of internal disequilibrium caused by a deficiency of aggregate effective demand over short periods of time.[2]

There is an important difference between the two conditions of internal equilibrium mentioned. The first condition is sought as an end in itself, since the more fully productive capacity is utilised, the larger the volume of income, savings and investment is likely to be. The second condition, on the other hand, does not *per se* constitute an economic end. The only justification for setting it as a necessary condition of internal balance is, as will presently be explained, the realisation that an environment of stable prices is more conducive to economic development than one of price inflation. The policies designed to stabilise prices will, however, generally have certain side-effects (positive or negative) on economic development, especially in the way they affect the level of activity and the distribution of income. It is clear, therefore, that these side-effects should be taken into account in assessing the *overall* impact of a price stabilisation policy on the economy.

The primary reason for seeking price stability is that inflation can hinder development in a number of ways, of which the following are in particular worth noting. *First*, as explained earlier (p. 40), price rises, whether generated by the failure of 'voluntary savings' to match investment or by a shortage in the supply of necessities in relation to demand, are likely to lead to a fall in real wages and to a redistribution of income in favour of profits; low paid workers, not protected by strong trade unions, tend to suffer most from inflation. Apart from its negative welfare implications, this type of income redistribution would

1.   In the case of developing countries this condition requires some modification (see pp. 215–16 below).
2.   Strictly, allowance must be made for changes in the volume of transitional and structural unemployment, but these are unlikely to be significant in the short run.

also tend to stimulate investment in the production of luxury goods leading to a 'lopsided' development (see pp. 8–10 and 59–60).

Secondly, inflation often has an adverse effect on the balance of payments on both current and capital accounts and thereby aggravates the foreign exchange constraint on development. A rise in domestic prices of a country in relation to those of its trading partners and competitors encourages imports and discourages exports unless the rates of exchange are varied simultaneously. Inflation also tends to stimulate imports of certain goods, such as precious metals, jewellery and works of art that contribute nothing to development, as a protection against the depreciation of the purchasing power of money. In addition, an outflow of capital may be induced by the expectation of relative inflation, since this provides an incentive to businessmen and other wealth owners to convert at least a proportion of their liquid assets into foreign currencies and into securities denominated in the currencies of countries which enjoy relatively more stable prices.

Thirdly, unless price rises are predictable, they introduce an element of uncertainty into the economy which may seriously impede rational planning of consumption and investment expenditures in both private and public sectors.

Finally, if inflation is allowed to continue unrestrained, there is a risk that it may accelerate and end in the social and economic chaos of hyper-inflation.

External equilibrium

There is no single, unambiguous definition of the term *external equilibrium*. In practice the term is generally used to describe one of three different conditions of the balance of payments of a country. In one version of the definition, external equilibrium signifies equality of receipts and payments on the combined current and long-term capital accounts of the balance of payments. In the other two versions, the flows of 'sustainable', or 'autonomous' (as distinct from 'compensatory') capital are substituted for that of 'long-term' capital in the above definition. According to these definitions, external imbalance would thus indicate a situation in which a deficit or surplus on the current account of the balance of payments was not entirely offset by the flow of one of the three categories of capital mentioned.

There would be no serious objection to any of the three versions of the definition mentioned, if the term 'equilibrium' did not in practice have a normative connotation, signifying a satisfactory situation. The fact that these definitions are generally used in this normative sense can only derive from the traditional neo-classical theory which postulates that *all* types of capital flow prompted by market forces are beneficial to both capital exporting and capital importing countries. This was, however, questioned earlier in this book where it was explained that the development potential of foreign capital varies with its terms and conditions, and that some capital imports may actually hinder rather than promote economic development. It would obviously be misleading to describe developing countries which rely on this type of capital flow for settling their current account deficits as being in equilibrium, in the sense of enjoying conditions favourable to economic development.

It follows from the above that in any assessment of the balance of payments position of a country, one must distinguish between the capital flows with a positive potential for development and those without. The distinction between different types of capital flow is made here solely by reference to their development 'potential', without regard to the important question of the 'utilisation' of this potential by the recipient countries, discussed earlier (pp. 159–62). For the sake of brevity, the capital imports with a positive development potential are designated as *desirable* and those with a negative development potential as *undesirable* capital flows. In addition, since very few developing countries, apart from some OPEC members, record persistent surpluses on current account, our analysis will be confined to situations involving only deficits on this account.

A country can then be said to be in external equilibrium, in the sense of being in a satisfactory state, when it can finance the entire deficit on its current balance of payments account through the importation of 'desirable' foreign capital. To identify the 'desirable' components of external capital, one would, of course, have to examine each component separately along the lines indicated earlier (pp. 145–59). The approach followed in most current economic literature, which implies that *all* 'long-term', 'sustainable', or 'autonomous' capital inflows are 'desirable', no doubt simplifies the problem of classification for statisticians, but it is far from adequate for the evaluation of the external position of LDCs as it affects their long-term development prospects.

There must clearly be a limit to the amount of 'desirable' foreign capital available to a country at any given time. This means that to maintain external balance, the authorities must contain the deficit on current account within the bounds prescribed by the availabiltiy of such capital. The inability of developing countries to do so has often forced the authorities into adopting one or both of the following courses of action detrimental to economic development. In many cases current account deficits have been financed by short- and long-term capital flows, many of which should be classified as 'undesirable' and hence harmful to development. In others, when governments have been unwilling, or more often unable, to procure adequate foreign capital to finance the external deficit, they have had to cut down imports by depressing production, thereby losing potential investment resources.

Apart from *persistent* external imbalances, LDCs, as we shall see, tend to suffer from pronounced short-term *fluctuations* in their export earnings which also hinder development (see pp. 226–7 below). *First*, uncertainty about the balance of payments position in the future renders rational planning of the utilisation of foreign exchange resources very difficult if not impossible. *Secondly*, surpluses earned when export earnings are high generally tend to induce the authorities to liberalise their import policy and to permit the import of certain inessential goods and services previously banned. Relatively high export earnings may also lead to a rise in the rate of investment above the level that is sustainable in terms of the long run capacity to import. On the other hand, deficits incurred when export earnings fall may compel governments to permit the inflow of 'undesirable' capital in the form of excessive short-term borrowing and/or to cut down essential imports.

The extent of economic disruption caused by instability of the balance of payments will vary with the amplitude of fluctuations in foreign exchange earnings in relation to foreign exchange reserves and with the availability of 'desirable' external credits.[3] Recognition of the harmful effects on development of the instability in export earnings of LDCs has prompted the Fund to establish its Compensatory Financing Facility, discussed in Appendix 6A; it has also led to the conclusion of a number of international commodity stabilisation schemes with which we shall not be concerned here.[4]

It was explained earlier that many developing countries suffer from what is known as balance of payments, or foreign exchange, constraint

3. For a detailed discussion of the disruptive effects of the balance of payments instability caused by a fall in export prices see Éprime Eshag, *Quantification of Disruptive Effects of Export Shortfalls*, UNCTAD, document TD/B/C.3/AC.3/23 (11 October 1968).
4. See, for example, UNCTAD documents *TD/Tin. 4/7* (15 May 1970) and *TD/Sugar.9/10* (17 October 1977) for details of the international agreements on tin and sugar, respectively.

to the growth of production (pp. 125–30). It is clear that such countries are not in a position to attain simultaneously external and internal equilibrium as far as full utilisation of productive capacity is concerned. Quite apart from 'structural unemployment' due to deficiency of capital equipment, they also have to endure idle productive capacity in capital and labour to maintain external balance. In such cases the condition for internal equilibrium related to the volume of aggregate effective demand, mentioned above, has to be somewhat modified. It must be construed as meaning the attainment of the highest level of activity that is sustainable in terms of the long-term capacity to import, as indicated by the trend in export earnings and in the inflow of 'desirable' foreign capital.

There is a close interrelation between internal and external balance. *First*, as shown below, in a large number of cases the two types of disequilibrium emerge simultaneously as a result of the operation of the same factors. *Secondly*, there is a causal link between the two types of imbalance, in the sense that the existence of one type often leads in due course to the emergence of the other. On the one hand, countries which experience a relatively faster rate of inflation compared with their trading partners and competitors will, as noted above, tend to experience a deterioration in their external account. On the other hand, external imbalances can lead to inflation when the authorities attempt to correct them through certain frequently applied measures, such as devaluation and import restrictions.

CAUSES OF DISEQUILIBRIUM

The orthodox (monetarist) approach to the question of equilibrium, which dominated economic thinking until the Great Depression of the 1930s, was simple and direct: generally the cause of rising prices and balance of payments deficits was thought to be the pressure of internal demand, in turn attributed to an excessive supply of money. It followed from this diagnosis that to combat inflation and restore external balances it was necessary and sufficient to curb the growth of internal demand through the control of the supply of money. Although, as shown elsewhere in the book (pp. 65–6 and 244–7), this simplistic approach continues to influence the thinking of many banking and financial circles, as well as of some economists and policy makers, it is now generally recognised that the problems of internal and external equilibrium, especially as they relate to developing countries, are much more complex. It will be shown that imbalances can be caused by a large number of factors, many of which have little or no bearing on the state of domestic demand or the supply of money.

We discuss below some of the more important factors which have, in our view, played a key role in engendering inflationary pressures and balance of payments difficulties in LDCs during the post-War years. These factors, although not entirely peculiar to developing countries, tend to play a considerably more important part in generating disequilibrium in these than in industrial countries. At the same time we shall omit some of the causes of imbalances which are more relevant to developed economies. No mention is made, for example, of external imbalances that may be caused by a failure of LDCs to keep in pace with their trading partners in the expansion of economic activity and in technological progress.[5]

In examining the causes and diagnosis of imbalances we have combined what has come to be known as 'structuralist' with the Keynesian income and expenditure approach outlined in Chapter 2. The structuralist approach, which seeks to explain the basic causes of imbalances in LDCs in terms of certain special characteristics of their production and foreign trade, was first given wide prominence in the post-War literature on development by the publications of ECLA.[6] Many of these publications contain detailed analyses of inflationary pressures and the balance of payments difficulties experienced by individual Latin American countries in which a prominent role is assigned to their structure of trade and production.[7] The importance of structural factors in this context has also been given further prominence by the writings of individual Latin American economists as well as by the publications of UNCTAD, established in 1964.[8] Equally significant was the pioneer work of Michal Kalecki in drawing attention to the important role played by structural factors in generating imbalances in both mixed and socialist developing economies during the post-War period, mentioned below.

5. For a short explanation of these and other causes of imbalances in developed countries, see Éprime Eshag, *Present System of Trade and Payments versus Full Employment and Welfare State*, Basil Blackwell, Oxford (1966), pp. 7–12.
6. See, in particular, United Nations, *Economic Survey of Latin America, 1949*, Sales No.: 1951.II.G.1, New York (1951), Part One.
7. See, for example, *Economic Survey of Latin America, 1951–52*, Sales No.: 1953.II.G.3, Part I, Chapter II: the 1954 *Survey*, Sales No.: 1955. II. G.1, Chapter I, pp. 20–38; the 1963 *Survey*, document E/CN. 12/696 (1 July 1964), Vol. I, Chapter II; and *Economic Bulletin for Latin America*, January 1956, Vol. I, No. I, pp. 45–8.
8. See, for example, Celso Furtado, *Development and Under-development*, University of California Press (1964), especially Chapter 5; and Oswaldo Sunkel, 'Inflation in Chile: an Unorthodox Approach', *International Economic Papers*, No. 10 (1960). For a more recent United Nations publication in which the role of structural factors in external equilibrium is illustrated, see Sidney Dell and Roger Lawrence, *The*

The structure of production

Of the many special characteristics of the structure of production in developing countries we discuss the three which, in our view, have rendered them particularly vulnerable to internal and external disequilibrium.

Supply of food

Perhaps the most important and persistent source of imbalances in LDCs has been a slow rate of increase in the supply of food and other wage goods in relation to the growth of domestic income. Because of the preponderant share of food in the consumption outlay of the great majority of the population of developing countries, we confine our analysis almost entirely to the supply of food.

Broadly, what has happened in most countries since the War is that the pressure of population against land, on the one hand, and the growth in employment opportunities in urban areas, on the other, has led to a steady migration of labour from rural to urban areas. The employment of unskilled and skilled labour has grown steadily in urban areas as a result of the expansion of construction and industrial activities as well as of private and public service sectors. This has produced a parallel increase in private incomes and in demand for food and other wage goods which has not always been matched by a proportionate growth in the supply of such goods.[9] The effect has been a persistent pressure of demand against supply leading to a rise in internal prices as well as to a deterioration in the balance of payments due to an increase in the imports of food and other necessities. Among the small numbers of food exporting countries, such as Argentina,

Balance of Payments Adjustment Process in Developing Countries, Pergamon Press (1980). This book, written under the auspices of UNDP and UNCTAD, is based on 13 country studies prepared by expert consultants in which the balance of payments problems encountered and the policies pursued by each of the countries concerned in the 1970s, but especially during 1974–8, are examined in depth. The country studies written in connection with this report are available from the UNCTAD Office, Palais des Nations, Geneva. The report is henceforth referred to as *UNDP/UNCTAD Report*. As indicated by the many references made to it, the data presented in this chapter owe much to the report in question.

9. It has been suggested that, because of low levels of food consumption among the poorer farm families, the migration of members of such families to the cities is likely to result in higher per capita food consumption by those remaining on the farms rather than in a proportionate increase in the shipment of food to the cities; see United Nations, *World Economic Report 1953–54*, Sales no.: 1955. II.C.1, New York (1955), p. 80.

similar developments have led to a fall in the surpluses of food available for export, again leading to balance of payments difficulties.[10]

The pressures on the balance of payments due to the growth in food imports has often resulted in devaluations of currencies, which have further aggravated inflationary conditions by raising the internal prices of imported goods. In many developing countries labour has, through trade union and official governmental actions, succeeded in raising money wage rates to offset, in whole or in part, the effect of price rises on real wages. Such wage rises, even when not entirely matching price rises, have generally exceeded increases in labour productivity and pushed up prices, often setting in motion a wage–price spiral of inflation.

Kalecki was the first prominent economist to draw attention to the importance of increasing the supply of food in line with the growth of wage income to prevent the emergence of internal and external imbalances in the course of economic development.[11] During his employment with the Secretariat of United Nations in the early 1950s, he directed a number of studies which demonstrated that inflationary pressures experienced in the socialist countries of Eastern Europe as well as in some other developing countries since the end of the War, were largely caused by a lack of balance between the growth of industrial and agricultural sectors, the former having expanded appreciably faster than the latter.[12] Particularly instructive as regards non-socialist countries was the detailed study of inflationary pressures in Chile between 1929 and 1953.[13] Although the factual information presented in this study is somewhat out of date, it does throw considerable light on the mechanism of inflationary pressures experienced by many developing countries in Latin America and elsewhere throughout the post-War period; it also gives some indication of the

10. See Éprime Eshag and Rosemary Thorp, 'Economic and Social Consequences of Orthodox Economic Policies in Argentina in the Post-War Years', *BOUIES*, February 1965, pp 5 – 7.

11. It has been seen that the rate of increase in the supply of necessities constitutes the primary constraint on the 'warranted rate of growth' in the development model subsequently published by Kalecki; see pp. 58–9.

12. See, for example, United Nations, *World Economic Report, 1951–52*, Sales no.: 1953. II.C.2. New York (1953), pp. 46–8; *World Economic Report, 1952–53*, Sales no.: 1954.II.C.1, New York (1954), pp. 49–52; and *Measures to Prevent Possible Inflation at High Levels of Economic Activity*, ECOSOC document E/2597 (12 May 1954). See also Sidney Dell 'Kalecki at the United Nations, 1946–54', *BOUIES*, February 1977, pp. 40–3.

13. See United Nations, *World Economic Report, 1953–54*, pp. 78–88.
   Although this study was initiated and partly supervised by Kalecki, it was written by a member of his staff and completed after Kalecki had left the United Nations.

type of data that is usually required for a meaningful analysis of imbalances in LDCs.

To assess the role played by the supply of food in engendering imbalances in individual developing countries, it would be necessary to examine each case in depth along the lines followed for Chile. There are, however, some broad indications that during the post-War period, food production has grown appreciably slower than real incomes and urban employment in most developing countries. This would suggest that supply of food is likely to have been a pervasive source of disequilibrium in many of them.

Table 6.1 shows the United Nations estimates for the annual rates of growth in certain relevant variables during the years 1960-75 for developing countries as a whole. It can be seen that GDP, which closely approximates to real income, rose almost twice as fast as agricultural and food production during this period. A rough indication of the growth in employment and in demand for food in urban areas is provided by the movements in the indices of industrial activity, wholesale and retail trade, construction and government consumption, all of which rose by over 6 per cent per year, compared

Table 6.1:   *Developing countries: annual average growth rates in population and in GDP and its selected components, 1960–75[a]*

(at constant prices, in per cent)	
Population	2.6
Gross domestic product	5.3
Agricultural production	2.8
Food production	2.8
Industrial activity	7.6
Construction	6.6
Wholesale and retail trade	6.1
Government final consumption	6.6

Source: United Nations, *Yearbook of National Accounts Statistics 1976*, Volume II, New York (1977), p. 127; United Nations, *Handbook of International Trade and Development Statistics, Supplement 1977*, Sales No.: E/F. 78. II. D.1, New York (1978) pp. 235 and 242; and FAO, *Monthly Bulletin of Agricultural Economics and Statistics*, January 1971, p. 17.
[a] Growth rates have been calculated from an exponential trend.

with an annual rate of growth of 2.8 per cent in food production. Considering that total population of developing countries rose at a rate of about 2.6 per cent per year, the per capita rate of growth in food production must have amounted to about 0.2 per cent per annum compared with a rate of increase of over 2.5 per cent in per capita GDP. Although income elasticity of demand for food is likely to be less than unity, the wide discrepancy between the two rates does indicate the pressure of demand for food against its supply. The rates of increase in food production vary considerably between countries, but it is interesting to note that in about 40 per cent of some 110 non-socialist developing countries and territories listed by the United Nations, food production actually rose more slowly than population during this period.

Production bottlenecks and sectoral demand pressures

Apart from the shortages in the supply of food, developing countries are likely to encounter other important production bottle-necks. Because of the inadequacy of productive capacity in these countries, discussed in Chapter 1, their structure of production is inevitably patchy and less diversified than that of industrial countries. This, combined with deficient transport and communication facilities, has also the effect of reducing the mobility of resources. Owing to these structural characteristics, developing countries tend to encounter in some sectors, serious bottlenecks in the supply of production inputs, such as skilled labour, raw materials, transport and power, while there is still widespread idle capacity in the rest of the economy. Attempts to bring such capacity into production by stimulating effective demand when some industries are operating at full capacity are likely to lead to price rises in the latter industries and to a growth of imports. These price rises may in time be transmitted to the rest of the economy if they result in a noticeable increase in the cost of living index and stimulate wage rises in excess of productivity growth, and/or if the goods supplied by the bottleneck sectors are widely used as inputs by other industries.

There is thus often a trade-off in LDCs between the rise of employment and production, on the one hand, and the increase in inflationary pressures and in current balance of payments deficits, on the other. The decision as to whether to allow effective demand to grow in such circumstances must depend primarily on the size and pattern of idle productive capacities and on the availability of foreign loans and credits of 'desirable' type to finance the external deficits.

It is clear that the higher the level of aggregate effective demand is allowed to rise, the larger will be the incidence of supply bottlenecks and the greater the number of goods rising in price. Inflationary pressures will gain strength, engulfing most sectors of the economy, and the balance of payments will deteriorate sharply if demand continues to grow when little or no spare productive capacities remain in the economy. In such conditions, the economy may properly be considered to be suffering from *excess aggregate demand* pressures, since the growth in demand leads primarily to a worsening of imbalances rather than to an increase in production.[14] Developed economies which enjoy adequate and more diversified productive capacities, tend to encounter such conditions at or near full employment levels of activity – conditions more commonly observed in war than in peacetime.[15] In LDCs, on the other hand, similar pressures are generally experienced long before all surplus labour is absorbed.

Size of harvests

Internal and external imbalances are quite often caused in developing countries by poor harvests due to such factors as droughts, pests, floods etc. A failure of food crops is likely to result in a rise of food prices and an increase of imports, whereas bad harvests of other agricultural primary products in individual countries, would have an adverse effect on their export earnings.[16] Compared with industrial countries, LDCs are more vulnerable to the vagaries of weather, lacking adequate agricultural infrastructure, such as flood control, irrigation and drainage schemes. Moreover, because agricultural production constitutes a larger share of total production in LDCs and accounts for a greater share of their export earnings, the economic disruption caused by bad harvests tends to be appreciably more serious for them.

The structure of foreign trade

Throughout the post-War period both the commodity composition and direction of foreign trade of non-oil exporting developing

14. Such conditions are at times designated as 'aggregate demand inflation'; see p. 39.
15. *Ibid.* See also p. 232 below.
16. It is, however, worth noting that, owing to the inelastic demand for primary products, poor harvests which significantly reduce the world supply of primary products, tend to be beneficial to developing countries as a group, individual countries whose production has suffered less benefiting more.

countries have contributed to the weakness and instability of their balance of payments. Until 1973 this was true of the oil-exporting developing countries also, but the success of OPEC in achieving a significant improvement in the terms of trade of oil since that year has transformed their position. Many OPEC members have since 1973 enjoyed substantial structural surpluses in their external account and, because of this, they are excluded from the discussion that follows.[17]

In summary, over 60 per cent of the imports of non-OPEC LDCs in 1978 consisted of manufactured goods, 80 per cent of which were bought from industrial countries.[18] On the export side, the great majority of these countries continue to depend heavily on the sale of primary products and many, like Ghana, Sri Lanka and Zambia, only on one or two such products. During the years 1978 and 1979, on average about two-thirds of their total exports were sold to developed countries, intra-trade accounting for about 20 per cent, and OPEC members and socialist countries for 6 per cent each.[19]

Regarding the commodity composition of exports, Table 6.2 gives a rough indication of the relative weight of manufactures and primary products in the exports of some 125 non-OPEC developing countries and territories. It can be seen that, in aggregate, manufactures accounted for 38 per cent of total exports of these countries in 1978, compared with 24 per cent in 1970. These aggregative percentages are, however, strongly influenced by the trade of four relatively small countries—Hong Kong, Singapore, South Korea and Taiwan, shown in the table, which together account for only about 2 per cent of the population of LDCs. The share of these countries in total export of manufactures, which amounted to 45 per cent in 1970, rose to about 60 per cent in 1978, by which date manufactures accounted for almost 80 per cent of their exports. This is despite the relatively low ratio of manufactures to total exports in Singapore, explained largely by its position as an entrepôt for primary products.

Excluding the above four countries, the share of manufactures in

17. For 1979, exports (FOB) of OPEC members are estimated at over \$200 billion and their imports (CIF) at less than \$100 billion; the value of exports (FOB) of all the other developing countries taken together was somewhat less than that of OPEC.
18. See United Nations, *1979 Yearbook of International Trade Statistics*, Vol. 1, New York (1980), Special Table B.
    'Manufactures' are defined as goods belonging to Sections 5 to 8, excluding subsection 68 (non-ferrous metals), of SITC, Revised. For details of the coverage, see United Nations, *Standard International Trade Classification, Revised*, Statistical Papers, Series M, No. 34, New York (1961).
19. United Nations, *1979 Yearbook, op. cit.*, and direct information from the Statistical Office of the United Nations.

Table 6.2: *Non-OPEC developing countries:[a] share of manufactures[b] in total exports, 1970 and 1978 (in $ million, FOB)*

	1970			1978		
	Total exports	Manufac- tures[b]	Manufac- tures as per cent of total	Total exports	Manufac- tures[b]	Manufac- tures as per cent of total
I *All countries*[c]	36,828	8,835	24	153,296	58,983	38
II *Selected countries*	5,849	4,093	70	44,154	34,880	79
1. Hong Kong[d]	2,037	1,949	96	8,684	8,344	96
2. Singapore[e]	1,554	427	27	10,134	4,534	45
3. South Korea	830	635	77	12,654	11,165	88
4. Taiwan	1,428	1,082	76	12,682	10,837	85
III (I *less* II)	30,979	4,742	15	109,142	24,103	22
IV *Other selected countries*	7,730	2,040	26	31,393	11,176	36
1. Argentina	1,773	246	14	6,394	1,672	26
2. Brazil	2,739	362	13	12,659	4,212	33
3. India	2,013	1,040	52	6,167	3,713	60
4. Mexico[f]	1,205	392	33	6,173	1,579	26
V *Remaining countries* (III *less* IV)	23,249	2,702	12	77,749	12,927	17

Source: United Nations, *Yearbook of International Trade Statistics*, 1975 and 1979, and direct information from the Statistical Office of the United Nations.

[a] Excludes centrally-planned countries.

[b] Manufactures are defined as goods belonging to Sections 5 to 8, excluding sub-section 68 (non-ferrous metals) of the SITC, Revised.

[c] Excludes re-exports from Hong Kong, estimated in total at $477 million in 1970 and $2,815 million in 1978.

[d] Excludes re-exports.

[e] Includes re-exports.

[f] Excludes exports of the customs bonded factories.

total exports of the rest of developing countries covered by the table would amount, on average, to no more than 22 per cent in 1978, as compared with 15 per cent in 1970. However, even these figures owe much to the significant progress in promoting export of manufactures made by a small number of countries, of which the four more important–Argentina, Brazil, India and Mexico–are listed in the table. The ratio of manufactures to total exports of these countries, taken together, rose from 26 to 36 per cent between 1970 and 1978, despite a fall in the share of manufactures in total exports of Mexico due entirely to the development of its oil industry and a steep growth in the export of crude petroleum during this period. As shown in the table, for the remaining countries and territories, which account for about one-half of the population as well as the exports of non-OPEC developing countries, the ratio of manufactures to total exports amounted to only 17 per cent in 1978 as compared with 12 per cent in 1970.

It is clear from the above data that, although developing countries have made some progress in reducing their dependence on the export of primary products, the great majority of them, including some of the so-called 'newly industrialising countries', like Argentina, Brazil and Mexico, continue to derive the bulk of their foreign exchange earnings from the sale of such products.[20]

The foregoing structure of trade of developing countries has tended to act as a source of disequilibrium in two important ways. *First*, the available data suggest that, during most of the post-War period, the ratio of prices of primary products, other than oil, to manufactures has followed a declining trend, resulting in a deterioration of the terms of trade of many LDCs.[21] The steep rise in the price of petroleum since 1973 has further contributed to the deterioration of the terms of trade of oil-importing developing countries. The loss of income due to this deterioration of the terms of trade has been a persistent source of weakness in the external position of most of these countries.

Several factors, all beyond the control of LDCs themselves, have been responsible for the decline in the ratio of primary product prices to those of manufactures, causing a deterioration in their terms of trade; the following three factors in particular are worth noting.

1. Owing to differences in market characteristics between manufactures and primary products, productivity increases in manufacturing

20. For a list of the countries classified as 'newly industrialising' by OECD, see p. 170, fn. 95.
21. See United Nations, *Statistical yearbook 1966*, New York (1967), Table 14; and *Handbook of International Trade and Development Statistics*, pp. 40 and 42.

industries usually result in higher wages and profits rather than in a fall in prices, as they tend to do in the case of primary products.

2. Export prices of primary products from LDCs have been adversely affected by a slow growth in foreign demand, due largely to: (a) the relatively low income elasticity of demand for some food crops, such as sugar, coffee and cocoa; (b) development of synthetic substitutes in developed countries for certain industrial raw materials, such as rubber and textile fibres, and (c) protection of domestic agriculture by industrial countries (see pp. 195–6).

3. Inflationary pressures in industrial countries have resulted in parallel rises in export prices of manufactures, whereas inflation in LDCs has had little effect on the world price of many primary products. The reason for this is that the international prices of those primary products for which there are no close substitutes in industrial countries are determined by the world supply of and demand for them rather than by their domestic prices. The least favourable position for developing countries is the one in which their industrial trading partners are experiencing simultaneously a cost-push inflation and economic recession, as they have periodically done since 1973. In such conditions, apart from facing increases in import prices, LDCs have also to suffer from a stagnation or fall in demand for their exports.

The *second* source of instability ensues from the fact that the bulk of exports of LDCs are, as noted above, sold to industrial countries. Because of this, economic booms and recessions in the latter countries tend to be translated into fluctuations in export earnings of LDCs. Moreover, owing to low price elasticities of demand for and supply of primary products, relatively small declines in the level of activity and in demand for primary products in industrial countries, have the effect of generating large falls in export prices and in foreign exchange earnings of developing countries, causing balance of payments difficulties. This can present a particularly serious problem for countries which rely heavily on the export of one or two primary products.

As far as the effect of fluctuations in export prices on internal balance is concerned, both a fall and a rise in export prices could in theory generate inflationary pressures in LDCs. On the one hand, a fall in export prices generally results in a balance of payments deficit, and this is often followed by such measures as import restrictions and devaluation, which push up internal prices. On the other hand, a rise in export prices will raise domestic income and expenditure which, if very pronounced, may not be matched by a parallel increase in the supply of goods and may thus have a similar effect on prices. The growth in the supply of goods may be hampered partly by a lack of adequate internal productive capacity and partly by the time-lag between the new import orders and the arrival of imports in the market.[22] In practice, however, these inflationary pressures have been much more rare than those caused by a fall in export prices.

In summary, most developing countries can be said to suffer in varying degrees from the chronic conditions of disequilibrium in normal circumstances because of the operation of one or more of the three structural factors mentioned – the slow growth in the production of food and other wage goods in relation to national income, production bottlenecks and the downward trend in their terms of trade. These factors tend to exercise a persistent and unremitting pressure in generating inflation and balance of payments deficits; for many developing countries this pressure is at present reinforced by the relatively large debt service charges in respect of the capital imported in the past (see Appendix 4B). The steady pressure towards the emergence of imbalances is from time to time mitigated, or wholly neutralised, by some favourable occurrence, such as an exceptionally good harvest, a significant short-term improvement in the terms of trade and a substantial inflow of foreign capital. On the other hand, the conditions of chronic disequilibrium are also periodically aggravated by the advent of adverse phenomena, such as unusually poor harvests and steep falls in the world prices of primary products, leading to balance of payments difficulties and to an acceleration in the rate of inflation.

DIAGNOSIS OF IMBALANCES

It is not always easy to identify all the factors responsible for generating imbalances and, where more than one factor is involved, it is even more difficult to impute to each an exact weight indicating its contribution to such imbalances. This is particularly true of LDCs for which the data are less reliable than for industrial countries. It is,

22. This time-lag, which in the normal course of trade extends over several months for most countries, may be lengthened considerably if the countries experience a steep and sudden rise in export earnings followed by a large increase in import orders. Apart from the delays caused by any inelasticities of supply in exporting countries, the distribution of goods within the importing countries may also be delayed by bottlenecks in their port and transport facilities. A recent example of this is provided by some members of OPEC, notably Iran, which experienced a steep and substantial growth in export earnings after December 1973; see, for example, INMIDEL, *Annual Report*, 1974/75, pp. 23–4.

nevertheless, possible even in the case of most developing countries to identify the principal causes of an imbalance by examining the quantitative and qualitative information available. Such a diagnosis should clearly form an integral part of the policy-making process in dealing rationally with internal and external imbalances.

We do not propose to give here a detailed prescription for the diagnosis of imbalances. The exact diagnostic procedure followed would, in any case, vary between countries, depending partly on the structure of their economies and partly on the availability of data. Our purpose is merely to provide a rough sketch of a rational approach to a policy-oriented diagnosis and to indicate the type of information that will generally be required for the purpose; the suggested approach is essentially Keynesian in nature.

Before embarking on the actual task of the diagnosis of an imbalance, it is essential to 'get a feel' for the country's economy by studying its recent political and economic developments, the structure of its trade and production, as well as its political and economic institutions, including its land tenure and its labour and business organisations. It is particularly important to ascertain the long-term trends in the production of and demand for necessities, notably food, and to identify important production bottlenecks existing in the economy. This background information should enable the analyst to form some impression of the degree of the stability of the economy i.e. its vulnerability to disturbances caused by short-term changes in supply and demand conditions.

Analysis of demand conditions

The analysis of 'demand conditions', namely the level of and changes in demand, immediately before and during the emergence of imbalances plays, as we shall see, a key role in a policy-oriented diagnosis. Apart from explaining the level and movements of economic activity, such an analysis can also clarify the role, if any, played by the growth of demand in generating inflationary pressures and external imbalances.

It is important to emphasise at the outset that the analysis of demand conditions, to be meaningful, must be conducted in terms of 'effective', or 'real', demand rather than in terms of 'nominal' demand, or of the 'supply of money'. Effective demand can be defined as 'scheduled', 'intended', or 'desired', expenditure *at constant prices*. The behaviour of effective demand has thus a direct bearing on production and prices at sectoral and aggregate level, analogous to those produced by a 'shift' in demand for a single commodity on its supply and price. It follows from this that a 'deficiency' in 'aggregate effective demand' should be measured in terms of the size of idle productive capacity and an 'excess' in terms of the prevalence and significance of production bottlenecks.

Movements in the so-called 'nominal' demand, which stands for expenditure *at current market prices*, on the other hand, vary partly with price changes, which, as we shall see, may at times take place for reasons unrelated to changes in 'real' demand and production. Because of this, the behaviour of 'nominal' demand is bound to be a rather unreliable indicator of changes in production and in the pressure of demand against productive capacity. As explained earlier, equally unreliable as an instrument of analysis for this purpose is the change in the 'supply of money' (see pp. 42–50).

The analysis of demand conditions should, wherever possible, be conducted through the Keynesian model of income determination discussed in Chapter 2. It would, as a rule, be best to start by examining the volume of what were termed 'injections', whether 'gross' or 'net', in the income equations, since movements in aggregate effective demand are usually *initiated* by changes in the volume of these variables; the term 'volume' is henceforth used to indicate values 'at constant prices'.

Taking, for example, the more familiar version of income equation (p. 38, equation 14a)

$$Y = \frac{G + I_p + X - a_1 - a_2 - a_3}{s_p + t + m}$$

the behaviour of private investment (I_p) can largely be explained by reference to the availability of spare equipment capacity, business attitude and expectations, and government fiscal and monetary policies. Fiscal policies also determine (directly) the volume of government investment and consumption outlays (G). Changes in the volume of exports (X) can be explained in terms of such factors as foreign demand, the size of harvest of agricultural exports as well as the elasticity of supply and competitiveness of non-agricultural exports. The analysis of the behaviour of the three injections, which represent the principal exogenous variables, should provide an explanation of the movements in the aggregate effective demand.

Although, in the short run, changes in the size of the multiplier, $1/(s_p + t + m)$, are unlikely to be very significant, we mention some of the more important factors that are likely to influence the three variables determining its magnitude. An examination of the taxation system and policies and of the distribution of income within the private sector, should throw some light on any changes in the marginal rate of taxation (t). The same factors, taken in conjunction with changes in consumer expectations concerning their future income and future consumer prices, should also help in the explanation of changes in the marginal propensity to save in the private sector (s_p). The more important factors to be considered in the examination of the behaviour of the marginal propensity to import (m) include changes in the pattern of production and of domestic expenditure, in the scope and severity of production bottlenecks and in the government import restriction measures e.g. tariffs, quotas, etc.

As far as the availability of data is concerned, one can make a meaningful analysis of changes in demand conditions along the above lines for almost all industrial and most developing countries. Many developing countries have detailed sectoral information on the pattern of production and employment, as well as estimates of GNP by industrial origin and by major categories of expenditure at constant prices; such information is adequate for a reasonably reliable analysis of the behaviour of demand at sectoral and aggregative levels.

But even for the countries which lack reliable national accounts and related data it is usually possible to collect sufficient information, quantitative and qualitative, to identify the major factors responsible for changes in the aggregate effective demand as well as to make a rough estimate of the magnitude of such changes. We list below some of the better known *indicators of movements in aggregate effective demand*; the great majority of developing countries will have at least some of them.

Internally, a growth in aggregate effective demand will be accompanied, almost invariably, by an increase in total production, employment, job vacancies and hours worked per week, and by a reduction in idle equipment capacity; a fall in demand will have the opposite effect. The same indicators used at a sectoral level provide information on changes in the pattern of demand and on the availability of spare productive capacity in different industries. For the industries operating at full, or near-full, capacity, an increase of demand will be reflected in a rise of prices and/or a lengthening of suppliers' order books, and a decrease of demand in an increase of idle capacity and a shortening of order books.

Externally,[23] an expansion of aggregate effective demand will be accompanied by a rise in the volume of imports of goods and services; a decline in demand will have the reverse effect. In examining this

23. See also p. 234 below.

indicator, however, it is important to make due allowance for any fortuitous movements in the volume of imports caused by autonomous factors, such as variations in the size of harvests. Unlike imports, the volume of exports need not be affected by movements in demand except when (a) the growth of exports is constrained by the availability of supplies, and (b) domestic expenditure on exportable goods and services is significant. Given foreign demand, when *both* these conditions are satisfied, a rise in effective demand will tend to reduce the volume of exports, and vice versa.

Inflationary pressures

In any analysis concerned with price movements, it is essential to distinguish between agricultural products, on the one hand, and manufactured goods and services, on the other. Prices of agricultural goods are determined by supply and demand conditions in the conventional textbook fashion and are subject to large periodic fluctuations. Because the supply of these goods is highly inelastic in the short run, relatively small changes in demand conditions often result in pronounced movements in their prices. Moreover, the year-to-year supply of agricultural products, especially in LDCs, being partly dependent on climatic conditions, is subject to significant variations, and this may also cause marked changes in their price because of the inelasticity of demand.

Prices of manufactures and services, unlike those of agricultural goods, are largely determined by their unit costs of production.[24] This means that inflationary conditions in these sectors of the economy result from an upward pressure of the unit costs and that a diagnosis of inflation must aim at identifying the factors responsible for such a pressure. We shall first consider briefly the likely effects of movements in demand on unit costs of production and then explain how other important factors, unrelated to demand conditions, could initiate inflation, either by pushing up unit costs of production, or by directly raising market prices.

Experience has shown that, over a large part of the trade cycle, an expansion of aggregate effective demand results primarily in the

24. In the language of elementary textbooks, to ensure the continuity of production, in the *short run* the minimum prices charged by producers must at least cover 'variable costs', such as wages and raw materials, per unit of output; retail prices must in addition cover indirect taxes. In the *long run* prices must be high enough to cover not only unit variable costs and indirect taxes but also unit 'fixed costs' as well as a profit margin (generally known as 'normal' profit) that satisfies the producers.

growth of production rather than in price rises. During the initial phase of recovery from a recession, when there is ample productive capacity to meet the growth of production, total unit costs are more likely to decline rather than increase owing to a fall in unit fixed costs; prices are, however, generally maintained stable, resulting in a rise of profit margins. With the progress of recovery, wage rates will tend to rise faster, the rate of rise varying with the bargaining power and policies of the trade unions. The effect of any increase in unit labour costs on prices will, however, for a time continue to be partially, if not entirely, offset by a fall in unit fixed costs due to the growth of production.

Generally, the upward pressure on prices in the course of economic recovery is likely to remain relatively weak until the idle productive capacities in the form of labour and/or equipment are largely exhausted and production bottlenecks begin to appear.[25] Thereafter, the continued growth of effective demand will be reflected increasingly in price rises and decreasingly in an expansion of production. This is partly because the growing shortages of labour and of idle equipment will tend to accelerate the rise in unit labour costs by pushing up wage awards, by increasing the share of overtime work and, at times, by reducing labour's physical productivity. In addition, as supply becomes more and more inelastic, producers are able to raise their profit margins by charging higher prices without running a serious risk of losing customers. In such conditions, the higher effective demand is allowed to rise, the more widespread the production bottlenecks and the stronger the inflationary pressures become. Price rises so generated by the pressure of demand against productive capacity can properly be designated as *demand-pull inflation*.

Unit costs and prices of manufactures and services may, however, rise for reasons which have no bearing whatsoever on either the level of or changes in effective demand. Moreover, such price rises may at times initiate an inflationary process commonly designated as *cost-push inflation*. It is important to understand the nature of this type of inflation, which has been experienced by many industrial and developing countries throughout most of the 1970s, because, as we shall later see, the policies required to deal with it differ radically from those required to cure a demand-pull inflation.

Prices of manufactures and services may rise because of an increase in the prices of imported inputs, such as raw materials, fuels and

---

25. As explained earlier, in LDCs, such bottlenecks appear at a relatively low level of activity in relation to productive capacity (see pp. 39–40 and 221–2).

equipment, and of imported consumer goods, brought about by a devaluation or by an increase in foreign prices. Similarly, a poor harvest would tend to push up the prices of food and of agricultural raw materials. Finally, an increase in indirect taxes, including tariffs, and a reduction of subsidies, would have the effect of raising prices. For the sake of brevity, these and any other factors not related to demand conditions which may cause price rises, are designated as *non-demand factors*.[26] It is clear that this type of price rise is not in any way related to the conditions of demand and can take place in a boom as well as a recession, and irrespective of whether effective demand is stagnant, growing, or falling.

Price rises caused by 'non-demand factors' would, however, generally have a once for all effect, but for the reaction of labour to them. The attempt of labour to safeguard its standard of living will result in wage claims and settlements which may exceed the growth of labour productivity. Such wage settlements will bring about a rise in unit labour costs and a further increase in prices, often setting in motion a wage-price spiral of inflation.[27]

It is worth noting in connection with this type of inflationary conditions that, *first*, the strength and duration of inflationary pressures will to a large extent depend on the attitude and bargaining power of the labour unions; the more successful is labour in maintaining real wages, the stronger the inflationary pressures. *Secondly*, failure of the unions to maintain real wages, while reducing the rate of inflation, will inevitably exert a contractionary influence in the economy. Thus, unless the authorities take measures to offset this influence, price inflation may be accompanied by a declining effective demand and by falling economic activity – a phenomenon observed in many countries in the course of the 1970s and sometimes called 'stagflation'. *Thirdly*, because of price increases, 'nominal' demand as well as the 'supply of money' may continue to grow despite stagnant or even falling effective demand and growing unemployment.

For monetarists, who regard the pressure of demand as the primary, if not the sole, cause of inflation, the phenomenon of 'stagflation' represents a paradox. But there is nothing paradoxical in it once it is

26. Because wage claims and awards are likely to vary with demand conditions, we do not include increases in unit labour costs among 'the non-demand factors' *initiating* a cost-push inflation.
27. For some reason, this process of inflation is usually designated as 'wage-price', rather than 'price-wage', spiral of inflation. The latter term, however, indicates more accurately the *origin* of a cost-push inflationary spiral of the type discussed here.

recognised that a wage-price spiral of inflation is, as we have seen, entirely compatible with conditions of rising, falling and stagnant effective demand.[28]

It can thus be seen that changes in 'nominal demand' and in the 'supply of money', by themselves, can provide little or no useful information on the causes of inflation. A meaningful diagnosis of inflationary pressures in manufacturing and service sectors must aim at identifying the factors responsible for the upward movement in unit costs. The work would entail a proper analysis of demand conditions, along the lines suggested above, as well as an examination of the behaviour of what are designated as 'non-demand factors'.

External imbalances

A balance of payments disequilibrium may at times result from adverse movements on *capital account*. Capital movements causing significant disturbances in external equilibrium can as a rule be readily detected and explained, and we shall not be concerned with the imbalances caused by them. A deterioration in the *current account* of the balance of payments indicates that the growth in the 'value' of exports has been less than that of imports. This may be the result of a worsening of the terms of trade and/or of a relatively slower increase in the 'volume' of exports as compared with the 'volume' of imports.

It is relatively easy to identify changes in the terms of trade and to estimate the impact of such changes on the balance of payments by examining prices of exports and imports. Changes in the volume of imports and exports, on the other hand, may be caused by a variety of factors, not so easily discernible, of which only some of the more important are listed here. *First*, as noted earlier (p. 230), movements in aggregate effective demand are likely to generate parallel movements in the volume of imports and may, in some conditions, affect exports. *Secondly*, the size of harvests plays an important role in determining the volume of both imports and exports of agricultural goods. *Thirdly*, trade in non-agricultural goods is likely to be influenced by changes in their production costs and in the rates of exchange which together

---

28. The phenomenon of 'stagflation', as observed in Argentina, was explained by the author as early as 1965 under the heading of 'A Model of Inflationary Deflation'. See Eshag and Thorp, *BOUIES*, February 1965, pp. 41–3. This study, which was conducted by the author with the assistance of Mrs Thorp, a colleague at the Institute of Economics and Statistics in Oxford, is available also in Spanish; see *Desarrollo Economico*, Abril-Junio, 1965, Buenos Aires.

determine the competitiveness and profitability of exports and of import-competing industries. *Fourthly*, changes in government measures related to foreign trade, such as tariffs, quotas and export subsidies, will generally have an impact on the volume of imports and exports.

It can be seen that most of the factors affecting the current account have little or no direct bearing on conditions of internal demand. This is particularly true of the terms of trade and the size of harvests, the two factors which play a key role in determining the balance of payments position of developing countries. It is also worth noting that external imbalances brought about by these two factors are in practice bound to have a contractionary impact on real national income and on the aggregate effective demand. This means that, unless governments take measures to offset this contractionary impact, such imbalances are likely to be accompanied by a slackening of economic activity.

It must have become reasonably clear by now that the diagnosis of inflation and of external imbalances is not as simple a task as it is at times supposed to be. The work entails, not only an analysis of demand conditions, which by itself is not an easy exercise, but also an examination of the behaviour of what have been labelled as 'non-demand factors'.

In some cases the diagnosis can produce reasonably clear and simple results. If, for example, imbalances are accompanied by a stagnant or declining demand at a time when the economy is not suffering from any serious production bottlenecks, it can be concluded with reasonable certainty that the imbalances are generated by one or more 'non-demand factors', which one should generally be able to identify without too much difficulty. At the other extreme, if demand is expanding and bottlenecks are widespread, it can safely be assumed that the pressure of demand against productive capacity has played some role in the emergence of imbalances; it should usually be possible to get a rough idea of the significance of this role by evaluating the part, if any, played by 'non-demand factors' in the process.

One should note in conclusion that an inflationary process 'initiated' by the pressure of demand may continue for long after such pressure has ceased to have any influence on prices because of a subsequent slackening of demand. This could happen, for example, if the authorities succeed in depressing demand through such measures as raising indirect taxes and devaluation which, by raising internal prices, set into motion a wage-price spiral of inflation. It is important to emphasise that in order to provide a remedy for this type of inflationary situation, it is the factors that are responsible for the *continuation* of the inflationary process, rather than the historical ones that *initiated* it, that have to be dealt with.

REMEDIES FOR IMBALANCES

In the long run, economic development, as defined in Chapter 1, constitutes the only remedy for reducing the relatively greater vulnerability of LDCs to internal and external imbalances. We need not dwell on this subject here since we have already examined (in Chapters 3–5) the ways in which fiscal and monetary policies can be used to promote development by enlarging and diversifying the productive capacity of developing countries. Here we shall be concerned exclusively with *short-term policy measures* required to deal with the imbalances that will inevitably be encountered in the course of the lengthy process of development. Quite apart from the adverse effects on equilibrium of certain mistaken policies that may be followed by developing countries themselves, such factors as poor harvests and sudden and pronounced deterioration in the terms of trade, which are almost entirely beyond their own control, are likely to result in periodic recurrence of imbalances.

Apart from exchange rate devaluation, discussed later (pp. 263–6), the short-term policy measures available to developing countries for dealing with the problems of imbalances can be divided into three broad groups: direct controls and selective measures; deflationary measures; and external borrowing. In examining these measures, it is necessary to bear constantly in mind the fact noted earlier (pp. 212–15) that the objectives of price stability and the balance of payments equilibrium are not sought as ends in themselves; the only reason for seeking them is to avoid the harmful effects on development that generally result from conditions of disequilibrium.

Since all measures taken to deal with imbalances are likely to have some side-effects on development, the usefulness, or admissibility, of such measures has to be judged by reference to two distinct criteria, namely, their *efficacy* in resolving the problems of imbalance and their *side-effects* on economic development. Some remedial measures may thus be rejected simply on the ground of their lack of efficacy, and others, although efficacious, may prove to be equally unacceptable because the adverse effects on development produced by them exceed those borne under conditions of disequilibrium. The question to be answered then is, 'how should LDCs deal with the various types of imbalances in the short run without seriously damaging their long-term development prospects?' It is clear that, because of the differences in institutional and other conditions between developing countries, measures that are found suitable for dealing with certain categories of imbalance in some of them may prove to be unsuitable to others.

Direct controls and selective measures:[29]

Most developing countries are in a position to ease, if not completely resolve, their problems of imbalances through direct controls and selective measures without hindering the progress of their economic development. Because of this, unless imbalances are generated by 'excess aggregate demand' (see p. 222), LDCs should generally resort, in the first instance, to these measures rather than to deflationary policies and foreign loans. We consider below some of the more important selective instruments of policy available for the purpose.

One of the *first* steps to be taken by countries facing external disequilibrium is a careful examination of the commodity composition of their imports with a view to tightening restrictions on, and even banning, the importation of all luxury and semi-luxury consumer goods as well as reducing certain non-essential government imports, such as armaments. Despite the various restrictions (high tariffs and quotas) imposed by most developing countries on the entry of non-essential consumer goods, the purchase of such goods continues to account for a significant proportion of imports in many of them. The emergence of a balance of payments deficit offers these countries the opportunity of tightening their import restrictions and of reducing useless government outlays. Additional relief to the balance of payments can be provided by discouraging the importation of capital goods and other inputs used in the production of luxury goods by domestic industries.

The instrument of import restriction was used by a number of developing countries which faced serious balance of payments difficulties following the steep rise in oil prices at the end of 1973. Of the 13 countries covered by the United Nations report mentioned earlier, the majority imposed or strengthened direct controls on imports. Brazil, for example, prohibited imports of some 300 items considered as 'superfluous', doubled tariff rates on about 1,200 items and raised the rates on 800 other items by 30 per cent. In India quantitative controls were made more restrictive and, except in certain priority industries,

29. The use that can be made of some of these measures to influence the pattern of investment was examined in Chapter 5 (see pp. 180–4).

import licences for industry were cut drastically. The Zambian Government withdrew all outstanding import licences for examination and selective revalidation.[30] The available evidence indicates that these measures had a swift effect in easing the balance of payments pressures experienced by the countries in question.

Secondly, balance of payments pressures can be relieved by selective instruments of policy aimed at promoting and diversifying exports, although these are likely to take longer than import restrictions to produce results. The ability of developing countries to increase export earnings through such measures varies with their potential for expanding non-traditional exports, notably manufactured and semi-manufactured goods, a potential which is likely to be greater among the semi-industrialised countries.

The United Nations report contains illustrations of the selective measures employed to promote exports by a number of countries included in the sample. In India, for example, these measures included cash subsidies, duty drawbacks, various tax reliefs and the linking of import licences to exports. Sri Lanka used a combination of measures to promote exports of gems and industrial goods which included a scheme permitting exporters to retain a certain proportion of their foreign exchange earnings in convertible rupee accounts. Selective fiscal and monetary measures to promote exports were employed also by Brazil, Jamaica, the Philippines and Uruguay.[31]

The *third* category of selective measures can be used to ease both inflationary pressures and balance of payments difficulties; it includes such measures as consumer subsidies, rationing and investment licensing, discussed earlier (p. 181). Rationing of food, combined with price controls, can in principle be used to reduce the hardships caused by a fall in the supply of food, due for example to poor harvests, as well as to ease inflationary pressures. In addition, subsidies of essential consumer goods, combined where necessary with rationing, would tend to weaken the wage-price spiral of inflation. Similarly, rationing and licensing systems can be used as a means of saving foreign exchange and of easing production bottlenecks through the reduction of luxury consumption and of inessential investment. For example, a scheme of petrol rationing that produces a significant reduction in pleasure motoring would result in savings of foreign exchange, while the licensing of new buildings which prohibits, or at least curtails, the

---

30. For further details, see *UNDP/UNCTAD Report*, pp. 50–1.
31. For further details, see *ibid.*, pp. 33–8. Brazil had, since 1965, relied heavily on selective measures to promote its non-traditional exports. For details of these measures see E.L. Bacha's study of Brazil, prepared for the above-mentioned *UNDP/UNCTAD Report*.

construction of luxury housing would ease the pressure of demand for construction materials. But although these instruments of policy can play an important part in moderating the gravity of internal and external imbalances, they are rarely employed by developing countries. The well-known difficulty of administering such schemes efficiently in LDCs only partly explains this attitude. As explained earlier, no less important a reason in many countries is the unwillingness of the authorities to interfere with the pattern of expenditure of the richer groups of the community in the interest of promoting development (see p. 181).

Industrial countries have a considerably wider scope than LDCs for using non-deflationary selective measures to deal with imbalances. This is partly because they have a more competent and reliable administrative machinery at their disposal and can implement such measures as subsidies, investment licensing and rationing more efficiently. Moreover, owing to their more diversified economies, it is easier for them to make the appropriate adjustments in the structure of production necessitated by changes in supply and demand conditions. Despite this, there has been a growing tendency on the part of many industrial countries since the mid-1960s to resort to deflationary policies.[32] We have suggested that, as in the case of LDCs, the *real* explanation for this development is political in nature, reflecting a shift in economic and political priorities from full employment to the promotion of the market mechanism (see pp. 52–3).

There can obviously be no assurance that selective measures such as those outlined above would always succeed in completely resolving the problem of *external equilibrium*. Countries that are unable to resolve this problem through these instruments of policy are compelled either to adopt deflationary measures to reduce the external deficit through a contraction of imports, or to resort to short-term external loans and credits to finance the deficit, or to do both. As we shall presently explain, however, no country is in any way 'compelled' to deal with a *cost-push inflation* through deflationary policies.

Global deflationary measures[33]

Briefly, restrictive, or deflationary, fiscal measures are aimed at limiting the government's budget deficit and borrowing requirement

32. The outstanding examples are the two Labour governments in the UK that came into power in 1964 and 1975, the Conservative government that succeeded the latter Labour government in 1979 and the US Administration that took office in January 1981. See also p. 241 below.
33. The term 'global', used in conjunction with policy measures, signifies 'non-selective', or 'non-discriminatory', measures.

by increasing direct and indirect tax rates and by cutting government outlays. Restrictive monetary measures are designed to control the supply of money through various means which limit commercial banks' advances to the private sector and raise market rates of interest; these measures include increasing commercial banks' reserve requirements, restricting the central bank's rediscounting facilities and setting a ceiling on its advances to government. As mentioned earlier, fiscal and monetary policies are closely interrelated, since the former have a direct bearing on the supply of money and on interest rates (see p. 28).

Judged by reference to the two criteria, namely the 'efficacy' and 'side-effects' of remedial measures, mentioned earlier, global deflationary policies, by depressing economic activity, are likely to curb imports and thereby contribute to an improvement in external balance. However, since the bulk of exports of most developing countries consists of primary products of which only a small fraction is internally consumed, a fall in domestic demand is unlikely to have a noticeable effect on export receipts. Deflationary measures are also likely to decelerate the rate of inflation by moderating wage claims and reducing the pressure of demand against productive capacity in bottleneck sectors.

From the point of view of the second criterion, namely the 'side-effects' of remedial policies, it is clear that global deflationary measures are highly suitable for dealing with the imbalances experienced under conditions designated earlier as 'excess aggregate demand' pressures (see p. 222 above). In such conditions, they would have the effect of reducing the upward pressure on prices and of improving the balance of payments position without significantly affecting domestic production. In the absence of such demand pressures, however, these measures are bound to result in a slackening of economic activity and a fall in domestic savings and investment.

Because access to foreign credits is often made conditional on the adoption of deflationary policies, as in the case of some IMF credits discussed later (pp. 257–9 and 273–4), countries may be compelled to adopt such policies to deal with their *external imbalances*, even when it is known that they will have damaging side-effects on production and employment. This is often the case with the poorer developing countries which have limited access to foreign credit.

There is, however, no need for a country to resort to a policy of deflation to deal with a *cost-push inflation*, notably a wage-price spiral of inflation. It is somewhat irrational to attempt to stabilise prices by depressing the level of production since, as noted earlier (pp. 212–13), price stability is not an end in itself, but a means to the promotion of production. A deflationary policy can be particularly damaging to countries which have well organised labour unions with strong bargaining power, where the authorities have to induce a deep and prolonged recession before achieving a significant moderation in wage claims and in the rate of inflation. Despite this, some major industrial countries have in recent years opted for strong deflationary measures. Monetarism and its companion doctrine of 'sound finance', which dominated economic thinking until the appearance of the *General Theory*,[34] have been revived and used to justify the economic and social hardships inflicted on the community through such policies. Apart from their adverse economic and social effects at home, monetarist policies in industrial countries have, as we have seen, created serious difficulties for developing countries by slowing down the growth of their exports as well as the inflow of official development assistance (see pp. 135, 140-2 and 165-6).

A more rational way of dealing with a wage-price spiral of inflation in both industrial and developing countries would be to adopt some form of incomes policy under which the unions would agree to moderate their wage claims in exchange for commitments on the part of the government to higher levels of employment and welfare benefits. The policy could also provide for the stabilisation of the prices of essential consumer goods through subsidies, and might at times entail rationing of such goods. It is clear, however, that an incomes policy of this nature is incompatible with the rigid budgetary and monetary targets prescribed by monetarists.[35]

Foreign loans

There are two main sources of foreign short-term finance available to developing countries – private and official. Private finance generally

---

34. It is, therefore, somewhat surprising to see the *laissez-faire* and 'sound finance' policies followed in the UK and the US since early 1979 and 1981, respectively, being at times described in the press as 'a gamble with *untried* policies'. These policies were closely followed throughout the nineteenth and early twentieth centuries when they produced periodic trade cycles, punctuated by major financial crises, finally ending in the Great Depression of the 1930s. Had they been a success, there would have been no Great Depression, no *General Theory* and probably no fascism and no World War II. One can only hope that this time history will not repeat itself in full.

35. A good illustration of this is provided by the breakdown in 1979 of the so-called 'social contract' between the Labour government and the unions in the UK due largely to the government's adherence to certain monetary and fiscal targets which prevented it from fulfilling its commitment to reduce unemployment.

takes the form of suppliers' credit granted by exporters to their customers, of loans from foreign banking and other financial institutions and of funds raised through the issue of bonds abroad. The principal source of short-term official finance is the IMF, which provides to its members a variety of credit facilities reviewed later. The relative importance of the two sources of credit in financing the balance of payments deficits of developing countries varies considerably from year to year and from country to country. As shown earlier, however, LDCs, as a group, have relied much more heavily on private than on the IMF credits for financing external deficits. (See Table 4.1).

The amount of short-term foreign private finance available to a developing country at any time depends largely on its credit rating, and because of this, the relatively poorer and less developed countries are likely to have a more limited access to such finance. A further important consideration is the domestic policies followed by the deficit countries. Generally, countries which adopt deflationary policies under the IMF 'stand-by arrangements', described below, tend to encourage the inflow of private capital from abroad.[36]

Compared with the IMF credits, private loans almost invariably carry higher interest charges and are often of shorter duration. Despite this fact, many developing countries with access to foreign capital markets, being unwilling to submit to the conditions imposed by the Fund, have at times preferred to borrow from private foreign sources rather than utilise the Fund's facilities, thereby undertaking a heavier debt service burden. This explains the relatively small use made of the Fund's 'conditional credit' facilities, described later (p. 257), during the balance of payments difficulties of 1974-9.[37] The pronounced increase in applications for this type of credit in 1980-1 does not signify a change of attitude on the part of developing countries. It is largely due to growing difficulties of obtaining credit from private capital markets and to the reluctance of some developing countries to increase their debt service ratios beyond the levels reached in 1979.

The policies chosen by different developing countries to deal with the balance of payments difficulties have in practice varied with their

---

36. See IMF, *Compensatory Financing of Export Fluctuation, A Second Report by the International Monetary Fund*, Washington, DC (1966), p. 38; and UNCTAD, *International Monetary Issues: Problems of Reform*, UNCTAD IV, document TD/189 (May 1976), p. 20.

37. See *IMF Survey* (5 June 1978), pp. 161-5, and IMF, *International Financial Statistics*, Yearbook 1981.

political outlook and economic circumstances. The United Nations report mentioned earlier suggests that three factors played a significant role in determining the policies adopted by developing countries during the period 1974–8. These were: the economic philosophy of the governments; the capacity to relieve the balance of payments pressure through selective measures and controls, such as those mentioned above; and access to international capital markets.[38] For example, the governments that came into power in Uruguay in 1974 and in Sri Lanka in 1977, attached high priority to a market-oriented economy and to reducing the scope of government involvement in the economy, and opted for deflationary policies rather than the tightening of direct controls.[39] In Brazil, on the other hand, the authorities expressly rejected a deflationary policy and instead resorted to selective measures and controls and to private foreign credits to deal with the balance of payments difficulties,[40] even though the growth in external debt has burdened the country with unusually heavy service charges mentioned earlier (p. 171). Other countries, like Jamaica and Tanzania, also resisted the application of global deflationary policies, but encountered severe limitations on their freedom of action because of inadequate access to external finance.[41] Generally, it is the less developed and poorer countries, which have a limited capacity for improving the balance of payments through selective measures as well as a low credit rating, that find themselves under greater pressure to resort to deflationary measures.

THE IMF MONETARY APPROACH TO THE BALANCE OF PAYMENTS

The approach to the problem of imbalances outlined above differs fundamentally from that followed by monetarists which, as noted earlier (pp. 51–3), has gained widespread popularity in recent years both in academic circles and among policy makers. We have already analysed the monetarist explanation of the problems of internal equilibrium (see Appendix 2A) and will, therefore, confine the present

---

38. See *UNDP/UNCTAD Report*, pp. 25–8.
   The availability of foreign exchange reserves does not appear to have played an important role in explaining the differences in policies adopted by the various countries. Generally, few non-oil exporting countries have adequate reserves to sustain a severe or prolonged pressure on their external balance such as that experienced in 1974.
39. *Ibid.*, pp. 27–8.
40. *Ibid.*, pp. 25, 45 and 66.
41. *Ibid.*, p. 67.

discussion to their approach to the balance of payments. We shall, furthermore, concentrate on the IMF version of the monetary approach which, as we shall see, differs in some important respects from that adopted by some members of the Chicago school.[42] The reason for this is that the Fund exercises significant influence on the economic policies of many of its members which from time to time draw on its resources.

The basic propositions of monetarism

The term 'monetarism' is used somewhat loosely here to embrace all analyses which rely heavily, though not necessarily exclusively, on the following two propositions in the examination of the balance of payments questions. The *first proposition* is that there are 'strong functional connections between money or credit creation and nominal income, and between income [meaning nominal income] and imports'.[43] The first part of this proposition, imputing a functional link between supply of money and nominal income, was discussed earlier where it was explained that it is theoretically illegitimate to infer a 'causal' link between the two variables on the basis of the observed 'correlation' between them (see pp. 65–8).

Equally illegitimate is the second part of the proposition, suggesting a causal link between 'nominal' income and imports. As noted above (p. 230) movements of 'real' income are likely to generate parallel movements in the volume of imports, but no such changes need necessarily follow movements in 'nominal' income. 'Nominal' and 'real' income may in fact move in opposite directions as often happens in periods of 'stagflation'. In the UK, for example, during the recession

---

42. The Fund's version of monetary approach presented here is derived largely from publications by senior members of its staff and associates. See, in particular, IMF, *The International Monetary Fund, 1966–1971*, Vol. 1, Washington DC (1976), (this volume of the publication is henceforth referred to as *The IMF, 1966–1971*); IMF, *The Monetary Approach to the balance of Payments*, Washington DC (1977), henceforth referred to as *The Monetary Approach*; and Carl P. Blackwell, 'Reflections on the Monetary Approach to the Balance of Payments', published in the *Proceedings of the Third Pacific Basin Central Bank Conference on Economic Modelling*, Vol. 1, The Reserve Bank of New Zealand, Wellington, NZ (1978); extracts from this paper appeared in *IMF Survey* (20 February 1978) pp. 52–5 and *IMF Survey* (6 March 1978) pp. 71–3. See also Joseph Gold, *Financial Assistance by the International Monetary Fund, Law and Practice*, IMF, Pamphlet Series, No. 27, Washington DC (1979), and *Conditionality*, IMF, Pamphlet Series, No. 31, Washington DC (1979).

43. See Blackwell, 'Reflections on the Monetary Approach', p. 13; words in brackets added.

of 1975, although 'nominal' national income rose by over 20 per cent, 'real' income declined, as did the volume of imports.

The question of the choice between 'nominal' and 'real' variables of income and expenditure has important policy implications and goes a long way to explain the difference between the monetarist and Keynesian approaches to demand management in general and to internal and external imbalances in particular (see p. 228 above). Because the data used in monetary models tend to be in 'nominal' rather than in 'real' terms, there is a general tendency on the part of monetarists to use the concepts of aggregate 'nominal' demand and 'nominal' income, as macro-economic tools of analysis. In doing so, they also often assume (explicitly or implicitly) that the same causal links exist between these 'nominal' variables and certain 'real' macro-variables, such as the volume of imports and of private consumption, as that found between the latter and aggregate 'effective' demand and 'real' income.

This practice has inevitably introduced a deflationary bias in policy prescriptions made by monetarists: a diagnosis made in terms of 'nominal' income and expenditure will, in periods of inflation, always tend to exaggerate both the level and the rate of growth of demand, at times calling for deflationary measures in the absence of any pressure of demand against productive capacities. The classical example of this is provided by the monetarist prescription of deflationary policies for some industrial countries of the West, such as the UK and the US, during the periods of 'stagflation' experienced from time to time since 1973.

The *second proposition* of monetarists is to regard the balance of payments as an essentially monetary phenomenon, in the sense of being determined by the supply of and demand for money.[44] This is based on the *accounting identity* which shows that any change in the overall balance of payments on current and capital accounts combined, as reflected in the change in international reserves, must necessarily be statistically equal to 'the difference between the change in the demand for money and the change in the supply of money of domestic origin'.[45] This identity constitutes a major plank in the strategy of most monetarists for dealing with external imbalances. It is argued that, for any given period, to keep the external account in balance and the change in international reserves to zero, it is only

44. See Blackwell, 'Reflections on the Monetary Approach', p. 13 and IMF, *The Monetary Approach*, p. 12.
45. See IMF, *The Monetary Approach*, p. 3; see also Blackwell, 'Reflections on the Monetary Approach', p. 13.

necessary to ensure that domestic credit creation is equal to the change in the demand for money.[46]

In most countries, domestic credit can be regulated by the authorities. The future demand for money has, on the other hand, to be estimated, and this is done on the basis of the anticipated change in nominal national income and on the assumption that the demand for money is a stable function, in the sense that income velocity of circulation is relatively constant, in the short run.[47] In other words, estimates of the future demand for money are derived from those of the anticipated changes in real GNP and in the average price level (indicating changes in nominal income) together with the value of the income velocity of circulation, derived from past experience. Given these estimates, all that the authorities need to do in order to obtain a target balance of payments is to place an appropriate ceiling on domestic credit creation.

Viewed in the light of our own analysis of the causes of imbalances, the most striking characteristic of the second proposition is its superficiality – it is concerned solely with the *symptoms* rather than the real *causes* of imbalances. It is, therefore, of little value for diagnostic purposes and can, in practice, easily lead to policy prescriptions that are irrelevant and at times harmful, economically as well as socially. From a theoretical point of view, the basic flaw of the proposition lies in its implicit assumption that external imbalances are not only *reflected in*, but are generally, if not invariably, *caused by*, excess domestic credit creation in relation to the demand for money, as defined by monetarists. It is as illegitimate to draw this conclusion on the basis of the accounting identity mentioned as it is to impute a chain of causality between the supply of money and prices on the basis of the quantity theory identity, discussed earlier (pp. 65–8).

It is important to emphasise that this criticism of the monetary approach is entirely unrelated to the question of the stability of the demand function for money; it is based on the universally recognised principle, noted above, that accounting identities and statistical correlations are neutral as regards causation. The same is equally true of the Keynesian, or national accounts, identities, which show that the external balance on current account is equal to the difference between domestic expenditure and GNP or to the difference between domestic investment and savings. These identities cannot *by themselves* serve any useful purpose for the diagnosis of imbalances and for the prescription

46. See IMF, *The Monetary Approach*, pp. 7–8.
47. *Ibid.*, p. 4.

of remedies, and, if so used, can lead to highly misleading conclusions. For example, the identity of savings and investment, *by itself*, provides no clear indication concerning the policies required to combat economic depression. It becomes useful as a tool of analysis only when taken in conjunction with the hypothesis that it is investment that generates savings and not the other way round, a hypothesis which is derived from the observed behaviour of market economies and is entirely unrelated to the identity itself. It was largely because of the failure to appreciate the significance of this chain of causation that, during the Great Depression of the 1930s, some industrial countries were led to adopt measures aimed at increasing investment by restraining public and private consumption.

IMF eclecticism

Although all groups of monetarists make some use of the two propositions mentioned, they vary in the extent to which they rely on them. 'Pure monetarists' can be defined as those whose diagnosis of external imbalances is based exclusively on these propositions. For them, all balance of payments deficits are due to excess supply of money of domestic origin in relation to demand for it, and to reduce the deficits it is essential to curb the supply of money; this, as we have seen, is analogous to the Chicago school approach to the problem of inflation reviewed in Appendix 2A.

According to the publications of some IMF staff members, although monetary models based on the two propositions constitute the starting point and foundation of the Fund's analysis of the balance of payments, its overall approach is not confined to these models and is 'eclectic' in character. The more important differences between the pure monetarists and the Fund's eclectic approaches, indicated by these publications, can be summarised under three broad headings.

The *first* difference, which is considered of crucial importance by some among the Fund staff, is that the IMF monetary approach, unlike that of pure monetarists, 'is never made in a purely mechanical fashion'.[48] Regardless of which monetary models are utilised, their results are 'supplemented by common-sense judgements about features of the economic process that can hardly be adequately represented in any manageable econometric model.'[49] It is suggested that discussions between the representatives of the Fund and the member

48. Blackwell, 'Reflections on the Monetary Approach', p. 23.
49. *Ibid.*

seeking Fund's assistance, generally followed by further dialogues in the Board of Executive Directors, provide abundant opportunity for taking into account 'qualitative considerations' and for 'modifying' and 'adapting' the original quantitative estimates obtained from monetary models.[50] In other words, the IMF approach involves 'a blending of experienced and objective judgement with quantitative analysis pushed as far as it can go (but no further)'.[51]

A similar account of the Fund's monetary approach is to be found in the official report of its operations during the years 1966–71.[52] According to this report, the Fund staff and the officials of a member planning to request a 'stand-by arrangement' sit together, in advance of the request, to prepare a 'stabilisation programme', described later (see p. 258). They make quantitative estimates of the total supply of the economy's financial resources and of the total demand for them.[53] Economic models indicating the relationship between credit creation and the balance of payments, as well as advanced econometric techniques, are then used to work out fiscal and monetary targets for inclusion in the programme.[54] The results obtained by these technical methods are, however, 'modified by judgement' and the ceilings and targets are 'adapted to the economic circumstances and financial institutions of the member concerned'. This is done in the course of 'continuing discussions between the member and the Fund, both at the management and staff level and at the Executive Board level'.[55]

It is rather unfortunate that, despite the great significance attached to the process of blending 'qualitative' considerations with 'quantitative' results of monetary models and to the 'modification' and 'adaptation' of these results, no information is provided on the techniques used for the purpose. It is, therefore, not possible to ascertain either the manner in which, or the extent to which, this is done in practice.

Secondly, unlike 'pure monetarists', the IMF does not confine its prescription for dealing with external imbalances to monetary, or credit, policies alone. 'Realistic' exchange rate policies, generally requiring devaluation as well as shifting of resources toward the external sector for deficit countries, represent important elements of

---

50. *Ibid.*
51. *Ibid.*
52. See *The IMF, 1966–1971*, pp. 364–8. See also Gold, *Financial Assistance*, Pamphlet Series, No. 27, p. 21.
53. See *The IMF, 1966–1971*, p. 365.
54. For further details, see *ibid.*, pp. 364–6.
55. *Ibid.*, p. 366.

the Fund's prescriptions for external imbalances.[56] Moreover, although the 'conditionality' embodied in the Fund's stabilisation programmes, discussed below, takes the form of 'credit ceilings', these ceilings reflect 'the monetary consequences of all financial policies' and not of monetary policy alone; in most programmes, the burden of adjustment may fall on fiscal policy and, at times, also on incomes policy.[57]

Thirdly, the Fund has, unlike 'pure monetarists', come to recognise that in some cases factors other than 'monetary mismanagement' may be responsible for the balance of payments difficulties.[58] These are, however, exceptional, or special, cases, for which the Fund has been willing to establish special credit facilities, with low degree of conditionality, such as the Compensatory Financing Facility and the Oil Facility described in Appendix 6A. As shown below, the Fund's general attitude, as reflected in the conditionality applied to upper credit tranches of its regular facilities as well as to the 'Extended Fund' and 'Supplementary Financing' facilities, continues to be based on the presumption that imbalances are generally caused by excess demand.

There can be little doubt that the Fund's 'eclectic' monetary approach is in some ways preferable to that of 'pure monetarists' whose policy prescriptions are based entirely on the results obtained from monetary models. Analytically, however, this does not amount to much, since it is not at all certain that the Fund's approach does, or indeed conceptually can, add up to a logically consistent and coherent system of analysis. In effect, what the Fund does, as a concession to common sense, is to introduce certain important non-monetary considerations to 'modify' or 'supplement' the conclusions reached through monetary analysis; what is required, however, is an approach in which these considerations form an integral part of the analysis. Indeed, it would be far more rational to use monetary statistics as a source of information 'supplementary' to other more important structural and income and expenditure data, along the lines indicated earlier in this chapter, than to start with monetary models, which are known to be based on untenable propositions, and then to modify the results obtained from such models by 'common-sense judgements'. To put it differently, in view of the questionable nature of the two basic propositions underlying the monetary approach, one may legitimately

56. See Blackwell, 'Reflections on the Monetary Approach', p. 25; see also *ibid.*, pp. 13–14, and pp. 264–5 below.
57. See *The IMF, 1966–1971*, p. 368.
58. See Blackwell, 'Reflections on the Monetary Approach', p. 14.

ask whether there are any rational grounds for using monetary models in the analysis of the balance of payments, even if they are, as in the case of the Fund, used only as a 'starting point' of the analysis.

According to the staff of the Fund, its monetary approach to the balance of payments was developed in the 1950s as a result of the staff's work on the balance of payments difficulties of developing countries, notably those of Latin America;[59] they give four reasons for adopting this approach. *First*, during the 1950s many LDCs lacked adequate national income data for the application of Keynesian income and expenditure approach, whereas monetary statistics were usually obtainable from the central banks, as were the balance of payments data. To quote the staff of the Fund, 'in view of the availability of these two sets of data in a large number of countries for which other statistical data was scarce, the thought naturally presented itself to develop a framework of analysis that could take full advantage of this data base'.[60]

The *second* reason was the desire 'to have available a framework for quantitative analysis that was sufficiently manageable (in the days before long-distance access to computers) to be serviceable during staff missions of foreign capitals. The monetary approach permits a meaningful approximate analysis of the relevant aggregates with the help of models that are small enough to be calculated with pencil and paper.'[61]

Thirdly, because LDCs have a relatively simpler financial structure than developed countries, the implication for their external account of excess domestic credit creation is 'more obtrusive'.[62]

Fourthly, a monetary approach was considered to be especially 'appropriate for many developing countries, particularly in Latin America, in which control over domestic credit was in fact relied on as a major instrument ... of demand management and balance of payments control'.[63]

It can be seen that the adoption of a monetary approach in the 1950s is explained, at least partly, in terms of the availability of monetary data and of the ease with which such data lend themselves to econometric analysis. These and indeed the other reasons given clearly have no bearing on the inherent merits of monetary approach and as such cannot by themselves justify the Fund's initial decision for

59. See IMF, *The Monetary Approach*, p. 7.
60. *Ibid.*, p. 6; see also *The IMF, 1966–1971*, p. 363.
61. See IMF, *The Monetary Approach*, p. 6.
62. *Ibid.*, p. 7.
63. *Ibid.*

adopting that approach. It would, in any case, be difficult to explain the continued adherence of the Fund to monetary approach now that all industrial and most developing countries have, as noted above, adequate data to permit a more meaningful analysis of the balance of payments (see pp. 230–1). We have in fact seen that even in the early 1950s the non-monetary data available for a country like Chile were sufficient to allow the United Nations Secretariat to identify the basic causes of imbalances experienced by that country.

It is true that the approach used by the United Nations and advocated here is more complex and would entail greater effort in determining the reasons responsible for imbalances. But considering the complex nature of all economic phenomena, it is difficult to see how one can devise a simpler method for their diagnosis to suit the convenience of econometricians. In practice, however, if the Fund were persuaded to abandon its monetary approach in favour of a more meaningful and realistic one, it would not have to start from scratch in gathering and analysing the relevant data on its members in the way the United Nations had to do for its Chilean study. The reason for this is that the Fund now has at its disposal a large number of country studies, including those prepared by its own and the World Bank staff as well as the United Nations, which contain detailed information on structural characteristics and on current economic developments of individual countries and which generally provide the bulk of the data required for the diagnosis of imbalances along the lines suggested by us earlier in this chapter.

It would, however, be wrong to assume that the sole reason for the Fund's adherence to a monetary approach is that it considers this approach superior, on 'technical', or 'theoretical', grounds, to the one suggested by us. It is in fact clear from the writings of some of its staff members that they are not entirely satisfied with some aspects of the Fund's monetary approach.[64] Perhaps the ultimate reason for the

---

64. Apart from the reservations expressed in Blackwell's paper, mentioned earlier, some writers have questioned the assumption of a stable income velocity of circulation of money as well as the monetarist hypothesis on the chain of causality between credit expansion and growth of imports (see J. Marcus Fleming and Lorette Boissonneault, in IMF, *The Monetary Approach*, pp. 139–45; see also Yung Chul Park, *IMF Staff Papers*, November 1970). Other members of the Fund have questioned the wisdom of relying heavily, if not exclusively, on 'aggregative' monetary policy and of neglecting 'selective' or 'qualitative' credit policies in developing countries (see Deena Khatkhate and Delano P. Villanueva, *World Development*, Vol. 6 No. 7/8, July/August 1978). The question of the 'applicability of a monetarist analysis to developing countries' was also raised in the IMF history of 1966–1971 (see *The IMF, 1966–1971*, p. 368).

Fund's reluctance to abandon the monetary approach is its inability to do so given the restricted role assigned to it in the international monetary system. That role, as we shall see, consists of managing a relatively small 'revolving fund' for the purpose of providing assistance to those of its members who find themselves in temporary balance of payments difficulties. Because of this, the Fund has to give high priority to safeguarding its resources, and this it does by making the use of most of its credit facilities conditional upon the adoption of deflationary measures. Since the monetary approach to the balance of payments serves to provide a 'theoretical' justification for prescribing deflationary measures, it is unlikely to be abandoned by the Fund as long as the role assigned to it remains unchanged.

It is somewhat unfortunate that the Fund has not explicitly acknowledged the fact that its continued adherence to a monetary approach is a matter of necessity, dictated largely by its special circumstances, but has instead defended it on its inherent merits. This has tended to boost the prestige of monetarism as a school of thought and, more seriously, to encourage as well as to provide a pretext to some governments to adopt voluntarily deflationary policies, in preference to other non-deflationary measures available to them, for dealing with imbalances (see p. 239 above).

We shall consider later how, in practice, the Fund uses its 'eclectic' monetary approach to deal with the balance of payments difficulties of the countries seeking its financial assistance. To provide a concrete impression of this procedure as well as of the scope of operation of the Fund, however, it will be useful first to present some factual information on its organisation, its resources and its credit facilities.

THE ORGANISATION, RESOURCES AND CREDIT FACILITIES OF THE IMF

The IMF was set up together with the World Bank at the United Nations Monetary and Financial Conference held at Bretton Woods, New Hampshire, in 1944, and it began operations in 1946. The primary reasons for establishing the Fund were to have an organisation to supervise the system of stable exchange rates agreed at the conference and to give short-term financial assistance to its members in balance of payments difficulties. The World Bank, on the other hand, as its official name, International Bank for Reconstruction and Development, implies, was set up to assist countries, through long-term loans, with their efforts in post-war reconstruction and in economic development. The establishment of two separate organisations entrusted with different functions has unfortunately tended to obscure the inevitable interaction, mentioned earlier, between the short-term measures concerned with the balance of payments and the long-term development strategy of the countries taking such measures (see pp. 236–7 above).

The organisation and resources of the IMF[65]

The constitution of the IMF is embodied in its Articles of Agreement ratified at Bretton Woods which describe, *inter alia*, its purpose, membership, organisation, management and operations.[66] Two important amendments have been made to the original Articles, the first in 1969 and the second in 1978. All amendments to the Articles have at present to be approved by three-fifths of the members, having 85 per cent of the total voting power. [67] This means that the US, which has approximately 20 per cent of total voting power, can alone block any modification of the Articles, as can a combination of the UK and any two other major industrial countries such as France, Germany and Japan.

The day-to-day activities and general policies of the Fund are under the overall supervision of the Executive Board, whose members are appointed or elected by member countries and whose votes are weighted by reference to the quotas of the countries appointing or electing them.[68] The Executive Board reports to the Board of Governors which represents all member countries, one for each country, usually consisting of their finance ministers or the governors of central banks.[69] The membership of the Fund has grown in line with that of the United Nations; by the end of 1980 it had some 140 members of which 120 consisted of developing countries. Almost all members of the United Nations, with the notable exception of some socialist countries, are members; Switzerland is neither a member of the United Nations nor of the Fund.

Quotas and SDRs

Each member country is allocated a *quota*, which determines: its subscription to the Fund; its drawing rights on the Fund; its voting

---

65. I am grateful to the Editor of the IMF for making 'technical' corrections to the earlier draft of this section.
66. See *The International Monetary Fund, 1945–1965*, Washington, DC (1969), Vol. III, pp. 185–214. This publication is henceforth referred to as, *The IMF, 1945–1965*.
67. See *Articles of Agreement*, Article XXVIII.
68. For further details, see *IMF Survey* (17 April 1978), p. 123.
69. *Ibid.*

power, and its share in the allocation of the Special Drawing Rights (SDRs) described below. The quotas have been determined primarily by calculations derived from formulae which take into account the members' national income, reserves, imports as well as export variability and the ratio of exports to national income. The procedure has in recent years been modified to give smaller countries a larger share in quotas, by giving less weight to national income and a larger weight to trade and to export variability.[70] At the end of 1980, some 20 industrial countries accounted for about 63 per cent of total quotas and the remaining 120 members for 37 per cent; among the latter, 12 oil-exporting countries had just over 10 per cent of total quotas.[71]

Quotas have been raised and reviewed periodically, at intervals of not more than five years, to take into account the growth in the value of the world trade as well as changes in the relative position of member countries. Increases in quotas have not, however, kept pace with the growth in the value of the world trade, largely because of the attitude of the major industrial countries, which determines the Fund's policies in such matters. At the end of 1980, total IMF quotas (SDR 59.6 billion) amounted to less than 4 per cent of the estimated value of the world imports during that year, compared to about 16 per cent in 1948.[72] This has, as noted later, had the effect of reducing the capacity of the Fund to supply financial assistance to its members from its general resources and is largely responsible for the establishment of some of the special facilities financed with borrowed resources, reviewed in Appendix 6A.

The scheme of *Special Drawing Rights* (SDRs) was established in 1969 under the First Amendment to the Articles of Agreement to augment international liquidity by supplementing the members' external reserves. The SDRs are unconditional reserve assets allocated, in proportion to quotas, to the members which wish to participate in the Special Drawing Rights Department; by 1980, all members of the Fund were participants in the scheme. The participant members accept an obligation to provide convertible currency, when designated by the Fund to do so, to other participants in exchange for SDRs up to an amount equivalent to three times their own allocation; only countries with a strong balance of payments position are as a rule so designated by the Fund.

The members whose holdings of SDRs are below the level of their original allocation pay interest on the difference, and those whose

70. for details, see *IMF Survey* (5 June 1978) pp. 166–8, and *IMF Survey* (18 September 1978), p. 294.
71. See IMF, *International Financial Statistics* (IFS), February 1981.
72. This was despite a 50 per cent increase in quotas towards the end of 1980.

holdings are above their allocation receive interest on the surplus. The rate of interest is determined by a formula based on short-term market interest rates in the US, Germany, the UK, France and Japan. By early 1981, total cumulative allocations of SDRs amounted to 21.4 billion – equivalent to about 1.5 per cent of the value of the world imports in 1980.

The SDR is also used as a unit of account in some foreign exchange transactions. Between July 1974 and the end of 1980, the value of the SDR in terms of the US dollar was determined on the basis of the weighted average of the dollar value of a basket of 16 currencies, but since the beginning of 1981 a basket of only five currencies – the US dollar, Deutschmark, yen, French franc and pound sterling – are used for the purpose.[73]

The IMF derives its resources from subscription, from borrowing and from service and interest charges.[74] Members of the Fund are required to subscribe to the Fund an amount equal to their quota. In the early years of the Fund's operations, 25 per cent of subscriptions had to be paid in gold and the balance in the members' own currencies. Since 1 April 1978, when the Second Amendment of the Articles of Agreement came into force, subscriptions can be paid partly in reserve assets, and partly in the member's own currency, or they can be paid entirely in a member's currency. *Reserve assets* consist of actual holdings of gold, SDRs, reserve position in the Fund and foreign exchange assets available to the monetary authorities to meet the balance of payments deficits. The amount by which the quota exceeds the Fund's holdings of the member's own currency was formerly called *gold tranche*, but is now known as *reserve tranche*, or *reserve position*.

To supplement the resource derived from subscriptions, the Fund is authorised to borrow from its members. As explained in Appendix 6A, such borrowing arrangements have been made to finance some of the special drawing facilities established by the Fund in recent years. Additional resources are obtained from service and interest charges made on the use of the Fund's credit facilities; drawings in reserve tranche, however, are free of such charges.[75]

---

73. For further details, see *IMF Survey* (12 January 1981) pp. 1 and 6, and *IMF Survey* (26 January 1981), pp. 20–1. At the end of 1980, 1 SDR was valued at 1.27541 US dollars.
74. Some additional resources were in recent years derived from profits on sales of the Fund's gold holdings, which were used to provide long-term loans to LDCs by the IMF Trust Fund described in Appendix 6A.
75. For details of the service and interest charges see *IMF Survey* (18 September 1978), p. 299.

The IMF regular credit facilities

The Fund's resources are made available to its members on a short- to medium-term basis only when they are in need of the balance of payments support. A member draws on these resources by *purchasing* other members' currencies in exchange for its own and is under an obligation to *repurchase* an equivalent amount of its own currency within a given period in media acceptable to the Fund. These consist of SDRs and of the currencies of other members specified by the Fund; sales by the Fund itself of a country's currency to other members has the same effect as a repurchase. It is clear that although the composition of the currencies held by the Fund change their total value remains unchanged overall as a result of such transactions. Although, strictly speaking, members do not 'borrow' from the Fund, but 'purchase' foreign currencies from it, and do not 'repay' loans, but 'repurchase' their own currencies, it is usual to refer to drawings, or purchases, from the Fund, as 'borrowing' and to repurchases as 'repayment of loans'.

The credit facilities provided by the Fund can be divided into two broad categories. *The first* consists of the facilities under the Fund's 'general reserve and credit policies', which, for the sake of brevity, are referred to here as *regular credit facilities*; the primary purpose of setting up the IMF at Bretton Woods was the provision of these facilities to member countries. The *second* category of facilities, known as *special facilities*, is briefly outlined in Appendix 6A. These facilities have been introduced at various dates since the early 1960s for certain specific purposes and include some which are of a temporary nature financed by the Fund with borrowed money.

The regular credit facilities are made available to members under two headings: *reserve tranche* and *credit tranche*. The former consist of drawings made against the reserve tranche position of a member, which, as noted above, equals the amount by which its quota exceeds the Fund's holdings of its currency, excluding the holdings which result from the use of certain special facilities mentioned in Appendix 6A. There are, in addition, four credit tranches, each equal to 25 per cent of a member's quota, under which drawings can be made, making the total possible holdings of a member's currency by the Fund under the regular facilities equal to 200 per cent of its quota.[76]

76. As explained in Appendix 6A, members may make additional drawings under certain special facilities established by the Fund. Following the new guidelines announced early in 1981, members' 'cumulative' access to the Fund's resources, excluding drawings under 'Compensatory' and 'Buffer Stock' facilities, would be up to 600 per cent of quota, and may in some cases exceed this limit (see p. 274).

A member's indebtedness to the Fund under regular facilities may thus be expressed in terms of the Fund's holdings of its currency as a percentage of its quota. A percentage of 75 or less, for example, indicates that a member has no drawings under the Fund's regular facilities; between 76 and 100 shows that it has outstanding drawings under the reserve tranche; between 101 and 125 denotes outstanding drawings under the first credit tranche, and so on. Members usually undertake to repurchase drawings under regular tranche policies in a period not exceeding three to five years. The Fund publishes each month detailed information on its holdings of the individual members' currencies as well as on their reserve tranche position and their drawings under special facilities.[77]

Conditionality of the IMF credit facilities

Drawings in reserve tranche are unconditional and can be made automatically, i.e. on the basis of an unchallengeable representation of needs; many countries include their reserve tranche position with the Fund as part of their official reserves. But drawings in credit tranches are subject to varying degrees of conditionality. Before drawing any part of its credit tranches, a member must obtain permission from the Fund, and its entitlement to do so is determined by the Fund after considering the member's economic position as well as its likely ability to resolve its balance of payment problems within a short period.

The conditionality applied by the Fund in authorising drawings in the first credit tranche is more liberal than that applied to *higher credit tranches* – the second, third and fourth. A member is not required to satisfy any specific conditions, designated as *performance criteria*, for drawings in the first credit tranche; the Fund need only be satisfied that the country has a programme representing reasonable efforts to overcome its balance of payments difficulties.[78] As explained in Appendix 6A, this type of mild conditionality is also applied to some special facilities, namely the Compensatory Financing and the Buffer Stock facilities; it was also applied to the temporary Oil Facility. On the other hand, drawings beyond the first credit tranche as well as under Extended and Supplementary facilities, described in Appendix 6A, are normally made by instalments and are conditional upon the observance of specific 'performance criteria'; such drawing rights are at times referred to as 'conditional credit'.

77. See, IMF monthly publication, *International Financial Statistics*.
78. See *IMF Survey* (12 December 1977) p. 382.

The procedure generally followed in formulating the 'performance criteria' is for the staff of the Fund, together with the officials of a member requesting a stand-by arrangement, first to prepare what is formally known as a *financial stabilisation programme* (but is often referred to simply as *stabilisation programme*, *financial programme*, or *adjustment programme*) which outlines the policies that the member intends to adopt to deal with its balance of payments difficulties. These policies and intentions are also set out in a *letter of intent* from the country's authorities to the Fund. The Fund then formulates the *stand-by arrangement* by reference to certain aspects of the 'letter of intent'; it selects some of the elements of the stabilisation programme that are formulated in 'quantitative' or other 'objective' terms to serve as 'performance criteria'.[79]

As explained later, performance criteria consist predominantly of fiscal and monetary targets phased over the period of the stand-by arrangement. At the end of each period the Fund checks compliance with the targets, and if the targets have been achieved, the corresponding fraction of the agreed drawing rights is released. If a member fails to observe the performance criteria, its 'right to make purchases under the stand-by arrangement will be interrupted without the need for a decision by, or even notice to, the Executive Directors'.[80]

Because the performance criteria are 'invariably objective in character, and require no 'subjective judgement' to ascertain whether they are being observed, a member knows at all times whether it is able to make purchases.[81] The stand-by arrangements thus serve also the purpose of assuring a member that during a given period it will be entitled to draw on the Fund's resources up to a specified amount without the review of its position and of its policies at the time of each drawing, provided it has observed the conditions of the arrangement. To ensure continuous supervision and to avoid abrupt decisions on the interruption of credit facilities, stand-by arrangements require countries to remain in 'close consultation' with the Fund during the period of the arrangements. This provides the Fund with an opportunity for examining the progress made in implementing stabilisation programmes as well as for the review of the conditions in which drawings could be resumed with the agreement of the Fund.

It is worth noting here that, historically, the 'stand-by arrangement' is an instrument of policy created by the Executive Board itself in the

79. Gold, *Financial Assistance*, Pamphlet Series, No. 27, pp. 13–14.
80. See *The IMF, 1945–1965*, Vol. ii, p. 533.
81. *Ibid.*

course of the Fund's operations; no suggestion of it can be found in the original Articles of Agreement of the IMF. Moreover, the entire concept of the stand-by arrangement has undergone a complete transformation as a result of successive decisions made by the Executive Board since 1952. Originally, its role was to provide 'a confirmed line of credit that gave a member an absolute right to make purchases subject only to those provisions of the Articles on ineligibility and the general suspension of operations' which were necessarily applicable to such purchases.[82] It has, however, now become 'the main instrument for conditionality' and, in particular, for ensuring that, beyond the first credit tranche, the Fund's resources will be made available to a member 'only if the member observes certain policies'.[83]

In March 1979, the Executive Board issued new guidelines on the use of Fund resources and stand-by arrangements, which replaced those formulated in 1968. The new guidelines permit the extension of stand-by arrangements beyond the normal period of one year, up to three years. They also specify that the Fund's adjustment programmes will pay due regard to social and political objectives, the economic priorities and the circumstances of members, including the causes of their balance of payments problems. In addition, performance criteria are to be confined to macroeconomic variables and to those criteria that are necessary to implement specific provisions of the Articles or policies adopted under them.[84] It is very unlikely, however, that the new guidelines will significantly modify the stabilisation policies, to which we now turn, as long as the Fund adheres to its monetary approach.

IMF STABILISATION POLICIES

One can get a clearer and more realistic insight into the Fund's monetary approach to the balance of payments by examining its 'adjustment policies', as indicated by the performance criteria and related policy measures contained in the stand-by arrangements and in the members' stabilisation programmes. As noted earlier (pp. 247–8) the writings of Fund staff suggest that the Fund's monetary approach, unlike that of 'pure monetarists', blends 'qualitative' judgements about a member's economy with 'quantitative' results obtained from monetary models. Judging on the basis of the infor-

---

82. *Ibid.*
83. *Ibid.* For a detailed discussion of the origin and the evolution of 'the principle of conditionality', see Gold, *Conditionality*, Pamphlet Series, No. 31.
84. See *IMF Survey* (19 March 1979) pp. 82–3.

mation obtained on the stabilisation programmes, however, it is clear that, whatever might be the precise techniques used for modifying the quantitative results, such modifications cannot go far enough to change substantively certain important common features of the Fund's policies. Of these, the two most significant, reviewed below, are the heavy emphasis placed on curbing effective demand and the promotion of the market mechanism, which, as noted earlier, are in our view causally related to each other (pp. 51–3).

Restriction of effective demand

Although the number and content of performance criteria included in stand-by arrangements vary from country to country, almost all stabilisation programmes aim at curbing effective demand. They provide for the use of global, or aggregative, monetary and fiscal measures, the net impact of which is to restrain and, at times, to depress economic activity.

In reviewing the contents of the programmes submitted to the Fund by a number of industrial and developing countries during the years 1966–71,[85] for example, it is reported that,

virtually all the programmes submitted to the Fund by members requesting stand-by arrangements in the upper credit tranches contained detailed quantitative ceilings on credit expansion. Most programmes contained separate ceilings on the extension of credit by the central bank to the government or to the public sector as a whole. Often credit expansion by the entire banking system was also subject to limits.[86]

In addition, 'direct fiscal measures – either additional taxes or cuts in aggregate public expenditure or both – were usually also stipulated in members' financial stabilisation programmes'.[87] There has been no noticeable change in this feature of the IMF stabilisation programmes in recent years: all stand-by arrangements in the upper credit tranches as well as drawings made up to 1981 under the Extended Fund Facility, described in Appendix 6A, have included performance criteria aimed at curbing the growth of effective demand through restrictive monetary and fiscal measures.

We have explained earlier that deflationary measures of the type mentioned constitute a proper instrument of policy for dealing with the imbalances caused primarily by what were designated as 'excess

85. These consisted of the stabilisation programmes of France, the UK, Brazil, Colombia and Indonesia; for details, see *The IMF, 1966–1971*, pp. 339–62.
86. *Ibid.*, p. 363. See also Gold, *Financial Assistance*, Pamphlet Series, No. 27, pp. 14–15.
87. See *The IMF, 1966–71*, p. 363.

aggregate demand' pressure, but that they are not strictly relevant to the other and more common types of imbalances experienced by LDCs (see p. 240 above). A recent example of the prescription of deflationary measures by the Fund in circumstances that could not rationally justify the adoption of such measures is provided by the stand-by arrangements made for some developing countries during the years 1974–8. According to the United Nations study mentioned earlier, the principal sources of disequilibrium during that period were: the sharp rise in the prices of oil and other primary commodities in 1974–5; the acceleration of the upward trend in the prices of manufactured goods imported from industrial countries; economic recession in industrial countries; and a growing wave of protectionism, directed particularly at imports from LDCs.[88] Despite these generally recognised facts, the logic of the IMF monetary approach required that the countries, such as Jamaica, Kenya, Peru, Sri Lanka and Uruguay, which applied for IMF assistance should adopt restrictive credit and fiscal measures to deal with their balance of payments problems.[89] It is also worth noting that these conditions were being imposed at a time when the Fund itself, recognising the special difficulties caused by the steep rise in petroleum prices at the end of 1973, had introduced the special Oil Facility, described in Appendix 6A, to help its members.

The deflationary feature of the Fund's policy has more serious and wider implications for the world economy, since the Fund's influence over economic policies of its members is confined almost exclusively to its deficit members. Countries enjoying persistent surpluses can in practice continue to accumulate foreign exchange reserves without being subjected to any effective pressure to take measures to rectify their imbalances. The only formal action the Fund can take against surplus countries is to invoke 'the scarce currency clause' of its Articles of Agreement, which would authorise its members to impose temporary import and exchange restrictions against surplus countries.[90] For a number of reasons, however, the Fund has never invoked this clause. During the immediate post-War years, when the US dollar was in short supply, it was not thought proper to invoke the clause against the US, which was providing substantial aid to Western Europe. Since 1962, the introduction of the General Arrangements to Borrow (GAB),

88. See *UNDP/UNCTAD Report*, pp. 126–7.
89. See *ibid.*, pp. 67–74. The stabilisation programmes of Peru during 1975–8 are discussed in greater detail in R. Thorp and L. Whitehead (eds.), *Inflation and Stabilisation in Latin America*, The Macmillan Press (1979), Chapter 4.
90. See *The IMF, 1945–1965*, Vol. III, p. 195.

described in Appendix 6A, has enabled the Fund to increase the supply of a potentially scarce currency by borrowing, so that it could not be regarded as 'technically' scarce. In practice, the GAB has thus had the effect of removing the need of exerting pressure on surplus countries to take corrective measures. There can be little doubt that the Fund's disapproval of trade and exchange restrictions in general and of discriminatory restrictions in particular, discussed below, has at least partly motivated the introduction of GAB.

The asymmetry in the pressure exercised by the Fund on its deficit and surplus members not only places the burden of the balance of payments adjustment almost exclusively on deficit countries but also implants a deflationary bias. on the world economy.[91] This bias is reinforced by the attitude of private banking and financial institutions which, like that of the Fund, generally tends to favour the adoption of restrictive fiscal and monetary measures by potential borrowers.[92]

The inherent bias of the present international monetary system in favour of deflationary policies has had the effect of directly restraining the growth of production and employment in both industrial and developing economies alike. The LDCs have, however, suffered also indirectly, as we have seen, from the deflationary policies of developed countries in two important ways worth noting. *First*, the growth of their exports has been retarded, partly because of economic recession and partly because of recession-induced barriers against exports in industrial countries, mentioned earlier (see pp. 142 and 195–6). *Secondly*, the policy of curbing public expenditure, prescribed by monetarists for dealing with inflation and external deficits, has resulted in a slowing down of the flow of economic aid to developing countries.

Promotion of the market mechanism

The second important feature of the Fund's stabilisation programmes can broadly be described as the promotion of the market mechanism by reducing the scope of government interference with the operation of market forces in both internal and external transactions. On the domestic front, the IMF discourages price controls and subsidies including those provided by financing the deficits of nationalised industries. Among the stabilisation programmes examined by the United Nations study, it was found that 'in at least two of the countries

91. See *UNDP/UNCTAD Report*, pp. 96–7.
92. For a more detailed discussion of this subject see Eshag, *Present System of Trade and Payments*, pp. 20–6.

studied, particular objections were raised by the Fund to the continuation at existing levels of subsidies on essential foodstuffs because of the heavy cost to the government budget', and 'in one case an effort was made to persuade a government to "dismantle" its system of price controls'.[93]

Regarding external transactions, the Fund does not consider trade restrictions an acceptable means of tackling balance of payments difficulties, although it is more lenient with trade than with exchange restrictions. Nevertheless, while recognising that certain long-standing trade restrictions 'may be difficult to remove in the short term, because of the effect that this will have on production and employment, the Fund requires that stabilisation programmes should provide for removal of restrictions newly imposed for balance of payments reasons, and for a renunciation of any further recourse to them'.[94] Stabilisation programmes, as we shall presently see, also often contain provisions to ensure that exchange rates are maintained at 'realistic' levels by allowing them to fluctuate freely without the intervention of central banks in the market and by avoiding restrictions on foreign exchange payments.[95] For the same reason, new multiple exchange practices and bilateral payments agreements are expected to be avoided.[96]

It is clear that some of the policies advocated by the Fund may at times conflict with the social and economic objectives of the member countries. The argument that 'the character of the Fund is determined by its technical tasks' and that it 'does not seek to modify the political or social policies of a member', advanced by the IMF Legal Department, is somewhat formalistic and misleading.[97] What matters in practice is not what the Fund 'seeks to do', i.e. its motivation, but what it 'actually does' in the course of performing its 'technical tasks'.

Foreign exchanges and devaluation

We have earlier questioned the relevance to LDCs of the *laissez-faire* philosophy to which this second characteristic of the Fund's policy can be attributed by explaining some of the important reasons for government intervention in the economy.[98] What has not been examined specifically and should briefly be considered here is the

93. See *UNDP/UNCTAD Report*, p. 112.
94. *Ibid.*, pp. 116–17; see also pp. 118–19.
95. See *The IMF, 1966–1971*, pp. 363–4.
96. See *UNDP/UNCTAD Report*, p. 107.
97. See Gold *Financial Assistance*, Pamphlet Series, No. 27, p. 20.
98. See pp. 11–20 and Chapter 5, especially pp. 173–86.

implication of that philosophy for the policies concerned with foreign exchanges.

The Fund generally acts on the assumption that a persistent deficit in the balance of payments is an indication that the country's rate of exchange is not 'realistic', i.e. is overvalued, and that, therefore, a devaluation is called for. A 'realistic' rate of exchange is presumably one which reflects 'the purchasing power parity' of the currency and thus ensures that the world prices of tradable goods cover their domestic costs of production. It is further implicitly assumed that a free market in foreign exchanges is likely to produce a *single* exchange rate which is 'realistic' in the sense described. There are a number of reasons for questioning the theoretical validity of these assumptions as well as the relevance of the policy prescriptions based on them especially as they relate to LDCs.[99]

First, as explained earlier in this chapter (pp. 234–5), adverse changes in capital flow as well as in short-term supply and demand conditions affecting current account, which need not necessarily be related to the level of exchange rates, can be responsible for balance of payments deficits; one cannot, therefore, assume that such deficits provide even *prima facie* evidence of an overvaluation of the currency.

Secondly, the rate of exchange in a free exchange market is determined by the *total* demand for and supply of foreign exchanges on current and capital accounts combined. It is true that receipts and payments on current account are determined partly, though not exclusively, by the ruling rates of exchanges and that an overvalued currency may at times be a major source of disequilibrium on this account. Movements of public and private capital, on the other hand, are strongly influenced by a variety of factors not directly related to the exchange rates, such as government policies on the importation of foreign capital, the relative rates of interest, profitability of direct investment and expectations of capital exporters concerning future political and economic developments at home and abroad. Because of this, there is little reason to expect that the free market rates of exchange need closely correspond to the purchasing power parity of the currency.

Thirdly, there are usually significant sectoral differences in developing countries between the productivity in and the relative costs of traditional and non-traditional export sectors as well as between these and import-competing industries. In such conditions there can be no

99. For a more general and detailed criticism of the Purchasing Power Parity Theory, on which the Fund's approach to foreign exchanges is largely based, see Eshag, *From Marshall to Keynes*, pp. 38–44.

single rate of exchange that can bring the unit costs of the products of all sectors producing tradable goods in line with their world prices. These differences in relative costs in fact by themselves provide a strong prima facie case for using multiple exchange rates and selective trade measures discussed earlier.

An additional reason for recommending the liberalisation of foreign exchange markets is that such a move is generally accompanied by a devaluation of the currencies of deficit countries which it is thought will contribute to an improvement in the balance of payments. Broadly, devaluation can influence the current balance of payments account through two channels. *First*, if wage and salary increases lag behind the price rises induced by devaluation, as they generally do, private consumption is likely to decline and, as noted earlier (p. 240), the balance of payments will improve largely as a result of a fall in imports. Viewed in this way, devaluation serves as a deflationary instrument of policy, supplementing other restrictive fiscal and monetary measures.

Secondly, devaluation has the effect of boosting the profits of the export sector and of raising the domestic prices of tradable goods. The influence exercised by such price changes and profit incentives on the balance of payments is less certain, since it depends largely on the elasticities of supply of and of foreign demand for exports as well as on the elasticity of demand for imports; the higher these elasticities are, the more the gains in the balance of payments from a devaluation are likely to be.

Regarding *exports* of developing countries, which consist largely of primary products, foreign demand for the sales of *individual* countries is generally highly elastic, but the supply is likely to be rather inelastic in the *short run*, largely because the internal consumption of these products generally accounts for a small fraction of their total output; a further reason is the inelasticity of supply of agricultural products. The *long-term* supply elasticity of primary products depends largely on the expectations of producers concerning the duration of price incentives. In countries where policies have been liable to frequent changes, it is unlikely that devaluation would produce a significant increase in fixed investment, and the long-term supply elasticity, like the short-term one, is likely to be rather low; this proved to be the case, for example, in Argentina during the years 1957–64, mentioned earlier (p. 12).

The elasticity of demand for *imports* depends partly on the commodity composition and partly on the availability of domestically-produced substitutes. For countries whose imports consist predominantly of essential consumer and producer goods without close domestic substitutes this elasticity too is likely to be low.

On the whole, the influence exercised by devaluation on current balance of payments account is likely to be more favourable in semi-industrialised developing countries than in the less diversified economies. For most developing countries, however, it would usually be difficult to find a strong case for using devaluation, in preference to other available measures, as a means of resolving the problem of external imbalances. The reason for this is that, even when a devaluation is likely to lead to an improvement in the balance of payments, it should generally be possible to attain the same result through selective measures, such as export subsidies and multiple exchange rates, mentioned earlier, without experiencing the adverse side-effects of devaluation on the level of activity, on inflationary pressures and on distribution of income. That the negative effects on development of a devaluation may in some instances exceed its positive contribution to the improvement of the balance of payments, is recognised by some staff members of the Fund itself.[100]

It is important to point out in conclusion that the foregoing critique of the two features of the Fund's stabilisation policies should not be construed as in any way indicating an objection to the principle of 'conditionality' *per se*; the objection is to the type of conditionality used by the Fund. Our criticism of these policies stems *solely* from the fact that the Fund's stabilisation programmes, being based on a monetarist diagnosis of imbalances and a predisposition in favour of the market mechanism, need not be, and in practice are not, always 'relevant' to the real problems faced by its members. There could, otherwise, be no rational ground for objecting to 'conditionality' *if* the conditions set were based on a meaningful diagnosis of imbalances along the lines proposed by us earlier in this chapter. Such a diagnosis would, in some cases, undoubtedly point to the need for restricting aggregate effective demand as well as government involvement in the economy (see pp. 24–5, 175 and 240 above). In many other cases, however, the measures indicated would consist of institutional and fiscal reforms aimed at restricting inessential investment and consumption outlays and at the promotion of essential investment through selective fiscal, monetary and other instruments of policy.[101]

100. See A.D. Crockett and S.M. Nsouli, 'Exchange Rate Policies for Developing Countries', *Journal of Development Studies*, January 1977.

101. No doubt many developing countries are likely to object to the type of 'conditionality' suggested here, as indeed are some industrial countries. It will be said that the proposed conditions amount to 'interference in the internal affairs' of the member countries, as if the 'conditionality' practised by the Fund was free of such interference (see p. 263 above).

CONCLUDING NOTE

It has been seen that inflation and balance of payments deficits can be caused by a variety of factors that need to be clearly identified before remedial measures are prescribed. A proper diagnosis of imbalances must take into consideration the structure of trade and production of the country as well as its economic and social institutions. It must, in addition, include an analysis of demand conditions within the framework of the Keynesian model of income determination; this approach involves the use of 'effective' demand as a tool of analysis. The monetarist approach to the diagnosis of imbalances, which relies heavily on the instruments of 'nominal' demand and the 'supply of money' in the analysis of demand conditions, has been shown to be based on theoretically untenable propositions. In practice it often leads to misleading conclusions by exaggerating the level and the rate of growth of demand, thereby imparting a deflationary bias to policy prescriptions.

We have suggested two criteria for judging the relevance, or usefulness, of measures taken to deal with imbalances, namely their 'efficacy' and their 'side-effects' on production and employment. On the basis of these criteria, it has been found that deflationary measures, of the type prescribed by the Fund, are highly relevant to conditions of 'excess aggregate demand' i.e. when the pressure of demand against productive capacity plays an important role in causing price rises and/or balance of payments difficulties. In such conditions, a contraction of demand will have the effect of moderating imbalances without causing an appreciable fall in economic activity.

Deflationary policies, even when 'effective' in curing imbalances, are, however, bound to have a significant negative 'side-effect' on production and employment if applied in conditions of deficiency in demand, and should for this reason be avoided whenever alternative non-deflationary policy measures are available. It has been shown that, in such conditions, inflationary pressures are likely to be of a 'cost-push' type and should be dealt with through some form of incomes policy and appropriate selective measures rather than through deflation. Selective fiscal and monetary measures as well as direct controls can also be used to reduce, if not entirely eliminate, the pressure on the balance of payments without depressing the level of activity.

Countries that are unable to resolve their balance of payments difficulties through selective measures and are not experiencing excess demand pressures require foreign credits in order to be able to avoid resorting to deflationary measures. The efficiency, or adequacy, of the international monetary system in promoting economic growth and development is to be judged primarily by its capacity to cater to the needs of such countries through private and official channels. The present system has proved to be inadequate in a number of ways, particularly as it affects LDCs.

Regarding private sources of finance, most developing countries have a limited access to international capital markets; this is particularly true of the poorer and less developed among them. Moreover, external private credits, being provided on relatively hard commercial terms, tend to give rise to debt service problems for the countries making use of them. (See Appendix 4B.)

IMF represents the chief source of official credit available to LDCs. We have seen, however, that the Fund's own resources, derived from subscriptions, are rather small in relation to its members' requirements for balance of payments support and that these resources have, in any case, to be managed as a 'revolving fund'. Because of this, the Fund has to give a high priority to safeguarding its own resources as well as those acquired by borrowing; the credit facilities that it can provide to its members without strict 'conditionality' are, therefore, highly limited. Apart from the Compensatory Financing and the Buffer Stock facilities, discussed in Appendix 6A, the low conditionality drawing facilities are confined to the first credit tranche, or one-fourth of the members' quotas, which in 1981 amounted to only $1\frac{1}{2}$ per cent of the 1980 imports for non-oil exporting developing countries; for industrial countries the ratio in question was even lower. All other drawings from the Fund are subject to strict conditionality, generally requiring the adoption of restrictive fiscal and monetary policies, and, except in conditions of excess aggregate demand, involving negative side-effects on production and employment.

It is thus clear that IMF, with its present terms of reference, cannot play a significant role in filling the existing gaps in the balance of payments support that can be and is provided by private financial institutions. To put it more precisely, given its constitution, the Fund is simply not in a position to play a major and effective role in promoting growth and development in the world economy. In our view, this would call for a monetary institution (be it a reconstructed IMF, or a new international monetary agency) which is empowered, and indeed mandated, by its constitution to exert direct and indirect pressure on industrial countries, which play a dominant role in determining the course of development in the world economy, (a) to maintain full employment and (b) to avoid excess aggregate demand pressures. This means that industrial countries would be required to correct persistent deficits as well as persistent surpluses on their external accounts without resorting to deflationary measures if and when these are likely to cause unemployment. Such a monetary institution would in effect be expected to play a role similar to the one envisaged by Keynes in his *Proposals for an International Clearing Union*.[102]

Developing countries as a whole would clearly benefit (through their exports) from such influence as the proposed international monetary agency would be able to exercise to promote full employment in developed economies. However, even with a high and growing level of activity in industrial countries, many LDCs are likely to continue to face serious balance of payments constraints on development. As noted earlier in the book, to ease these constraints such countries would have to be provided with special balance of payments support with varying degrees of concessionality (p. 144).

It is, of course, realised that there is little or no prospect at present of introducing fundamental changes in the international monetary system along the lines suggested here. Such suggestions are unlikely even to be seriously considered, still less acted upon, as long as the major industrial countries which control the IMF, continue to invoke the pre-Keynesian orthodox dogmas to justify the policies which accord a higher priority to the promotion of the market mechanism than to full employment. The prospects of establishing an international monetary agency geared to promoting full employment and economic growth are, therefore, even bleaker in 1981 than they were at Bretton Woods in 1944 when Keynes's 'Clearing Union' proposals were found unacceptable by the US Government; only a pronounced reversal in the present order of priorities of the political and economic objectives mentioned can improve these prospects.[103]

APPENDIX 6A: IMF SPECIAL FACILITIES[104]

Since the early 1960s, the Fund has introduced a number of facilities for the provision, in special circumstances, of short- and medium-term

---

102. See Cmd. 6437. For a brief review of and comments on Keynes's scheme see Eshag, *Present System of Trade and Payments*, pp. 32–5.

103. Such a reversal in policy will largely depend on the political pressure of the broad sections of the population (the unions and the middle classes) who bear the brunt of the sacrifices imposed on the community by the orthodox monetarist policies. Academic criticism of these policies, such as the criticism presented in this chapter and in the Appendix 2A, are, as we have explained earlier, of secondary importance (see pp. 22–3 and 52–3).

104. I am grateful to the Editor of the IMF for making 'technical' corrections to the earlier draft of this appendix.

finance to its members. The primary reason for the introduction of these special facilities has been the realisation that the Fund's regular credit tranche facilities, discussed in the text, are far from adequate to meet some of the essential needs of its members. We have seen that regular credit facilities are limited to 100 per cent of the quotas and that these have lagged considerably behind the growth of international trade (see p. 254 above). Moreover, only drawings in the first credit tranche (one-quarter of the quota) are subject to 'mild', or 'low', conditionality, all other drawings being subject to 'strict' conditionality. Special facilities are thus designed to increase the capacity of the Fund to provide credit (with 'low' as well as with 'strict' conditionality) to its members.

We give below a brief description of the special facilities established by the Fund.[105] It will be seen that the first two facilities mentioned – the Compensatory and the Buffer Stock facilities – are designed to provide low-conditionality loans to developing countries, as did the third – the temporary Oil Facility – for a time to both industrial and developing countries. The Extended and Supplementary facilities, on the other hand, serve to provide the members with conditional credit, similar to that available under the higher regular credit tranches. Drawings under the Compensatory and Buffer Stock facilities are additional to those under regular tranche policies and do not affect a member's 'reserve position' in the Fund; the same was true of drawings under the Oil Facility.

Compensatory Financing Facility (CFF)

This facility was introduced in February 1963 largely in response to the repeated demands of the United Nations.[106] It is the first important step taken by the Fund in acknowledging that countries, particularly primary exporters, may require special assistance because of a shortfall in their export earnings due to factors beyond their control. Before providing such assistance the Fund must be satisfied that,

(a) the shortfall is of a short-term character and is largely attributable to circumstances beyond the control of the member; and

105. Special facilities are subject to periodic changes and modifications; our description pertains to early 1981. Changes in these facilities are regularly reported in the *IMF Survey* and in the Fund's *Annual Reports*; a short up-to-date description of all Fund facilities can be found in its monthly publication, *International Financial Statistics*.
106. For reference to some of the United Nations publications, see for example, IMF, *Compensatory Financing of Export Fluctuations, A Report by the International Monetary Fund*, Washington DC (1963), pp. 1 and 5–8.

(b) the member will cooperate with the Fund in an effort to find, where required, appropriate solutions for its balance of payments difficulties.[107]

To identify what are to be regarded as export shortfalls of a 'short-term character', the Fund, in conjunction with the member seeking to use the facility, establishes estimates regarding the medium-term trend of the member's exports; these estimates are based partly on statistical data and partly on the qualitative appraisal of the country's export prospects. As in the case of the drawings under the first tranche of the Fund's regular facility, the condition that 'the member will co-operate with the Fund' is interpreted rather liberally for drawings under this facility. This has rendered the CFF the primary source of low-conditionality credit to some LDCs. Drawings under the CFF are, as in the case of regular facilities, repayable within 3 to 5 years, or earlier if the member's balance of payments and reserve position permit.

The CFF has been revised and liberalised three times since its introduction, first in September 1966 and later in December 1975 and in August 1979, no doubt partly in response to the persistent pressures of LDCs through UNCTAD.[108] The amount of outstanding drawings under this facility, which were initially limited to 25 per cent of a member's quota, have been increased by successive steps to 100 per cent and the ceiling on annual drawings has been abolished.[109] Developing countries have, nevertheless, for long been pressing for further liberalisation and improvement of the CFF. In this they have received the support of the Brandt Commission[110] which has urged the Fund: to remove the quota-based limits to drawings under the facility; to expand the scope of the facility to include other important cases in which balance of payments difficulties are due to factors beyond the country's control, such as increases in import prices and harvest failures; and 'to make repayment terms flexible, so that they are linked to changes in the borrowers' capacity to repay'.[111]

The Commission recognises that to implement these proposals the

---

107. *Ibid.*, p. 25.
108. See, for example, UNCTAD, *Trade and Development, Final Act and Report*, Sales no.: 64. II. B. 11, (1964) p. 52; *Commodities*, UNCTAD IV, document TD/184 (May 1976), pp. 14–15; *International Monetary Issues: Problems of Reform*, UNCTAD IV, document TD/189 (May 1976), p. 21.
109. See IMF, *Compensatory Financing of Export Fluctuations, A Second Report by the International Monetary Fund*, Washington, DC (1966), pp. 40–2, and *International Financial Statistics*, February 1981, p. 5.
110. See *North-South: A Programme for Survival*, Pan Books, London and Sydney (1980), pp. 217–18.
111. *Ibid.*, p. 218; see also Sidney Dell, 'The World Monetary Order', *Third World Quarterly*, October 1980, p. 714.

CFF would require much greater funding, which it estimates at \$12 billion – three times its present size. Given the Fund's limited resources, it is not certain that it is at present in a position to treble the funding of the CFF. It has, however, agreed to consider the establishment of a 'food import facility', probably within the framework of the CFF, which would provide assistance to members, especially low-income countries, 'suffering from crop failures or sharp rises in food import prices'.[112]

The Buffer Stock Financing Facility

This facility was established in June 1969 and may be used by countries experiencing balance of payments difficulties for the purpose of financing their contributions to international buffer stock agreements; drawings may be made up to 50 per cent of quota. As in the case of the CFF, drawings under this facility are subject to 'low' conditionality and have to be repaid within three to five years. The loans advanced through this facility have been on a much smaller scale than those provided under the CFF; by the end of 1980 total drawings under it amounted to about SDR 100 million, compared with SDR 5.9 billion under the CFF.

The Oil Facility

This was a temporary low-conditionality facility provided by the Fund to assist both industrial and developing members to meet the impact on their balance of payments of the steep rise in petroleum prices that took place towards the end of 1973. Two oil facilities, one in 1974 and the other in 1975, amounting to SDRs 6.9 billion, were made available and fully utilised by May 1976. Repurchases under the Oil Facility are made in equal quarterly instalments and have to be completed within seven years. The resources used in providing this facility were borrowed from the members of OPEC and from some industrial countries with relatively strong balance of payments position. The facility, in effect, served to channel part of the balance of payments surpluses of these countries to deficit countries.

Subsidy Account: In August 1975, the Fund established a Subsidy Account with the objective of reducing the effective rate of interest payable on drawings under this facility by 25 countries considered to have been 'most seriously affected' by the rise in petroleum prices. The

112. See the statement of the Managing Director of the IMF at the 1980 Annual Meeting of the Board of Governors, on 30 September 1980.

annual rate of interest payable by these countries was reduced by about 5 percentage points, from 7.7 to 2.6 per cent. The Account was funded by contributions from industrial countries and members of OPEC.[113]

Extended Fund Facility (EFF)

By introducing this conditional credit facility in 1974, the Fund explicitly acknowledged that 'serious balance of payments difficulties', requiring medium-term loans, can be caused by 'structural' factors. The facility, to quote the Fund, 'assists members with economies suffering from serious balance of payments difficulties resulting from *structural imbalances* in production, trade and prices or economies characterised by slow growth and an inherently weak balance of payments position'.[114] Before making this facility available to a member, the Fund has to be satisfied that its resources are required for longer periods and in larger amounts than are available under the regular tranche policies. 'In addition, the member is expected to present a programme setting forth the objectives and policies for the whole period of the extended arrangement, as well as a detailed statement of the policies and measures that it will follow in each 12-month period to meet the objectives of the programme'.[115]

Drawings under the EFF are phased over periods of up to three years, and may not exceed 140 per cent of quota, or, together with drawings in the credit tranches, may not exceed 165 per cent of quota. Repayments are expected to begin not later than 4 years and are to be completed not later than 10 years after the date of purchase. They are made under *extended arrangements* and are subject to performance criteria similar to those specified in stand-by arrangements reaching into upper credit tranches, discussed in the text (see pp. 257–63). The criteria in question usually include fiscal and monetary targets as well as measures related to the liberalisation of trade and exchanges, although it is not certain that these provide the best means of monitoring progress in 'structural' adjustments, for which this facility was designed.

Supplementary Financing Facility (SFF)

This facility is financed with borrowed resources. It was provided for in August 1977 although it did not come into force until February 1979,

---

113. See United Nations, ECOSOC, *Committee for Development Planning, Fifteenth Session,* document E/AC. 54/22 (16 March 1979) p. 29.
114. See IMF, *IFS*, February 1981, p. 5; emphasis added.
115. *IMF Survey, Supplement on the Fund,* September 1979, p. 10.

by which date agreements had been concluded with a number of industrial countries and the members of OPEC to make a target amount of resources (not less than SDR 7.75 billion) available on call to the Fund.[116] Like EFF, this facility is intended to assist members facing serious balance of payments difficulties which need resources in larger amounts and for longer periods than are available to them under regular tranche policies.

The SFF is used only in support of stabilisation programmes under 'stand-by arrangements' reaching into the upper credit tranches, or under 'extended arrangements'. Drawings under the SFF are thus 'subject to the relevant policies of the Fund, including those on conditionality, phasing and performance criteria'.[117] An arrangement which involves the use of the SFF will normally cover a period of more than a year and may extend up to three years. Drawings under this facility are to be repaid in equal semi-annual instalments that begin not later than three and one-half years and are completed not later than 7 years after the date of purchase; charges levied are equal to the rate of interest paid by the Fund on the loans raised to finance the facility, plus a small margin.[118]

Following the completion of quota increases in December 1980, the Fund announced new guidelines on access to its resources which will significantly enlarge the amount of conditional credit available to the members within the framework of the SFF.[119] 'The new guidelines provide, generally, for members to have an annual access to Fund resources of up to 150 per cent of their new quotas or up to 450 per cent over a three-year period. Members' cumulative access, net of scheduled repurchases, would be up to 600 per cent of quota'.[120] Such drawings will be additional to any made under the Compensatory Financing and Buffer Stock facilities, as well as to those outstanding under the Oil Facilities.[121] The guidelines also 'allow for flexibility in application' so that in some cases members will be able to borrow larger amounts than those indicated by the above limits.[122] To finance these enlarged facilities the Fund has tentatively set itself an annual borrowing target of SDR 6 to 7 billion.[123]

116. For the list of the countries involved and their loan commitments, see IMF, *International Financial Statistics.*
117. See *IMF Survey, Supplement on the Fund*, September 1979, p. 10.
118. For further details see *IMF Survey* (5 March 1979) p. 75; and *IMF Survey* (23 March 1981) p. 93.
119. See *IMF Survey* (26 January 1981) pp. 17 and 21; and *IMF Survey* (23 March 1981) p. 1.
120. *IMF Survey* (26 January 1981) p. 17.
121. *Ibid.*
122. *Ibid.*, p. 21.
123. *Ibid.*, p. 17.

Subsidy Account: Early in 1981 the Fund announced the establishment of a Subsidy Account to reduce the cost of using the SFF for its low-income developing members.[124] The aim is to allocate SDR 1 billion to the Account, of which SDR 750 million will be derived from the expected repayment of loans granted by the Trust Fund, described below, and the remainder from voluntary contributions and other sources. The Fund has listed 69 low-income countries which will be eligible for a subsidy not exceeding 3 per cent per annum and a further 14 countries which will receive one half of the subsidy.[125]

The Trust Fund

The Trust Fund was established in May 1976 to provide loans on concessional terms to low-income developing countries with balance of payments difficulties to support their programmes for balance of payments adjustment. The resources used for providing these loans originated from profits made on sales of the IMF gold holdings, from the income received on such profits pending their disbursement and from contributions of member countries.[126] The Fund has decided to terminate this facility at the end of April 1981, or soon thereafter. Of the resources received from the repayment of loans advanced under the Trust Fund, SDR 750 million will, as noted above, be transferred to the SFF Subsidy Account and SDR 1.5 billion will be used to provide balance of payments assistance to low-income developing countries under arrangements broadly similar to those that were available under the Trust Fund.[127]

General Arrangements to Borrow (GAB)

Only eleven industrial countries participate in this facility which is administered by the Fund. In January 1962, a four-year agreement was concluded with ten industrial members and Switzerland under which these countries agreed to lend to the Fund up to $6 billion in their own currency to supplement the resources available for drawings by the participants in the agreement.[128] The agreement, known as General Arrangements to Borrow, has been renewed periodically and the most recent renewal is due to expire in October 1985. The maximum credit available to the Fund through the GAB amounted to about SDR 6.8 billion at the end of 1980.

124. See *IMF Survey* (12 January 1981) pp. 1 and 9–13.
125. For details, see *ibid.*, p. 11.
126. Between June 1976 and May 1980, the Fund sold 25 million ounces of gold which yielded a profit of $4.6 billion, *ibid.*, p. 10.
127. *Ibid.*
128. See *IMF Survey* (18 September 1978) p. 294.

INDEX

Names of the authors and institutions appearing in footnotes are generally followed by the titles of their publications and thus serve as a bibliographical guide to the book; each title is indexed only once, when first mentioned. Periodicals and regular reports published by institutions have not been indexed.